Getting the
WORD
Across

Getting the
WORD
Across

Speech Communication for
Pastors and Lay Leaders

G. ROBERT JACKS

William B. Eerdmans Publishing Company
Grand Rapids, Michigan / Cambridge, U.K.

© 1995 Wm. B. Eerdmans Publishing Co.
255 Jefferson Ave. S.E., Grand Rapids, Michigan 49503 /
P.O. Box 163, Cambridge CB3 9PU U.K.

Printed in the United States of America

00 99 98 97 96 95   7 6 5 4 3 2 1

ISBN 0-8028-4152-X

TABLE OF CONTENTS

Acknowledgments

Thanks to:

The Best TA's In the World:
Graham Robinson, TA #1, who said, "RJ, you ought to write a book!"
Doug Learned, TA #2, who said, "Just do it!" and kept encouraging me
    and praying
Brent Strawn, TA #3, who said, "No shame!!!"

Lois Haydu, who read every single word and told me to take out the parts she didn't like
Chuck Bartow, who kept me on fire with collegial enthusiasm
Rob Lanchester and Janet Weathers, for more collegial support and helpful suggestions
Jim Kay, who was unbelievably encouraging
Nora Tubbs Tisdale, who said "It's just like you're talking to us!"

Students and friends who lent an eye and an ear:
Jack and Sharon Brown, who said, "This is not only instructive, it's devotional!"
Doug Cushing, who read it and made wonderfully helpful suggestions
Tom Edwards, who said, "This will be a blessing to the Church!"
Rob MacSwain, who said, "Did I spot a cliché?" (I took it out, Rob!)
Steve Shaffer, who said, "Made me think of 'I, not I, but Christ' and 'Lord, make me an
    instrument of thy peace'—we are only <u>instruments</u> of grace."
Jon Swanson, for editorial eye and computer savvy

Wonderful friends who have been so supportive with their encouragement and prayers—who
    said, "What on earth are you doing with yourself during your sabbatical?" and really
    cared

Don Reiff and Fred West, for their part in answered prayers for an IPA font—and special
    gratitude to Wycliffe's Summer Institute of Linguistics

Chris Carpenter, who graciously fielded all my stupid questions about computers

Princeton Theological Seminary, for sabbatical time for writing

My children, Stephen, Elisabeth, and Daniel, for the grace God manifests through (and to) them

My wife Rosanne for her very special support and exquisite proofreading

TO THE LORD OF MY LIFE, WHO HAS BLESSED ME WITH ALL OF THE STUDENTS WHO HAVE TAUGHT ME SO MUCH

Foreword

The Bible is not a dead letter but living literature. In *Getting the WORD Across*, G. Robert Jacks keeps us aware of that. In worship, with the Scriptures, God in Christ, by the power of the Spirit, brings people alive to divine truth and seals that truth upon their hearts. Of course, worship leaders and preachers do not make that happen by their speech. Instead, their speech bears joyful witness to that happening. Their speech is—or ought to be—sensible, intelligible, simple, direct, imaginative and purposeful. Above all, it is—or ought to be—*disciplined*, for its task is not to call attention to itself. Artful speech is transparent, not opaque. The *Word of God* is seen, heard, touched and felt *through* it.

Back in the late sixties, in a lecture on preaching, Paul Scherer cautioned: "Don't ask for whom God's Word is meant. It is meant for you." So worship leaders and preachers do not speak the Word as if it were meant for everybody in general and nobody in particular. It is meant for *them* and for all those who listen to them. It is Personal Word and Personal Presence. The proclamation of the Word of God *is* the Word of God, and proclamation begins with the speaking and hearing of the Scriptures. The speaking of the Scriptures, therefore, demands the same prayerful preparation as the speaking of sermons. We bring God our best effort, not our worst, for to count on God to make up for a casual, inattentive and indifferent handling of the divine Word (which God *will* do for the sake of the divine Name) is not humility; it is arrogance.

Having set out what is at stake in speaking and hearing God's Word, Professor Jacks provides "hands on" lessons in disciplined, interpretive speech. In these lessons, Jacks speaks to us directly, personally, with humor and sensitivity, seeking always to build us up and not to tear us down. The lessons are appropriate for the veteran preacher who wants a review of the basics. Yet they also are appropriate for the beginning lay reader who may seldom speak or read in public—except in church—and who may never have had any training in speech at all. The myriad of illustrations and exercises are well-chosen and carefully explained. Jacks does not simply tell us what to do. He also shows us how to do it. The lessons in emphasis, in phrasing, in imagery, and gesture are compelling. The detailed, yet readily accessible treatment of pronunciation, articulation and voice management is a gem. In my judgment, we have here one of the best and briefest treatments of voice and diction available in print. What a pleasure it is to be able to learn so much so quickly, and to have such a good time while doing so!

Getting the WORD Across is a humble offering. Its author, a minister, practical theologian, trained musician, scholarly interpreter and translator of the liturgical drama and pastoral theology of Swedish theologian/playwright, Olov Hartman, does not show off his erudition. He puts it all to subtle and understated use for the sake of his students, his "congregants" as he likes to say. G. Robert Jacks is a servant of the servants of the Word. He has been that at Princeton Theological Seminary for twenty-eight years. Now he has opened up his classroom to any who want his help. It is a place of prayer, of fun, of learning. Welcome!

Charles L. Bartow
Carl and Helen Egner Professor of Speech Communication in Ministry
Princeton Theological Seminary
Princeton, New Jersey

Preface to the Prefaces

Jesus said, "Peace be with you! As the Father has sent me, I am sending you." And with that he breathed on them and said, "Receive the Holy Spirit." (John 20:21-22)

Prayer: O Lord, let my life be a hymn of praise to you—every word, every thought, every deed a moment of trusting and obeying—that it all may be to your greater glory. In Jesus' Name. Amen.

People do notice.

And they sometimes talk about it. Or write about it.

Mark Twain did. Wrote. In 1880. About *it*. And this is what he said:

> The church is always trying to get other people to reform; it might not be a bad idea to reform itself a little, by way of example.... The average clergyman could not fire into his congregation with a shotgun and hit a worse reader than himself, unless that weapon scattered shamefully. I am not meaning to be flippant and irreverent, I am only meaning to be truthful. The average clergyman, in all countries and of all denominations, is a very bad reader.[1]

So—there *is* a *need* for this book.

You need it if you're a <u>*seminary student*</u> who's probably *a beginning reader*. That label isn't at all meant to be pejorative. It simply means you probably haven't had experience *reading aloud in public*. Like they do a lot in some European countries. Like they don't do a lot in our country.

You need it if you're a <u>*pastor*</u> who had maybe only one unit on speech communication in the middle of a course devoted primarily to homiletics. Or even if you *had* a speech course and it didn't take. And you find yourself fumbling and stumbling as you read, or winding up with a sore throat or a missing voice after conducting a service or two.

You need it if you're a <u>*layperson*</u> who's been asked to read the Word of God in church on Sunday and you're scared because you've never done it before. The main thing I want to do for *you* is to reassure you that you *can* do it, and do it *well*, and in the process it's going to bless you and you're going to be involved in a splendid ministry of blessing others through the reading of the Word.

So hang on! Two more Prefaces to get through, and then we're on our way. Enjoy!

And *God bless*!!!!!!

---

[1]*Mark Twain, A Tramp Abroad, Vol. II (Hartford: American Publishing Company, 1880), p. 92. (Please don't fault old Mark for his non-inclusive language. He wrote it back in 1880 when people didn't know any better. Besides, his point is well taken. Please take it.)*

Preface I: A Word To Lay Readers

In _The Book of Lists_[1], guess what's number one among the greatest fears? It's _"speaking before a group."_ More fearful even than the fear of dying![2] And you feel safe, because there's no way you'd be caught alive or dead _speaking before a group_. Right?

Guess what again? The pastor's just called you up and asked you to read Scripture in next Sunday's service!

Gotcha!!!

Of course you're going to hedge. "But I can't read Scripture—I'm not _ordained_!" Wrong. There are plenty of ordained people who can't read Scripture worth a hoot. I know I'll get in trouble for saying that, but I'm going to say more, as I get wound up, about reading Scripture _well_—so hang in there with me. I won't mention a lot of the other kinds of hedges you could come up with. You're creative enough without my giving you suggestions.

Of course you're going to think "I'll be scared!" and you're dead right. You will be. Anyone who has to stand up in front of anyone else and do anything usually gets scared. Just ask me. Sometimes those butterflies are the size of a house. But you can get comfortable with the task. You can—more or less—relax. Let me help you:

> ## _"Relax!!!"_

Didn't help, did it? Sorry!

Anyway, you can do the job. It doesn't have to be life-threatening, or even threatening at all. In fact, it's a major blessing. It can be a profound spiritual experience. Just think of it. _You_ have been asked to read _God's Word_! Now, if God didn't think you could handle it, God wouldn't have seen to it you were asked.

What you're blessed with is a ministry of reading. Someone's taken *the priesthood of all believers* seriously and asked you, a layperson, to help lead in worship. Isn't that glorious? And you can do it, really. And do it well. Part of my ministry is to try to help you. So please read on.

---

[1]*David Wallechinsky, Irving Wallace and Amy Wallace. The Book of Lists. New York: William Morrow and Company, Inc., 1977, pp. 469-470.*
[2]*The fear of speaking before a group is followed, in order, by the fear of heights, insects and bugs, financial problems, deep water, sickness, death, flying, loneliness, dogs, driving/riding in a car, darkness, elevators, and escalators.*

Preface II: A Word To Pastors & Pastors-To-Be

I want to take you to task.

(NOTE: If, by the time you finish reading, this doesn't apply to you, you're off the hook. And good for you! Please join me in taking to task others to whom it *does* apply.)

What am I talking about? I'm talking about the short shrift most worship leaders make of the *reading of Scripture*. We spend lots of time each week working on our sermons. But how much time do we spend preparing to read the Scripture lessons? Be honest. Preparing for the reading aloud—the oral interpretation or vocal exegesis, if you will—of the Scripture. I'm not going to ask you to write me or telephone me or E-mail me and let me know. But you know. And your congregation can guess. And guess what? *God knows!*

Do you think it's fair to spend a lot more time preparing *our* words (the sermon) than we do on *God's* word? And does it make sense that the Word-as-proclaimed is going to wow them if it's based upon a haphazard Word-as-*read*? Do you really think your preaching is more important for the people to hear than the reading of God's Word? Diatribe. Diatribe. You get the point.

I love reading Scripture aloud. To think God can use me as an instrument through which God's holy Word comes to life is a profoundly thrilling spiritual experience. For years (twenty-eight, as of this writing) I've tried to instill that same love in my students. I've tried to teach them to believe the most important part of the worship service is the Scripture reading. I've tried to get them to think of the reading as "the gem in the setting of the worship service."

I think I've gotten through to some. I know I got through to a student I'll call "Todd." He appeared at my office door one afternoon, about six years after he'd graduated from Princeton Theological Seminary. He wanted to tell me about "the parish from Hell" as he called it. He'd just left there for another position. What made the one parish so frustrating was the senior pastor who wanted to do everything in the worship service himself—so it could be done *right*! The only thing he didn't care about doing—the one thing he let Todd do—was reading the Scripture lessons.

Todd told me that story, and then he said, "RJ, he didn't know what a precious gift he'd given me! He gave me 'the gem in the setting'—and he never even knew it!!"

So, pastor, that's what I'd like to get you to believe. And I want you to take *the priesthood of all believers* seriously enough that you'll ask lay leaders to participate in the service with you. Let them have a go at "the gem." And both of you treat it, please, with the respect and awe and wonderment and thank-you-Jesus exaltation that it should have.

God has put into *your hands* and now into *your voices* the life-giving, life-changing Word that turns the world upside down. Think about that!

Pray and shout and be dazzled and thank God about that too! Amen!

Prologue

I love the story of Elisha and the Shunammite woman. Look it up in 2 Kings 4:8-37. To me it's a powerful story about the miraculous power of a great God. I read it once at an ordination service for a former student, a good friend. And then I preached a sermon about the things God did through his faithful servant Elisha. When the service was over, another seminary professor commented on how "real" and "alive" my Scripture reading was. He said, "It was as if you were there." Well, I *was* there. That story is so alive in my imagination. I identify with the love the Shunammite woman feels for the man of God. I minister through his promise that God would be faithful. The tragedy of the little boy's death catches in my throat. And I fight to catch my breath and keep tears from welling in my eyes at the wonder of the child's resurrection at the hand of a God-trusting Elisha. The story never ceases to be "new" to me, no matter how many times I read it.

On another occasion, I preached at the dedication of a new sanctuary. I chose that 2 Kings passage as my Old Testament lesson, and it was the wellspring from which my sermon rose. The event was one of those affairs-of-presbytery where a whole gaggle of ministers (they called it a commission) was gathered to participate in the service. Someone called to worship, someone else invoked, another person read this Scripture and another that Scripture. And I think you can tell what's coming. And you're right. The person who read *my beloved Old Testament lesson* had obviously given little thought or preparation to this part of his ministry. His voice fell right back down to the page where his eyes were glued, his diction was sluggish, he mispronounced words, and there was no apparent understanding or care about what he was reading. I was saddened. Saddened because he'd done injustice to a beautiful passage of Scripture. Saddened even more that he was communicating something about the Word of God he didn't realize he was communicating. And that message was, "This has not touched my heart, nor is it going to touch yours." Furthermore, the sermon I'd wanted based upon that awesome, lovely passage, wound up being built upon an utter shambles. To me it was a devastating experience. The Word of the Lord had not come to life in our midst. It had been desecrated in our very presence.

That's when I decided it was *crucial* to instill in my students this one Absolute: *always prepare thoroughly, lovingly, prayerfully, intelligently, your Scripture reading. It should be the gem, the hub, the red thread, the brightest possible moment in any worship service.*

It's my hope and my prayer that you will buy into this fixation of mine. Maybe "passion" is a better word. I love reading Scripture. Not long ago, I felt singularly blessed when a student-brother-friend asked me to travel to Michigan to participate in his wedding. There were three ministers there—one from his home church, his college pastor, and me. I was to be the minister of the Word: to read the Old Testament lesson, the Epistle, and the Gospel. I tell you, I felt like the king of the hill. Sure, these other pastor guys were doing important stuff like uniting these two in marriage. But *I* got to read God's Word! Talk about a blessing, an honor, a privilege, and all that!!

So I'd like to share this passion with you. "You" may be a layperson who's been asked to lead in a worship service. Or a seminary student who's trying to sort out all the stuff all the other professors think is of utmost importance. Or a pastor who's never been trained to read Scripture aloud (or told that the Scripture reading was unmitigatedly *bor*-ing).

Love reading the Scripture. Take to heart the preciousness of the task God's given you: to give voice to God's own part in the conversation between God and the people gathered there to adore their Creator. Praise God that he trusts you to be faithful in this glorious task!

✠Ad majorem Dei gloriam✠

✠Go for it!✠

PART ONE

The
WORD
Springs to Life

There Is a God—And You're Not It!
Transparency and Technique
Not the Law & the Gospel!—Just Some DOs & DON'Ts
Presence
Rubrics
Your Face Is Showing!
Oral Interpretation of Scripture
Explore the Word
Here's What's New and Important: Emphasis Matters
Putting It All Together: Phrasing Matters
Internalizing

There Is A God—And You're Not It!

[The Lord] said to me, "My grace is sufficient for you, for my power is made perfect in weakness." Therefore I will boast all the more gladly about my weaknesses, so that Christ's power may rest on me. That is why, for Christ's sake, I delight in weaknesses, in insults, in hardships, in persecutions, in difficulties. For when I am weak, then I am strong. (2 Corinthians 12:9-10)

Prayer: Lord of all, keep me honest with myself. I serve you not because I'm worthy to serve you, but because you are worthy to be served. When you give me a blessing, it's not because I'm so important I deserve your blessing, but it's because you want me to bless others. Let me always remember to humble myself under your mighty hand, that you may lift me up in due time. And may I always cast all my anxiety on you, knowing you care for me. I thank you, Lord, for that promise. Amen.

You're not perfect. You're only human. You're even—if I may say it—a bit inadequate. Yes, I will say it: *you are inadequate*!

That doesn't sound like a very nice thing to say to you, does it? Especially not when I'm trying to bolster your courage, give you some confidence, and tell you you can go out there and do a bang-up job of reading Scripture and glorify Almighty God in the process.

But it's true. You are inadequate.

You're inadequate because the Lord God made you that way. If God had made you adequate, you'd be God and not you. But there's only one God, and it's not you. And since you're not God, you're something less than God and God's God and you're you and that's that. And the main reason God made you inadequate is so that you'd have to realize you're not up to snuff and you've got to depend on God. I thank God all the time when I'm given tasks too big for me to handle (which is just about everything) because then I have to fall back on God's grace. And there's nothing God likes to do better than to bestow grace on you. And you'd better believe that. Really, you'd better believe that because God says it's so. God told me. And now I'm telling you.

I'll get off the soapbox now and tell you why I'm saying these things to you.

It's because, being human beings, we most of the time get things all mixed up. Or upside down. Or backwards. And this is especially true when it comes to doing any kind of speaking in public. Remember, I said it's number one of all our great fears. When you and I have a speaking task to do, what are the three basic components of that job? Simply, they are *ME, MY AUDIENCE* and *MY MESSAGE*. And that's usually the order in which we rank them according to importance. When we have the task of public speaking ahead of us, we set up a sort of hierarchy of things that are going to concern us. Very naturally, our hierarchy of concerns usually goes like this:

Last fall, on the first day of each class, I asked my students to complete this sentence:

"If God is to use my *voice* and my *presence* in ministry, I will need ..."

A lot of the answers were in the "I will need to depend on God" ballpark. But one just really hit the nail on the head when it came to honesty. That was Jeff's. Jeff wrote:

"If God is to use my *voice* and my *presence* in ministry, I will need to pray for God to provide me a butterfly net so that I can catch the butterflies in my stomach that hatch five minutes before preaching."

Now that's the real human condition: butterflies usually as big as SST's hatching in our stomachs sometimes even at the *thought* of speaking in public. So very naturally I'm going to put ME at the top of the list of my concerns. Am I going to read the text well? Am I going to trip and fall getting up from my chair and stepping up to the lectern? Is my tie straight? Are my earrings too gaudy? Will my voice crack? Will I lose my place? And I could fill pages with all the possible terrors that await ME as I get up to speak. That's natural. That's being very human. Acknowledging the butterflies—and realizing they're not going to go away. Every speaker I've ever known, no matter how many times that person has spoken, has felt those butterflies. It's a given. So there it is, top of the list, my major number one concern:

ME

Then there's the second level of the hierarchy of concerns: MY AUDIENCE. Those people out there. The ones who are going to judge me. Waiting there like vultures ready to swoop down and fly off with the carrion of the job I'm going to do. People I know. My grade-school principal. The lady who lives down the street. The guy I know from work. They know I'm no public speaker, and they're going to rip me to shreds! They're going to see my knees shaking. They're going to die laughing when I make all the mistakes I know I'm going to make. Oh, God, why did you let me get myself into this??? Why???? I love reading the comic Calvin and Hobbes. Calvin gets so paranoid over everything, and that's just like me most of the time. Well, any time it comes to doing something cataclysmic like *speaking publicly*. Surely, this is the equivalent of all the monsters Calvin *knows* are lurking under his bed. So, and this is still being human, right in the middle of my hierarchy is my second greatest concern:

MY AUDIENCE

And then, at the bottom of the hierarchy, comes MY MESSAGE. Almost forgot about that! Got so caught up in the first two items. Let's see, my message. It's right here in the bulletin. I hope they didn't change it on me after they asked me to read from Colossians, chapter 3. Oh, whew! It's still the same one I've been practicing all week. And so on. And you get the picture. Our very natural, very human tendency is to stack things this way:

ME
MY AUDIENCE
MY MESSAGE

Because very naturally, we are very human. I'm not going to tell you you can overcome that. You're still going to be human. Inadequate. Butterflies. Panic City.

But there is something you can do about it. You can give it up—give it over to God. You can say, "OK, Lord, I'm fully aware of what I'm up against and it has me terror-stricken but I'm going to give the whole thing over to you because you can deal with it and I can't and I need your help. Amen." Or something like that. And you know what God can do? God can tell you what you can do with your hierarchy of concerns. God can tell you to take your hierarchy of concerns and turn it upside down. Better still, *God* can take your hierarchy of concerns and turn it upside down *for* you. Because this is a God who does that sort of thing. The very Word God's asked you to read can turn the world upside down. Jesus the Word Incarnate can turn the world upside down. And if God can pull that off, God can certainly do something about your speaking in public. God's going to say, "OK!" and hand back your hierarchy so now it looks just like this:

MY MESSAGE
MY AUDIENCE
ME

Just think of the difference that makes! Now, what's *really* of primary importance is MY MESSAGE: the Word of God. Big blessing. Major news of utmost magnitude. Wow! Spotlights and trumpets and fireworks and fanfares and red carpets! *REALLY important!* I'm sure you get the picture.

Next in importance is MY AUDIENCE. Those people out there. That throng. They're hungry. They're hurting. They're dying to hear God's Word. God's Word is going to feed them. God's Word is going to make them whole. God's Word is going to bring them to *life*! God's Word *is* life! Wow again! Something phenomenal is about to happen to them!

And then, what's left? Oh, yes. ME. I'm the one who's so very blessed God thinks I can handle the situation. God thinks I can get up there and share *GOD'S MESSAGE* with *GOD'S AUDIENCE*. And now when I look at that hierarchy, I can see I'm not really all that important. Sure, the *task* is important. But if I suddenly drop dead before I'm supposed to jump up and read the Scripture, someone else could get up and read it. My grade-school principal. The lady who lives down the street. The guy I know from work. The janitor. Anyone. That's what God thinks of my ME-first hierarchy. God thinks it just plain doesn't have to be that way. Look at it again the way God wants it to be:

MY MESSAGE
MY AUDIENCE
ME

But I have to surrender it to God. I have to trust. I have to ask for God's grace. And then I think, together, we can pull it off. I mean *I know* we can pull it off!

So I'd better face it: I'm inadequate. But I'm going to praise God that God made me that way. Because God's got enough adequacy for himself and me too and anyone who asks for it.

Go ahead. Ask.

Transparency and Technique

[God said to Moses] "So now, go. I am sending you to Pharaoh to bring my people the Israelites out of Egypt."
But Moses said to God, "Who am I, that I should go to Pharaoh and bring the Israelites out of Egypt?"
And God said, "I will be with you. And this will be the sign to you that it is I who have sent you: When you have brought the people out of Egypt, you will worship God on this mountain."
Moses said to God, "Suppose I go to the Israelites and say to them, 'The God of your fathers has sent me to you,' and they ask me, 'What is his name?' Then what shall I tell them?"
God said to Moses, "I AM WHO I AM. This is what you are to say to the Israelites: 'I AM has sent me to you.'"
...Moses said to the Lord, "O Lord, I have never been eloquent, neither in the past nor since you have spoken to your servant. I am slow of speech and tongue."
The Lord said to him, "Who gave man his mouth? Who makes him deaf or mute? Who gives him sight or makes him blind? Is it not I, the Lord? Now go; I will help you speak and will teach you what to say."
(Exodus 3:10-14, 4:10-12)

Prayer: Holy Lord, I know I'm a lot like Moses. When you call me you put a major responsibility upon me and I don't want to mess up. Keep me, Lord, from making excuses about why I can't do what you want me to do. Instead, let me trust you when you say to me, "Now go; I will help you speak and will teach you what to say." I do trust you, Lord. You are faithful. I love you. I thank you. Amen.

Transparent. I have no notion where it came from. But the word *"transparent"* has come to be of major significance to me. When you think about ordinary human men and women—vessels, sometimes cracked or chipped or broken—taking on the task of reading the Holy Word of God, that word "transparent" just seems to make so much sense. It's not *my* word people have come to hear. They've not come to direct their attention on "a wretch like me," but on the "amazing grace" that calls me to the task of reading God's Word. If that's the case, then my task is to be *transparent.* *To get myself out of the way so the Word of God can be alive for me and those who hear me read. To speak so that through my voice the voice of God can be heard. To be a window through which others can see God's presence in our world.*

So what does that mean? If it's the Word of God I should get myself totally out of the way? How? Does that mean I shouldn't mess with it at all but just read it in a flat monotone and never ever try to *"interpret"* it as I read it aloud?

Uh-uh. No. No way. If you read it in a flat voice you *are interpreting it.* If you read it that way, what you're saying is "This is the Word of God and I think it's as boring as sin because all it can get out of me is this flat monotonous drone." You may not *think* you're interpreting it. But that's the message you're getting across. And talk about getting yourself out of the way. Think about this. You're so much in the way that you've turned off the very people who just heard you from thinking there's anything at all *meaningful* or *interesting* or *alive* about the Word of God. Hear? *The Word of God!*

If you take getting yourself out of the way seriously, you need to work at it. And pray at it.

> Variations on a theme. My ministry for the past three decades has been, in part, one of teaching: how to use the voice, interpretative skills applied to reading Scripture and leading worship, and the like. In all these years of teaching, I've heard comments like these addressed to the matter of learning technique:
>> "In my tradition, we don't interpret the Scripture reading. We just read it 'straight' and let God interpret it for the listeners."
>> "But I don't want to look phony and display a lot of technique. I just want to be natural."
>> "But God called me, so God must be able to use me just exactly as I am."
> Every day I pray a little prayer that goes something like this: "Lord, I thank you that you love us enough to accept us just as we are. But I thank you more that you love us too much to leave us that way."

Technique. You need to be aware of all the things that could get in God's way. Like using a voice no one can hear beyond the first row. Like muffled consonant sounds that garble words. Like misplaced pauses and awkward emphases that keep people from making sense out of what you're saying. There are various *techniques* a good reader or speaker has to learn. But remember, you don't learn technique in order to go out in public and display technique. The polar opposite of the abovementioned drone is the person who's so aware of his craft that he displays it like a flashy salesman. You learn technique so you can sublimate technique, not show it off. You learn it so it becomes a part of you. A part that's unselfconscious. A part that makes God say about your reading, "Well done!" I didn't say *other people* are going to say that. You're not doing this for other people. You're doing it for the One whose Word you're sharing with those other people.

Try this for an analogy. A concert pianist is planning to play a concerto by Sergei Rachmaninoff. As part of her preparation she goes through a bunch of piano exercises by Hanon and Czerny to give her the dexterity and skill (technique) she needs. She's never going to go out on stage in Carnegie Hall and play Hanon and Czerny. But because she's mastered Hanon and Czerny her

Rachmaninoff will be brilliant! Note a couple of things here. First of all, she's not thinking even the teeniest tiniest bit about Hanon and Czerny when she's playing Rachmaninoff. She's concentrating 100% percent on Rachmaninoff. Second of all, she didn't prepare for her concert by sitting in a comfortable chair and reading Sergei's score. She got up. She went to the piano. She sat down. And she practiced Rachmaninoff. Lots. Good enough to present it in public.

You do have to master technique. But you don't get up on Sunday to read from the Gospel of John and stand there thinking about voice and diction, because if you do you're going to communicate something other than the Gospel of John. You're going to communicate that you're a person who's concentrating on voice and diction. Whatever your mind is focused on is what you're going to communicate. So do whatever technical work you need to do on voice and diction. During the week. But then on Sunday focus at least 100% on the Gospel of John and pray for grace that the work you did on voice and diction will kick in. It will, eventually. Remember who you prayed to. And remember who gives the grace you asked for. And please hear me. *You need to practice. Out loud.* You can't just sit there and go over it in your head. You need to do some of that, for sure. But you also need to stand up, check your breathing, and go through the paces. You *need* to do that. If you don't, it will show. And I sure won't come back next week to hear you.

Instruments of Grace. Someone once said that the best singer (caution: I'm changing the analogy!) is not the one who sings the song well, but the one who lets *the song sing itself through her*. In the first case, the singer gets all the glory. In the second, the song gets the glory. See how that applies to what you're doing when you read God's Word? You're trying to let *it* take over. Don't even *you* try to get yourself out of the way. Leave that to God. Grace again. Give yourself to the Word as you prepare it. Then give yourself and the task of reading totally to God. Absolutely surrender the situation into the hands of God. God's not going to let you down. That's a promise.

Just remember: *any* time *anyone* reads the Word aloud, there is *interpretation* going on. God is using us clay vessels as instruments. I've often told my students to think of themselves as musical instruments. Well-tuned, they can sound like a Stradivarius. Untuned, they might sound like a ten-cent-store special. You and I need to work a bit on self-tuning. But ultimately we need to hand the instrument over to the Lord to *play* us. I like the sentiment in Wayne Watson's song *The Touch of the Master's Hand*. Even an old dusty violin up for a two-dollar bid can pull in a couple of thousand after it's been loved by the Master's Hand. Another way of saying this would be to affirm that there is interpretation going on every time we read, but *it shouldn't be our interpretation at all*. William Cowper (1774) said it best in the hymn *God Moves in a Mysterious*

Way, when he wrote: "God is His own interpreter and He will make it plain." It's wonderful when God lets that happen *through us*.

Not the Law & the Gospel!—Just Some DOs & DON'Ts

Your word is a lamp to my feet and a light for my path.
I have taken an oath and confirmed it, that I will follow your righteous laws.
I have suffered much; preserve my life, O Lord, according to your word.
Accept, O Lord, the willing praise of my mouth, and teach me your laws.
Though I constantly take my life in my hands, I will not forget your law.
The wicked have set a snare for me, but I have not strayed from your precepts.
Your statutes are my heritage forever; they are the joy of my heart.
My heart is set on keeping your decrees to the very end.
I have hidden your word in my heart that I might not sin against you.
Praise be to you, O Lord . . . . (Psalm 119:105-112, 11-12a)

Father, I don't know where you are taking me, but I rejoice that you do lead me by the light of your Word. Thank you for the wisdom only you can give, the truth that is the joy of my living. I praise you that you trust me to proclaim your Word to the hungry hearts and minds of my brothers and sisters. I freely give myself to you that your Word may dwell within me. In the name of the Lord Jesus. Amen.

Much of what I've taught my students about reading Scripture has come from my experience as a pastor and leader of worship. Some of it has come from erudite editions on the oral interpretation of literature. But not much. A lot of it is just plain common sense. Problem is, we don't always use that common sense. For example, when our task is teaching or preaching based upon the Word, we sometimes fit a passage into the category of RATIONAL THOUGHT and neglect the other facets of a passage. So let's start here, and look at some possible *DOs and DON'Ts* to guide us as we prepare to read.

First of all, there's more to a passage than the rational knowledge it contains. Yes, it's important to go to the commentaries and find out what all the best minds have to say about the passage. And yes, it's important for you to grasp ratiocinatively (look that one up) the words you're reading. But remember, you're not just *reporting* objective information. If it's really the Word of God, and if it's really God's Word speaking to *you*, then you have to reveal to your hearers something of your *investment* in that Word. In other words, it's not just any old *words*, it's the holy *Word of God* you're giving voice to. Let it speak to your head. But let it speak to your heart too. To your gut. Where you live. Pray, as you study it, that it will reveal itself to you and come to life within you in such a way that it will reach into the lives of others.

Summary:

Don't limit your encounter with the passage to one of *rational thought* only (as if you were going to "report" the material but had no particular investment in it.)
Do seek a oneness with the text until you get a "gut feeling" for what it's saying. Let it move from head to *heart*. *PRAY THAT IT WILL COME TO LIFE THROUGH YOU.*

✠　　✠　　✠

Try to approach your passage with a totally open mind. Preachers sometimes go looking for a passage to use as a "proof text" (they wouldn't call it that, but they'd do it) for whatever message they wanted to convey. All of us need to be careful that we haven't judged beforehand what we're going to let a passage say to us. Open your mind and your heart to the passage and let the Lord say a few things to you before you start talking back. Prepare yourself to be creatively led by the Holy Spirit. Prepare to encounter exciting thoughts, astonishing tales, moments that may move you to tears—or cheers! Prepare to *enjoy*—yes, have *fun* with your encounter with God's Word! First of all, just sit there and read the passage. Now reread it. Do it again. And again, until it starts to whisper in your ear, "Yeah, I'm talking to *you*!"

Whenever I read Scripture in worship I'll look at every translation I can get my hands on: the RSV, the NRSV, the KJV, the NIV, the Jerusalem Bible, the New English Bible, and anything else I can find. What I'm looking for is not any one particular set of words, but *the substance* those various sets of words are trying to give voice to. Words on the page are nothing but dry ink. It's the *life* (the thought, the story, the feeling) those words are pointing to that I want to get hold of. I'm not called to master a particular set of words. I'm called instead to be mastered by the Word.

One other thing I've found helpful is to read the passage in my Swedish Bible. You may know German, or French, or Spanish or some other language that will give you insights not found in any English language translation. Here are a couple examples of "light bulb moments" I've gotten from the Swedish.

(1) The story of Belshazzar's Feast (Daniel, chapter 5, KJV) begins like this:

> Belshazzar the king made a great feast to a thousand of his lords *and drank wine before the thousand.* (italics mine)

The KJV is very polite, and so are we when it comes to not suspecting there could be much of anything *earthy* going on in the Bible, and so we probably imagine the scene to be one of polite wine-sipping with hors d'oeuvres and canapes. But the Swedish translation gives us another picture. The phrase "and drank wine before the thousand" in Swedish is: "och höll dryckeslag med de tusen"—literally, "and had a drinking bout with the thousand." Totally different picture, folks! This was not some polite scene. Imagine Hagar the Horrible getting sloshed and you come closer to what was going on!

(2) A little way into the same story, a new character comes into the story:

> Now the *queen*, by reason of words of the king and his lords, came into the banquet house.

Belshazzar's wife? No, his mother. Which you'd find out if you looked in a commentary or two. Or simply read the passage in Swedish where the word for "queen" is "kungamodern": *queen mother.* The Swedes are very specific about relationships. For example, *farfar* and *farmor* = paternal grandfather and grandmother; *morfar* and *mormor* = maternal grandparents. Does that make a difference to Belshazzar? Yes. To the story? Yes, because his *mother* sends him searching for the prophet Daniel who was hanging out during the reign of his father Nebuchadnezzar, so she knew from firsthand experience what she was talking about. Besides, when you read her lines, you ought to be able to distinguish who you are as that character—his mother, and not his wife.

(3) Elijah, on Mount Horeb (1 Kings 19:12, RSV), hears "a still small voice" and in that voice is the presence of the Lord. Haven't you always imagined that that little voice was God saying something like, "Shape up, Elijah, and get your act together"—or some such bunch of *words*? In the Swedish, that "still small voice" is "en sakta susning": *a gentle sighing.* Isn't that wonderful? No words at all, just a sighing. You know what I immediately connected with when I read that? Romans 8:26, (RSV):

> . . . We do not know how to pray as we ought, but the Spirit himself intercedes for us with sighs too deep for words.

It's the sighing of the presence of the Holy Spirit!

Summary:

Don't approach Scripture with a closed mind, unwilling to give it any but the preconceived interpretation you have *superimposed* on it, telling it what it's supposed to be saying.
Do approach Scripture with an open mind. Read, *reread*, and *reread again*. Let *it* say something to you. Try various translations, other languages.

✠   ✠   ✠

All Scripture should not *sound* alike. If you could record several readers, some reading Scripture and others reading any secular material, and then distort the content so you could hear only the speech rhythms, do you think you could tell which readers were reading Scripture and which were not? I'll bet a penny you could. For some odd reason, when we read Scripture we often leave it on some high and lofty shelf labeled "The High and Holy Word of the Lord" and we never get down to earth with it. God's Word didn't stay up on a heavenly shelf. He became incarnate. And that's what our readings should do. You don't want to go from "natural mode" into "pontifical mode" just because you're reading the Bible. Remember it's the Word-come-down-to-earth, the Word among us and for us. Read it as you would any other literature. Look up words you don't fully understand and pronunciations you're not 100% sure of. (There's certain to be someone in your audience who will *know* you've mispronounced that word!) Paraphrasing is one of the best ways of making the "words" your own. When I was a pastor in an inner-city church in Indianapolis, we had a Friday morning Bible study that was remarkable. A passage was chosen, and each of us wrote our own paraphrase of it, using none of the original words (except for proper names, articles, etc.). Then we'd share our own "translation" of the passage with one another. What a great process for making the Word become a part of *you* so that as you read the text your mindset is on *telling us* the Good News!

Summary:

Don't prepare to *read Scripture* as though all Scripture sounded alike (and unlike a sensitive reading of any other literature). Best if you don't even think "I'm *reading Scripture*" but instead think "I'm *telling the story*" or "I'm *sharing the thoughts*." For God's sake, don't pontificate!
Do approach with a literate mind. What *kind* of literature is this? Look up words you may not understand, pronunciations you're not *sure* of (check a good dictionary of the Bible). Get hold of *connotative* as well as *denotative* meanings. Translate words into fresh, living ideas. *Paraphrase*, putting the ideas into your own words.

✠   ✠   ✠

When we read *any* kind of material *aloud*, it's easy for us to fall into certain speech patterns we don't normally use (e.g., were we to *say* the same thing rather than reading it). This can be a special problem when we read Scripture aloud. Two of the most common patterns are *"holy tone"* and *"teacups."*

First, there's **_holy tone_**. Possibly because we're influenced by certain models, or because we think God's "holy Word" should somehow *sound* "holy" (however you do that!) we lapse into a "holy tone" (sometimes called *stained glass voice* or *monastery moan*). It's hard to reproduce this in writing, but it would sound something like this:

"Heeeear the Word of Gawwwd as written in the book of Gennnnnesissss . . . "

You can get the general effect if you stick your head inside an empty wastebasket and say

"Innnnn the begiinnnnnnnng, Gawwwd created the heav'nnnnnnnns annnnd the earrrth . . . . "

It's as if you'd suddenly ceased being a normal human being and stepped up to read the Bible with

the word GOD stamped on your forehead.

Next, **_teacups_**. Just imagine a cupboard shelf with a row of upside-down teacups on it. It would look something like this:

/ \ / \ / \ / \ / \ / \ / \ / \ / \ / \ / \ / \ / \ / \ / \ / \ / \ / \

If you can translate that visual image into *sound*, imagine a rising pitch with every / and a falling pitch with every \. It easily becomes an inflection pattern we get locked into when we *read*. We wouldn't normally use it in *speaking*, but it can become a major pitfall for many beginning readers (and a lot of old hands, too). At the beginning of a phrase the pitch rises, and then falls again at each pause (usually each comma). Look, for example, at this passage from Isaiah 9:6:

For to us a child is born, to us a son is given; and the government will be upon his shoulder, and his name
will be called "Wonderful Counselor, Mighty God, Everlasting Father, Prince of Peace."

The very way it's laid out on the page in most Bibles might alert one to the problem. Most of the time it's written like this:

For to us a child is born,
    to us a son is given;
and the government will be upon
        his shoulder,
    and his name will be called
"Wonderful Counselor, Mighty
        God,
Everlasting Father, Prince of
        Peace."

With a little imagination (or maybe a very vivid imagination!) you can almost see the "teacups" coming. The pitch goes up, and then comes down—up then down, up and down, like this:

```
        us a              a son        government will be              name will
    to      child is   us      is       the          upon his    his        be
For             born, to         given; and              shoulder, and          called


        ful Coun          ty              ing                    of
    der      sel     /    God      last  Fa          /      Peace
"Won             or, Migh     \, Ever         ther, Prince      \."
```

Because a falling inflection generally indicates the conclusion of a thought, *sound*-wise, this pattern has the effect of one dishing out conclusion after conclusion. Any feeling of progression or building towards a climax is totally lost. If you can catch yourself falling into this pattern, try simply keeping the inflection in suspension until you come to the very *end* of the thought, and then let the inflection fall.[1]

> I once was working with a student who simply couldn't *hear* the difference between a rising and a falling inflection. In fact, we were working on this Isaiah passage. Finally I got him to *sing*: "for to us a child *'Maria...',*" to the tune of the song from *West Side Story*. Once he heard that rising pitch interval in the first three notes of the song, he caught on to the idea of rising inflection.

A lot of folks get into the teacup pattern in preaching, and it sounds—well, *preachy*! Don't tell yourself when you read Scripture, "Now I'm going to try to sound like a pastor." (Say what?) Or like a teacher, or evangelist, or any other "type" of communicator. Just be yourself, and let the word come alive through you. Use your imagination to internalize the text. Jump in feet first, and give it your all.

Summary:

> Don't submit Scripture to your habitual speech or reading patterns. (Watch out for *stained glass voice* or *monastery moan*, inflection patterns such as *teacups*, and so forth.) Don't try to fit every passage into some "theological bag" or confine it to whatever image you may have of a minister / communicator. Submerge your personality to become a servant of God's Word. Do read Scripture with imagination. If it's a *story*, let the drama come alive, in technicolor, in your mind's eye. *See it happening*, and try to communicate that *picture* to your listeners. Are you sharing *thoughts? Think the thoughts*, and bring them to life—thoughtfully. Is it heavily *emotional? Feel the feelings*, voicing them as you respond to them.

When I get up to read Scripture in the worship service, I need to remember it's God's Word to *all* of us, including me. Maybe even *especially* me, chief of all miserable sinners. God doesn't do things by accident, remember. God just plain doesn't do coincidences! Whenever the Word is read or preached, it's addressed to everyone—not just to the folks out there in the congregation, but to the reader and preacher as well. I need to ask myself, Why has the Lord put this text at this moment in my hands? To share with others? Certainly. But he must think I need it most of all. He must want to implant this particular message in my heart and my mind, for some reason known only to him. So even as I lead others in worship, I can't forget I myself am a part of the worshipping community. I know it's hard to focus on worshipping sometimes when I'm up in the chancel and my mind is on what's coming up next in the service and do I do it or does someone else do it? But I don't want the fact that I'm helping lead worship right now to become for me a distancer that sets me apart from the very Word I'm sharing with others. It is God's message to *me*. I need to hear that Word speaking to me. I need to be receptive to that Word. I need to know it's no ordinary bunch of words. I need to be excited by what God's saying to *me*. If I'm not excited, that's going to show in my reading. This is especially true of those passages I've known since I was a tad. I need to look them over with an extra careful eye to see what's new there I haven't noticed before. *Nothing* is old hat here. God's Word is always new and always renewing. How am I going to respond if I really *believe* these words I'm speaking?

Summary:

Don't read Scripture as if its message were intended for everyone in the congregation—but not for *you*. It's probably intended *especially* for you, or God wouldn't have "happened" to put the passage in your hands. Ask yourself as you study the passage: What is God trying to get through to *me* in this particular passage?

Do read with a receptive mind. Read it as though it were written for *you*, as though were reading it for the first time. Expect it to inspire and excite you—then think what it could do for your listeners! Read it with a responsive mind. Ask yourself: What would I do if I took this seriously? Would I *see* persons or situations differently? Would I *do* anything differently?

✠   ✠   ✠

In only a tiny way am I "responsible for" the Word I'm going to read. Of course I want to do it well. I don't to make a spectacle of myself and flub my way through the reading. I'll need to speak up, enunciate, understand what I'm saying, pronounce words correctly, and master as well as I can any other technical aspects of the job God's asking me to do. I could even get a master's degree or a Ph.D. in speech communication. In terms of my preparation, there's no overkill. But I need to remember, *I'm not "responsible for" this Word. God is.* Once I've given my all in the way of preparation, I need to give the job back to God. My job now is to become *TRANSPARENT to the Word.* Not *responsible*, but *RESPONSIVE*, so God can bring that Word to life within me. I'm not called to an act of performance so much as I'm called to an act of devotion, of surrender, of total abandon to the Living Word of God.

Summary:

Don't think of yourself as being "RESPONSIBLE for" the Word. *GOD is, not you!!!!!*
Do let yourself be "RESPONSIVE to" the Word! LET IT COME TO LIFE IN YOU! Better yet: *LET IT BRING YOU TO LIFE! Pray some more!!!!!*

---

[1] *"Teacups" can totally frustrate the life and motion of ideas being presented. Each falling inflection stops the flow of ideas as surely as someone traveling down a highway and braking to a stop every thirty seconds. Ideas move and progress. As we give voice to them, our voices should reveal that movement and progression. The ending of the well-known Philippians 2:1-11 passage is an excellent example of the difference "teacups" can make. With falling inflections (\ \ \) the ideas lie fallow:*

> Therefore God exalted him to the highest place\ and gave him the name that is above every name,\
> that at the name of Jesus\ every knee should bow,\ in heaven\ and on earth\ and under the earth,\
> and every tongue confess\ that Jesus Christ is Lord,\ to the glory of God the Father.\

If, however, you leave the inflections alive (~ ~ ~) until the ending, the ideas move and progress to a glorious crescendo of praise:

> Therefore God exalted him to the highest place~ and gave him the name that is above every name,~
> that at the name of Jesus~ every knee should bow,~ in heaven~ and on earth~ and under the earth,~
> and every tongue confess~that Jesus Christ is Lord,~ to the glory of God the Father.\

Presence

He went to Nazareth, where he had been brought up, and on the Sabbath day he went into the synagogue, as was his custom. And he stood up to read. The scroll of the prophet Isaiah was handed to him. Unrolling it, he found the place where it is written:

> "The Spirit of the Lord is on me, because he has anointed me to preach good news to the poor.
>
> He has sent me to proclaim freedom for the prisoners and recovery of sight for the blind, to release the oppressed, to proclaim the year of the Lord's favor."

Then he rolled up the scroll, gave it back to the attendant and sat down. The eyes of everyone in the synagogue were fastened on him, and he began by saying to them, "Today this scripture is fulfilled in your hearing." (Luke 4:16-21)

Prayer: Lord, as I stand up to read your holy Word, guide me by your Holy Spirit, that through me your Word may come to life and be fulfilled in those who hear it. Let it be for us all the good news that frees us and heals us. In the strong Name of Jesus I pray. Amen.

It may sound contradictory, after saying the reader of Scripture should be *transparent* to the Word, to suggest you be a positive *presence* as a reader. Is the reader anything more than a voice speaking God's Word? Would a tape-recorded message be just as good? Obviously not. Whether you're ordained or a lay reader, you as Scripture reader are *ministering* through your reading. Therefore, there are several things to keep in mind regarding how you relate to your congregation.

> eye contact
> memorizing
> gesturing
> stance
> use of hands

Eye Contact. If your congregation does not read the Bible along with you, it's especially important to acknowledge your listeners as you speak. Look directly at them when you announce the Scripture lesson. Look at them—as much as possible and as much as is comfortable—as you read. If your congregation is accustomed to reading while you read, it still doesn't hurt to be an alive presence as you read. If you totally ignore them, you're likely to give less to your reading than you want to. And if you read well and expressively, they may come to prefer to look and listen as you read rather than following along in their Bibles.

A number of things need to be said about _eye contact_. A lot of people are puzzled about how to do it. And to be honest, some people do some pretty funny things in the name of eye contact. There's the "panner," swooping across the audience like a camera doing a panoramic view of the Great Plains. And there's the person who looks like someone watching a Ping-Pong tournament. Then there's the person who always favors the left side or the right side of the audience (and who'd probably be terribly surprised to look over at the non-favored side and see they'd all gone home!). You don't want to get all glassy-eyed and look like you're trying to take in the whole listening audience at once. Nor do you want to establish direct eye contact exclusively with one individual—(especially not when you're reading a line like "You snakes! You brood of vipers! How will you escape being condemned to hell?" or "Depart from me, you who are cursed, into the eternal fire prepared for the devil and his angels"—unless you know that individual _very well_). What I try to do is look up at a group of about three or four people, which looks a little more personal than the panoramic gaze, and move randomly through the audience so it doesn't look like I'm tracking in a particular pattern. And then for those really intense "repent or you'll burn in hell" moments, look down at the text and just read.

Head Movement. In addition to the side-to-side movements that can drive listeners up the wall, there's the robin-going-after-the-worm movement where the head goes bob-bob-bobbin' up and down to get the words and then look up. It looks something like this: ᴠᴠᴠᴠᴠᴠᴠᴠᴠᴠ. Tall people with short lecterns typically have the problem, but most of us indulge in it now and then. The trick is to have as direct a line as possible between your eyes, your text, and your audience. Try to get the text up as high as possible (pushed up to the top ledge of the lectern) or hold your Bible high enough (I'll say more on this in a moment) so you can look down and up with your _eyes only_ with as little gross head movement as you can manage. Try tucking the chin in slightly so the back of the neck is elongated. It should enable your movements to look more like ～～～～～～～ than like ᴠᴠᴠᴠᴠᴠᴠ. (One way to check whether or not there's too much head movement is to have someone videotape you and then play it back on fast forward. It really sets off any extraneous head, hand or body movements.)

What Kind of Passage? To a large extent, when and how you use eye contact depends upon the _kind of passage_ you're reading. With a passage that's predominantly _mental_ (like one of Paul's epistles), I'd try for as much direct eye contact as possible. What you're doing is sharing, directly, Paul's thoughts with your listeners. With an _empathic_ passage, I'd tend to look under or over the eyes of my listeners (or just plain not look up at all). I don't want to look directly at you and say, "O Lord, our Lord, how majestic is your name in all the earth!" or you're likely to have identity problems. With a *story* or *narrative* passage, you're going to keep busy playing narrator plus a whole cast of characters. When you're reading a narrative line, you're speaking directly to your audience as a storyteller would. But when you're reading the words of one of the characters, you've left off speaking to your audience and are now giving voice to the character (generally speaking to another character). So you want to look "in scene" (as if you'd suddenly become part of the story and were *character A* speaking to *character B*) and not at your audience. Look at a brief portion of the Naaman story for instance. The narrator is saying (directly to the audience):

> Naaman, commander of the army of the king of Syria, was a great man with his master and in high favor, because by him the Lord had given victory to Syria. He was a mighty man of valor but he was a leper. Now the Syrians on one of their raids had carried off a little maid from the land of Israel, and she waited on Naaman's wife. She said to her mistress,

At this point, the reader gives voice to the "little maid" and says:

> "Would that my lord were with the prophet who is in Samaria! He would cure him of his leprosy."[1]

As the reader, you want to stop glancing at your audience at this point. Otherwise it will appear as if Mrs. Naaman is moving around wherever your eyes happen to land, which will appear very odd. If you glance down, you make Mrs. Naaman about three feet tall. If you glance up, she's suddenly a basketball player. Your best bet is to look (rightish, leftish or forward) *on your own eye level (above the eyes of your audience)* at the imagined Mrs. N who is in the imagined scene with you. (Alternatively, you could simply keep your eyes on the text.) Of course, the more characters the more complicated it can get, but you simply want to *suggest* the character(s) looking at the other character(s). Remember, you're not *acting* the character, you're simply suggesting the scene with the characters in it.

<u>Open vs. Closed Circuit</u>. Whether you opt for eye contact or not, being prepared to open yourself up to your audience as you read is an important part of your preparation. When you first begin practicing reading aloud, try this: Mark your passage into phrases you can easily and comfortably memorize. That's right, I said "memorize!" Don't try, for goodness' sake, to memorize:

> Belshazzar the king made a great feast to a thousand of his lords, and drank wine before the thousand.[2]

It's too long. Unless God has blessed you with a phenomenal memory, you'll never make it—and you'll lose your concentration on *what* you're reading because you're worried about *how* you're going to get through it. Instead, break it up:

Belshazzar the king //	[now look up and say it to your lamp shade]
made a great feast to a thousand of his lords //	[same]
and drank wine before the thousand. //	[same from here on]
Belshazzar, whiles he tasted the wine //	
commanded to bring the golden and silver vessels //	
which his father Nebuchadnezzar //	
had taken out of the temple which was in Jerusalem //	
that the king, and his princes //	

his wives and his concubines //
might drink therein.

Let's talk about what's happening here. First of all, it's going very slowly and you're going to be very frustrated and want to rush it. Don't. If you go through this procedure once a day for a week before you read it on Sunday, you'll gradually pick up speed. It's important to go slowly enough so you can *trust yourself* you're going to get it right (without fudging and looking back down at the text). Using a tape recorder to monitor yourself can be helpful here. Read your passage through and then play the tape back to double-check yourself for accuracy. In addition to the pace feeling slow, it will feel to you that with all those pauses the reading is sounding very broken up. To your listener, it will not sound that way. Your listeners will appreciate the fact that you're giving them time to appropriate what they're hearing *as they're hearing it* simply because your pace is more relaxed. Eventually you'll sense that too when you listen to your tape recording. With this technique, you'll notice a number of nice things happening. You probably won't sound like you're <u>reading</u> (as in your first shot at a Dick and Jane book) because you're not looking at the *words* as you speak them—you're speaking them from inside your *brain* instead, and your speech should take on the rhythm and flow you'd use in naturally relating the material to someone else. Then you'll find when you do read on Sunday you know the passage so well (after all, you've been memorizing it in bits and pieces) you'll have done a fantastic job of *internalizing* it—and that's what it's all about, really, isn't it? And all of this is going to be true whether you ever actually look up on Sunday morning or not. Your reading is going to be better!

So look up when you can, but don't feel as if the world's coming to an end if you don't. And there are definitely times when you should *totally ignore eye contact*, for the sake of the flow and movement of the reading. For example, the indented lines above:

which his father Nebuchadnezzar had taken out of the temple which was in Jerusalem

function as an "aside" within the main thought:

Belshazzar, whiles he tasted the wine, commanded to bring the golden and silver vessels . . .
that the king and his princes, his wives and his concubines, might drink therein.

As you read, you'll want to move fairly quickly through that aside to keep the main thought alive. Similarly, if you're reading something where the action, the thought, the mood is sprightly, *move with the material* and don't bother with eye contact. In any case, use your best judgment. Try to be as present as you can, but don't let the Word suffer just because you're trying conscientiously to have eye contact.

Memorizing Scripture. Now let's go back and pick up a few loose ends I left hanging along the way. First, a word about ***memorizing.*** The process described above uses memorization as an end to learning the material well enough that you can look up now and then when you want to. You may also want to memorize the *ending* of a passage so you can look up and speak it directly to the congregation. A couple of examples of the effectiveness of this would be:

> Wait for the Lord; // <u>be strong and let your heart take courage; yea, wait for the Lord</u>.* *(Psalm 27, RSV)*

Here, in the last line of the psalm, the psalmist breaks off speaking to himself and "opens up" to the congregation the invitation to "be strong and take heart and wait for the Lord." (*Underlined words indicate where you'd look up.) Here's another:

> So he went down and dipped himself seven times in the Jordan according to the word of the man of God; // <u>and his flesh was restored like the flesh of a little child, and he was clean</u>. *(2 Kings 5:14)*

At the end of the Naaman story, your looking up to tell the congregation God's healing miracle took place can be a wonderfully powerful testimony (and not *just* the last line of a reading). You'll find numerous places like this in Scripture readings where the Word just wants to open itself out to your listeners and proclaim itself to them. What a joy when God lets this happen *through you!*

Now, suppose you're wondering about memorizing a whole passage. Maybe you weren't, but you might sometime. If it's a short piece (like Psalm 23 which you probably memorized as a child anyway), go for it if you want. But I wouldn't try to memorize an entire Scripture reading to be done during the worship service on Sunday morning. Why? For one thing, half of your concentration will be on the material and the other half on not forgetting. For another, it's likely to come across as a *tour de force* which calls more attention to itself ("Oh, look, she's memorized the Scripture reading—isn't that wonderful?") and to what a neat memorizer you are and takes away from our attention on the Word of God. Maybe you want to risk it, but I'd look out for thunderbolts from on high if I did that! Okay, memorize the Sermon on the Mount and present it Wednesday at Family Night, if you want to. That's fine. But don't do anything in the service of worship that's going to call attention to you and drag our attention from glorifying and praising God.

<u>*Gesturing*</u>. Something needs to be said about <u>*gesturing*</u> during a Scripture reading. There are always a few expressive souls who want to gesture while they're reading. The problem with this is it looks funny, at least most of the time. There you are with your head down, reading the text, and your arms are going east and west, and you look positively *disembodied*. So I wouldn't use gestures unless some spot in the material suggests looking up, away from the text, and putting your whole self into it. In over a quarter century of teaching, I've seen that done effectively—*once!* This was during a chapel service years ago, when Princeton Theological Seminary's Dean Elmer Homrighausen was reading from Acts, chapter 26. Dean Homrighausen (everyone called him "Homey") was a marvelously expressive person to begin with, and this exuberance naturally carried over into his reading of Scripture, which was always electric. These

were the words he was reading:

> And Agrippa said to Paul, "In a short time you think to make me a Christian!" And Paul said, "Whether short or long, I would to God that not only you but also all who hear me this day might become such as I am . . ."

and then the Dean looked up, paused, held his fists out, wrists together, and finished:

> ". . .—except for these chains."

You talk about powerful! But it takes a giant like Homey and a lot of the Holy Spirit to pull that off. Best to wait until you're a spiritual giant before you try this.

(Here's a suggestion: If you are a gesturer, or if you flat out can't keep your hands still, buy a pair of lead gloves. Just kidding! Here's a *serious* suggestion: Imagine you're preparing and doing the reading on *radio*. Then the only kind of "gesturing" you can do is *vocal gesture*. In other words, let the Word come alive through your voice only. It is a wonderfully rich instrument and God loves to use it!)

Another loose end that *has* to be dealt with is the amount of <u>*time for preparing the reading*</u>. Note that I began talking about working with eye contact during *a week's preparation* of the reading. Now I'm not naïve. I know that sometimes pastors get busy or lazy or whatever, and don't know until the week's partly gone what passages are going to be read. But I hope that doesn't happen very often, because you really need to live with a passage for as long as possible in order for it to come alive as you read it. So if you're going to read the passage yourself, pastor, we'll presume that *your* level of proficiency will enable you to get it all together in a matter of days. But if you're giving the passage to a layperson, or a student assistant, or someone else to read, please don't wait until the last minute. A week's preparation is not too long. The less amount of time a reader spends with the Word, the less fair it is to the reader, the listeners *and to the Word itself.* You think about whether God's going to be happy with you if you let that happen very often!

<u>*Stance*</u>. How you stand can add to your comfort and your listeners'. If you have a very narrow base (both feet together) you'll be as wobbly as one of those weighted balloon toys that go "boing" when you bop them. If your feet are too wide apart, you'll look like a stevedore or the Jolly Green Giant. If your feet are slightly apart but evenly behind the lectern, it's very easy to sway from side to side and make your listeners seasick. If you keep them slightly apart (your feet, that is, not your listeners) with one slightly behind the other you'll find it nearly impossible to sway, you'll have a good firm stance, and you can "lean into" or "back off" depending upon the intensity of the material you're reading. Try in general to keep the body in balance. If you stand as if you've "backed off" from your audience, you'll look a tad timid. This is called the "Help me!"

stance. If you stand with the body thrust forward, you may look as if you want to attack them. Especially if you stand with hands gripping the sides of the lectern, body jutting forward in "lunge" position, you're likely to look menacing. All of us hope you don't *intend* to look that way. If you lean your upper body on the lectern it looks as if you're too tired to stand up and the ushers may rush to your assistance. Your best bet is to stand tall, as if you're simply *relaxing upward towards the ceiling*. Try it. It's a most comfortable, relaxed position, and you'll be relating towards your listeners with a stance that looks good, friendly, and welcoming. (Furthermore, it's a stance that will help your breathing and your projection. But that's another chapter!)

Use of Hands. What about your <u>hands</u>? It looks and feels most natural if you just rest them lightly on the lectern where they're available to turn pages, keep your place, etc. If you need a reminder to keep the body aligned for good diaphragmatic breathing (see the chapter on breathing), place your hands beneath the front ledge of the lectern and *lightly* lift up. If you lift too strenuously, you'll be pushing the lectern over into the front row. I wouldn't do that. Just a gentle lift will do the trick. It will probably look awkward if you let your hands dangle at your sides. It creates a sort of Neanderthal image. If you stand with hands folded in front of you it may look as if you have to go to the bathroom. If you're very tall and the lectern can't be raised high enough for you, try holding your Bible in balance in one hand and turning pages with the other. It would not be a good idea to try this with that big lectern Bible. If you've typed your passage (as I often do for ease of reading) don't lift pages as you turn them. Subtly slide them to one side so they're not visible to your listeners.

With regard to every aspect of your physical presence, remember the word *transparent*. You want people to look not *at* you but *through* you to God and God's Word. You're not up front so everyone can admire how beautiful you look, no matter what your mother thinks. You're not there to call *any* kind of attention (good or bad) to yourself. Nor are you trying to prove what a great reader you are. What are you there for? You're there to testify to what a great God God is and what wonderful good news God's Word is for us! It's a ministry in which God blesses you. It's a ministry in which God uses you to bless others. Praise this great and faithful God!

<u>Let's sum up some of these suggestions</u>:
— As a reader, *be present* to your listeners. Don't do a "closed-circuit" reading, you and the text doing your thing and ignoring everyone else.
— Use *eye contact* appropriate to the kind of passage you're reading.
- <u>Mental</u>: *direct eye*

- <u>Empathic</u>: *indirect*
- <u>Narrative</u>: *direct on narration, "in-scene" on characters' lines*

— *Practice* your reading looking up from the text as you speak. The reading will flow more naturally and not sound "read."

— When the material moves in such a way that eye contact is difficult, *stay with the material.*

— The Scripture reading in worship is a *reading; you don't need to memorize it.*

— As a rule, *don't gesture* while you're reading.

— *Preparing a reading takes time.* Allow yourself a week, if possible.

— Don't let awkward *stance* or use of *hands* detract from the reading.

---

[1] *The story of Naaman the leper is from 2 Kings 5:1-14. I'm using the RSV here, since that's what I've used to teach this passage for several years. It's a fantastic story about how God can work wonders with us when we humble ourselves before him and let him lift us up!*

[2] *This story, Belshazzar's Feast, is found in the book of Daniel, chapter 5. The story runs over thirty verses, and I've been teaching a "cut" version that's helpful in introducing students to narrative or "story" passages of Scripture. This is from the KJV, which is a challenge to all of us since we don't speak "that language" any more. It's like talking Shakespearean. And, yes, it* does *say funny things like "whiles he tasted the wine," so stop thinking that's a typo.*

One other thought: Please don't look at the KJV examples and say, "Well, that's just the KJV's problem!" Modern translations have just as many hurdles and glitches to work through. Most of the examples I'm using are from the RSV or NRSV or NIV. Besides, don't develop an "attitude" towards the KJV. You may not want to use it all the time, but don't overlook the beauty of its language -- and the fact that a lot of your listeners will be more <u>familiar</u> with the KJV than with other translations.

Rubrics

On the morning of the third day there was thunder and lightning, with a thick cloud over the mountain, and a very loud trumpet blast. Everyone in the camp trembled. Then Moses led the people out of the camp to meet with God, and they stood at the foot of the mountain. Mount Sinai was covered with smoke, because the Lord descended on it in fire. The smoke billowed up from it like smoke from a furnace, the whole mountain trembled violently, and the sound of the trumpet grew louder and louder. Then Moses spoke and the voice of God answered him. (Exodus 19:16-19)

In that day the Lord will thresh from the flowing Euphrates to the Wadi of Egypt, and you, O Israelites, will be gathered up one by one. And in that day a great trumpet will sound. Those who were perishing in Assyria and those who were exiled in Egypt will come and worship the Lord on the holy mountain in Jerusalem. (Isaiah 27:12-13)

Prayer: Lord, you've called me to lead others in worshiping you. Help me take care of all the "important" elements. And help me just as much to consider the real importance of those "incidental" elements by which I guide people in their worship. For even as the trumpeter called the Israelites to tremble in fear in your presence, I am calling others to hear your Holy Word. And even as the shofar is sounded to usher in your day of redemption, I am calling others to an awareness of your redemption for their lives. Great and faithful God, I praise you and thank you and bless you that you trust me with this holy ministry. In my redeemer Christ's name I pray. Amen.

As worship leaders, you and I have the task of doing some things all worship leaders do, routinely, which too often come across *sounding* terribly routine. And that's the **rubrics** involved in every worship service done from the time you first participate in leading worship until the time you retire to Acapulco or Jesus comes, whichever happens first.

And what are "rubrics"? Traditionally, they're the little red words in a missal (or any liturgical book) that tell you what to do in conducting a worship service and how to do it. They're the little sentences with which we announce what's coming up next. The call to worship, the prayer, the Scripture reading, the offering—whatever. Things like:

> *Let us worship God.*
> *Hear the Word of God....*
> *Let us pray.*
> *Let us offer unto God....*

They're the things you will be saying Sunday after Sunday, Wednesday night after Wednesday night, week after week, year after year. And they will very very very soon become "old hat" to you. Things like reciting the multiplication tables in the fourth grade. Things like repeating the Lord's Prayer and the the Apostles' Creed and the Pledge of Allegiance and your social security number and your telephone number and your address and your birth date and your ATM secret code and things like that. And if you let them, they will become meaningless and stale and rote and totally worthless when it comes to leading people into the wonders and mysteries and delights of worshiping God the Father Almighty.

Calls to Worship. Let's begin with what we begin with when we begin a worship service—the Call to Worship. The way you say "Let us worship God" can inspire your listeners to respond, "Oh, wow! Here comes something terrific!" or "Oh, jeez, do we have to go through this again?" You call the shots. You set the tone. When you say "Let us worship God," you can communicate either "Let's do something fantastic and wonderful and awesome and better than Robert Redford" together or "Let's go squash ants in the gutter." It's all in your tone of voice. And in what's going on inside of you when you say the words. If you _think_ worshipping God is a fantastic and wonderful and awesome thing to do, then don't be afraid to let that come out in the way you _say_ "Let us worship God." Put in an exclamation point or three or a zillion at the end of that sentence and let it be a sentence that makes people respond "Hey, okay! That's a great idea!" As a worship leader you're engaged here in roughly the same kind of activity as the shofar-blower calling the Israelites to tremble before the presence of God at Mount Sinai. Or the muezzin at the top of the minaret calling untold thousands to stop what they're doing and worship Allah. So don't be coy or shy or low-key or low-blood-sugar about it. Say it with zest and zeal and zip. Say it as if you expected something absolutely fantastic to happen. And then maybe something fantastic _will_ happen.

And don't be afraid to do some "coaching" as a worship leader. I remember once, leading a congregation in a responsive call to worship, when I called "time out" and had them start again. Once more—with feeling. The call to worship began with me saying, "This is the day which the Lord has made." And then the congregation said, "Let us rejoice and be glad in it." Only they said it as if they were some corporate entity saying, "My gerbil just died." So I stopped them. And said, "Let's start again and say what we're saying as if we really meant it. Think about what you're saying: 'Let us _rejoice_ and be _glad_ in it!'" Of course, I felt like I was waving pompoms in their faces. But it just didn't seem right to me that they were saying those joyous words as if they were repeating a dirge. And I didn't think God liked it very much either. So we started again. And this time, they had smiles on their faces and smiles in their voices and they said the words as if they were going to have a really bang-up time. And I think God smiled a little too.

___Hear the Word of God.___ When you announce the Scripture lesson or lessons, you're going to set up a sense of expectation or non-expectation in the way you do it. If you say "Hear the Word of God as it is written in the Gospel according to St. Luke" as if you were saying, "Let's go have the angioplasty surgery and get it done with," you're bound to get a "Here we go again" response from your listeners. How about bearing in mind that this may be the very *first time* some of your listeners have ever heard the Good News about Jesus? And it may be the very *last time* you had a chance to share that Good News with them. Would that make a difference? Don't you sense some sort of urgency or excitement or "wow-ness" about sharing the Word of God with people? If you do, then let it come through in the way you invite them to listen to that wonderful Word of life!

A few more words about introducing the Word. Do you say "Hear the Word of the Lord" or "Listen for the Word of the Lord" before you read? Take into consideration what's happening at this moment in the worship service. You as a leader of worship have the authority to announce that the Word of the Lord is about to be heard. What you're saying is, "God is about to speak. Those who have ears, let them hear." God is taking the initiative and speaking to us, whether we understand fully or like what we hear or not. Whatever the case, we're going to *hear the Word of God.* Now if the Scripture reading is simply a volley of words in which some arcane meaning can be discovered only by some spiritual *cognoscenti*, then I guess I'll listen up and see if I can figure out which among all those words is the real Word of God. And then after it's all over someone will say, "Will the *real* Word of God please stand up?" And I'll turn to the person sitting next to me and say, "Shucks, Maude! I missed it again!" And she'll say, "Me too! I thought for sure it was a couple of them words in the second verse," and we'll walk out of the sanctuary saying, "Well, better luck next time." In case you can't tell, I vote for "Hear the Word of God."

And, presuming the Scripture lesson is identified in the worship bulletin, please don't think it necessary to tell us that the Old Testament lesson for today is from the book of Habakkuk, chapter 2, verses 8b through 19a. We can read that for ourselves. All you need to say is that it's from the book of Habakkuk. And pronounce it right.

Then there's the matter of what to say at the end of the Scripture reading. My preference is simply to end the reading (with a healthy pause, of course), look up at the congregation and announce: "The Word of the Lord," to which the people of God respond, "Thanks be to God!" But there are other closure statements that may be more comfortable and familiar to your worship tradition. Just be sure to think about what you're saying. Do you really want to say, "May God add a blessing to this reading" or is the reading of the Word in and of itself already a blessing? If you want to use the blessing idea, how about, "May God *bless to our understanding* this reading" or something like that? I once heard this: "Here ends the reading of the Scripture lesson. If you respond to these words they will become for you the Word of the living God." A little wordy, perhaps, but it does make you think. Believe it or not, there have been several occasions on which I've heard "Here ends (or *thus ends*) the Word of God." To which my response has to be, "Heaven help us!"

Let Us Pray. Maybe you mean it to communicate "Let us talk with our Lord and Savior Jesus" or "Let us enter into the throne room of the God who created the heavens and the earth." But what comes across is "Let us cry into our beer because God is dead and this is God's funeral." Can you not get into your voice the tone of joy and awe and mystery and wonder that leads us into God's gracious presence? I can't tell you *what* tone of voice you should use or *how* you should speak these words, but I can tell you whether or not you move me into expecting to experience something so totally extraordinary that I should fall to my knees and then rise up in victory. And if you don't have some kind of expectation that something fantastic is about to take place, I'm sure not going to conjure up that kind of expectation for myself.

As a worship leader, you have the authority to say, "Let us pray." It's not bossy. It's not a command. It's a bidding from you to the congregation to engage in prayer. (Incidentally, if we're asked to *join together* or *unite together* in prayer, are we about to become colluders in a repetitive redundancy?) What's wrong with "Shall we pray?" which sounds, perhaps, a little more democratic than "Let us pray"? There's probably nothing terribly *wrong* with it, except that it sounds as if you're asking us to vote. And there are likely to be some folks who won't *feel* terribly much like praying and you'll get voted down. It's roughly the equivalent of "Prayer, anyone?" and you're likely to find no takers. And then there was my wonderful, dear Canadian seminary classmate who invited us to "snuggle up to God in prayer." (Presumably after we'd all gone home and gotten our booboos and our teddies.)

And when you do lead in prayer, could you please let us hear what you're saying? Granted, you're talking to God and not to your congregation. But you're talking to God *on behalf of* your congregation. It's not as if you were telling God "I've got a secret" and shutting the rest of us out. If you're speaking to God on the behalf of all of us, for goodness' sake let all of us hear what you're saying to God. Chances are we're not going to stand up and challenge you and say, "Uh, God, I'd rather ask something a little different," but you are praying *for* us and *with* us and it would be very kind of you to let us in on the conversation. It is a corporate prayer. Let the corps hear what we're saying.

Let Us Offer Unto God. Same as above. Don't make it sound as if you're saying "You *must* pay the rent!" and expecting us to respond "I *can't* pay the rent!!" Let it convey the overtones of "The Lord loves a cheerful giver," and "Look what God has given to us! Now's our chance to give something back to this wonderful gracious God!!!"

Let Us Sing. Ditto. The announcement ought to be something roughly equivalent to "Let's hear it for *GOD!!!*" rather than the equivalent of "Will the owner of a Chevrolet Impala, license number ZXY231, please report to the parking lot. You left your lights on." Come to think of it, an announcement like that might just convey a bit of urgency. Shouldn't we be a little more *urge*-ent in singing praise to God?

Benediction. You are now about to send us all forth with a blessing from God. There are several matters to consider in doing this. First of all, are you ordained or a lay person? Traditionally, the ordained blesser blesses *you*, while the lay blesser blesses *us*. Like this:

> *Ordained*: May the grace of the Lord Jesus Christ, and the love of God, and the fellowship of the Holy Spirit be with *you* all.

> *Lay*: May the grace of the Lord Jesus Christ, and the love of God, and the fellowship of the Holy Spirit be with *us* all.

Note also that a *benediction* is not the same as an *ascription*. An ascription begins with, or contains, words such as "now unto him," or "unto the Father," or "unto God" followed by whatever it is that's being ascribed to God. This ascription, from Jude 24-25 (NIV) is typical:

> To him who is able to keep you from falling and to present you before his glorious presence without fault and with great joy—to the only God our Savior be glory, majesty, power and authority, through Jesus Christ our Lord, before all ages, now and forevermore! Amen.

Even though it "blesses" us with the nice things God is doing for us (e.g. keeping us from falling), its ultimate intention is to ascribe eternal glory, majesty and power and authority to God. This is usually followed by a benediction, such as the one above (from 2 Corinthians 13:14, NIV).

Finally comes the question about what to do with your hands. You have probably seen just about everything, most of which creates the impression that the one pronouncing the benediction doesn't know what to do with his or her hands. This is probably because the one pronouncing the benediction *doesn't* know what to do with his or her hands. There's the timid hand-barely-up gesture that says "I think I know the answer but I'm not really sure." And the "Heil Hitler!" gesture with the outstretched arm and hand in a kind of salute. And the one-hand-in-front with the other hand raised giving a "Can I please be excused?" gesture. And then there is the "Come fly with me" gesture with both arms outstretched à la Superman ready for takeoff.

The gesture I was taught (and the one that makes the most sense liturgically and theologically, I think) is that of the extended right arm, bent gracefully at the elbow, with right hand outstretched, fingers together, and gently cupped. It is the equivalent of the motion one would make in the *laying on of hands* at an ordination. Only now it is extended in blessing over the entire congregation.

And of course the words are pronounced thoughtfully and with meaning. The worship leader is in the act of bestowing a blessing from God Almighty upon these people who have come to worship. And to be blessed in order to be a blessing to others.

Beginnings and Endings. As you *begin* any part of the worship service—whether it be a call to worship, a Scripture reading, a prayer, a sermon, or announcements of any sort—try to do three things:

(1) Acknowledge your audience with a "Hello out there" glance before you start to speak. Otherwise you'll be speaking down to the lectern or pulpit, or into some impersonal sea of faces. These are your brothers and sisters in Christ. Be friendly!

(2) Breathe. Get the breathing process going correctly by *consciously* beginning diaphragmatic breathing. *As you take in that breath, take in the idea you're about to speak so you don't run the risk of "engaging mouth before engaging brain."*

(3) Expect God to do something—through you, to you, with you, and with everyone who's gathered there for worship.

At the *conclusion* of any part of the worship service, keep these things in mind:

(1) You've completed whatever element of the service you have needed to "perform." Now you're blessed with another moment of acknowledging the church family. If you have a concluding statement to declare (such as "This is the Word of the Lord"), don't make it a throwaway line. Announce it for the wonderful thing it is, as if you were saying "Can you believe that's God's good news for you and me?" (In other words, if you've begun with a sense of expectation, now you're communicating—perhaps nonverbally—that God is faithful and has blessed us again.)

(2) Use a healthy pause to put a "frame" around each part of the service. Otherwise the whole service can flow together into an amorphous blob, rather than a sequence of worship happenings with some order and individual meaning and purpose. Your adrenalin will probably kick in as you stand "up front" to do your thing. Don't let it push you over

the speed limit!

Caveat. Do not try to say any of these rubrics with zest or zeal or zing or zip *unless you feel that zest and zeal and zing and zip* in your heart and spirit and down to your toes. If you try to come across as the cheer leader leading worship when there's no spirit of cheer down deep inside you, you're going to come across as one big major phony. So if you're feeling like a deadhead, go ahead and talk like a deadhead. We're going to sense that anyway. But if you're feeling on fire with the Spirit of God, don't hesitate to let that Spirit fire up the way you lead us into worship. We *need* to feel that. Oh, how *desperately* we need to feel that fire inside us as we approach the throne of God! So if you're feeling that Spirit of joy and enthusiasm, please share it with us. And if you're not feeling it, get down on your knees and pray that that Spirit will revive your spirit and that that revival will spread into the hearts and minds and lives of everyone who hears you say, *"Let us worship God!!!"* If you ask it, *it will happen!*

Your Face Is Showing!

Now Stephen, a man full of God's grace and power, did great wonders and miraculous signs among the people. Opposition arose, however, from members of the Synagogue of the Freedmen (as it was called)—Jews of Cyrene and Alexandria as well as the provinces of Cilicia and Asia. These men began to argue with Stephen, but they could not stand up against his wisdom or the Spirit by whom he spoke.
Then they secretly persuaded some men to say, "We have heard Stephen speak words of blasphemy against Moses and against God."
So they stirred up the people and the elders and the teachers of the law. They seized Stephen and brought him before the Sanhedrin. They produced false witnesses, who testified, "This fellow never stops speaking against this holy place and against the law. For we have heard him say that this Jesus of Nazareth will destroy this place and change the customs Moses handed down to us."
All who were sitting in the Sanhedrin looked intently at Stephen, and they saw that his face was like the face of an angel. (Acts 6:8-15)

Prayer: O blessed Lord, to think that you can fill mortal beings with your grace and your power! To think of your great wonders and miraculous signs in our very midst! As I lead others in worshipping you, inspirit me with your wisdom that flies in the very face of human wisdom. Give me courage to believe and speak the Gospel that tears down the temple and fulfills the law and the prophets. And even though no one will say of me, "That one has the face of an angel," let me be so filled with your grace that those who see my face may see right through me to your holy Presence. Let me be to others the presence of the Risen Christ. In the name of the Word made flesh who dwells among us to save us, even Jesus Christ our Lord. Amen

This is just a little bit on how we present ourselves from the neck up. That's the part of us that most people are interested in, and we ought to be aware of what it is that we're presenting to others.

If you ever have a chance to see yourself on videotape, jump to it. It will give you a no-holds-barred view of what your face is saying. And sometimes it doesn't say the same thing your mouth is saying.

The Happy Face. Some people come across as such nice people they must take "nice pills" every morning when they get up. They always have a wonderful friendly smile. And that's great. As long as what you're saying is something to smile about. I've seen students get up and preach about "sin and degradation" with such a big smile you'd think sin and degradation was just the best thing you could ever imagine! So be careful that your face doesn't say "Isn't that wonderful, folks?" when your voice is talking about something you shouldn't be smiling about.

The Deadpan. Some people are so stone-faced, you can't tell a thing by their facial expression about how they feel about what they're saying. You can't tell whether they're happy or sad or what. Usually, unfortunately, they don't convey much feeling with their voices either. Think about your message. How do you feel about it? Let us see in your eyes the fire or the light or the sorrow or the anger or whatever it is you're talking about! I've often videotaped students reading from Galatians, chapter 6. When they get to verses 7 and 8, they read (RSV):

> Do not be deceived; God is not mocked, for whatever a man sows, that he will also reap. For he who sows to his own flesh will from the flesh reap corruption; but he who sows to the Spirit will from the Spirit reap eternal life.

Invariably, you get someone announcing we're going to have eternal life as if he was announcing the sinking of the Titanic. (And usually, in the same session, you'll have old Smiley-Face announcing that "we're going to reap *corruption!! Whoopee!*")

The Fuzzy Face. A dear friend of mine used to wear a full beard. This man has the most wonderful sense of humor, and along with it the knack for telling a knockout joke with all the finesse of the best standup comic you ever heard. Plus a phenomenal sense of wit and wisdom. After he'd sported his beard for several years, he decided to shave it off. When he did, people started saying things like, "Eliot, we could never tell before whether you were kidding or were serious! Now we can tell—we can see it in your face!" So if you have a beard, or even a mustache, you need to be aware that facial hair can *mask* your facial expressiveness. Even if you're a person who's naturally expressive, that fuzz on your face will tend to turn everything into understatement. Which means that if you want your face to reveal what's going on in your head, you're going to have to try harder.

But Don't Try Too Hard. While you do want a modicum of awareness of your facial expressiveness, you don't want to come across as plastic—whether that's in the form of a painted-on smile or some sort of grimace over the sin and degradation you're warning us about. For goodness' sake, don't choreograph your manuscript or your margin with notes like "smile here" or "look worried." You'll only succeed in coming across as over-rehearsed, non-spontaneous, canned, and probably phony. If you know you tend to smile (or frown or be deadpan) all the time, put a little yellow sticky thing up in the top corner with a note to yourself. But don't let facial awareness be all-consuming. Remember, what's going on in your head is what you're going to communicate. You can be reading Scripture for all you're worth, but if you're thinking about what to do with your face, people will say, "She's thinking about what to do with her face!" Therefore, do not rehearse in front of a mirror. It will lead to the ultimate in self-consciousness. You'll wind up mugging. Just you and the mirror going at it together. That's a lot different, by the way, from working with a video camera turned on you. You can, if you try, ignore the camera and communicate with the real or imagined audience in front of you—while the camera just "happens" to look on.

More Than Words. Something must be said here about the *power* of facial expressiveness. Words can of course move people to action, to tears, to faith, to rejoicing. But if the face and eyes are not communicating along with the words—*or even when there are no words*—then something's lost in the translation. Let me give you a couple of examples. You'll think of a lot more.

Example One. The end of the story of Peter's denial (Luke 22:61-62, RSV):

> And Peter remembered the word of the Lord, how he had said to him, "Before the cock crows today, you will deny me three times." And he went out and wept bitterly.

Scenario One: The reader speaks the words intelligently, but there is no facial expressiveness, and the ending sounds something like: "And he went out and wept bitterly here ends the reading of God's holy Word."

Scenario Two: The reader, visualizing the story as she reads, sees Peter as he remembers the Lord's words.

> And Peter remembered the word of the Lord, how he had said to him, "Before the cock crows today, you will deny me three times."

Her eyes reflect the horror and compassion she feels for Peter and what he's done. She watches as he goes out. Sees him weeping.

> And he went out and wept bitterly.

Her eyes mirror the agony in his eyes. She continues to watch as the scene fades very slowly to black. Then her entire body relaxes a bit. She focuses upon her audience: "Here ends the reading of God's holy Word."

Example Two. The end of Psalm 27 (vv. 13-14, RSV):

> I believe that I shall see the goodness of the Lord in the land of the living!
> Wait for the Lord; be strong, and let your heart take courage; yea wait for the Lord!

Scenario One: Reader reads the words intelligently and with some expression, but there's no expression on the face except for wondering what comes next in the service. Ends with: "The Word of the Lord" as he reaches for his hymnal.

Scenario Two: Reader experiences in his heart the goodness of the Lord as he reads:

> I believe that I shall see the goodness of the Lord in the land of the living!

As the words are expressed, he is smiling. He's saying, "You betcha I believe!!" *With his eyes!!!* He looks directly to his audience with the longing of a parent or a pastor.

> Wait for the Lord; be strong, and let your heart take courage ...

He pauses, gathering in the entire congregation with his eyes.

> ... yea wait for the Lord!

He continues to look at them. With his eyes, he's saying "Just *do* it!!" After a moment, he speaks: "The Word of the Lord!" Another moment later, he hears the organist begin playing a hymn. He reaches for his hymnal.

Example Three. The end of the Naaman story (2 Kings 5:14, RSV):

> So he went down and dipped himself seven times in the Jordan, according to the word of the man of God; and his flesh was restored like the flesh of a little child, and he was clean.

Scenario One: Same, basically, as the others.

Scenario Two: Reader doesn't know what's going to happen, but is telling us as she sees Naaman go on down to the Jordan. She watches as he steps into the water. Continues to watch as he emerges. Her eyes glow with surprise and delight and wonderment and whatever else you want to think of as she notices Naaman's *cured*. And after she tells us

> and his flesh was restored like the flesh of a little child, and he was clean

her eyes stay with the scene for a moment and reveal what she's thinking—which is probably a combination of "Glory, hallelujah!" and "Yippee!!" and "Thank you, Jesus!" and "God does it again!!"

All I want to say is, the people in each "Scenario Two" are going to make people believe a lot more in grace and glory and blessing and, well, God than the "Scenario One" people whose eyes don't speak out.

Quirks. All of us have little facial habits, most of which we're probably not aware of. We may smile or frown too much, or "smack" our lips (or what I call "ironing" our lips—kind of pressing them flat), or squint or look bug-eyed, or lots of other things. Seeing ourselves on videotape can reveal to us what we're doing so we can change what we don't like. There are a lot of little quirks we can and should change. You don't want to play with your hair, or scratch your nose, or try to get a piece of spinach off your teeth, and you won't be tempted as long as you remember to keep your hands away from your face as much as possible. That "as much as possible" is a necessary caveat, since those of us with spectacles may find them slip-sliding down our noses and need to push them back up into place. If this happens too often, though—like between every syllable—you might try Elmer's glue. Or a thumbtack. Or maybe get your glasses adjusted so they fit a little better. Overall, it's not a bad idea to keep in mind that *you and I* are going to be most critical about those things we see *ourselves* doing—probably a lot more so than our audiences. So if you notice something about yourself that you're quite sure is going to get in the way of your most effective communication, then by all means do something about it. However, try to rest assured that *all of us* have little habits—facial and otherwise—that accrue from the fact that we're human and generally annoying in a lot of ways anyway. And *our* habits will probably bother *us* a lot more than they will our audiences. So fix what you think really needs to be fixed, and don't worry about the rest. Audiences can be most forgiving. On the other hand....

Adornment. Discretion is the better part of something when it comes to how much we should decorate ourselves when we're the object of an audience's attention. Especially if you're leading worship, you might want to err in the direction of being conservative. No black lipstick or green eye shadow. And probably no diamond in the nose. (Doesn't that hurt, anyway??) Choir directors used to tell the women in their choirs not to wear earrings. I don't know what they're saying nowadays in the age of pierced ears. Something subtle might be okay, but steer clear of something that looks like a Waterford chandelier in the grand ballroom. And speaking of pierced ears, what about guys? Do you stand out just a little bit with that one-inch gold hoop sticking out of your left earlobe?[1]

As with all other aspects of our communication skills, awareness is a key factor. So go ahead and become self-conscious (preferably for a brief season) about how and what you communicate from the neck up. But then try to forget about it. What's most important is that you communicate what's in your heart and in your head. Again, I'm preaching *passion*. If you believe in the Word and the words you're speaking to us—if you experience the joy, the grace, the very wonder that God's goodness has been lavished upon us—if you really believe that, then just let go. It'll come through in your voice and in your whole persona. And in your face. *We'll see it in your eyes!*

After all, look what they said about Stephen!

---

[1] *My brother Doug had this comment to make about earrings and such:*

> *Is your need to wear big, gaudy jewelry so great you're willing to let it get in the way of people hearing the Word of God? Is your identity as a stylish preacher more important than people focusing on the message? Because that's what happens when you show up with a nose ring, or whatever. It doesn't matter that it shouldn't matter. In reality, it does. Be a servant! Be a slave to Christ. Give up your own identity so it becomes more like Christ's.*

To which I could add only this: Amen!

Oral Interpretation of Scripture

The hand of the Lord was upon me, and he brought me out by the Spirit of the Lord and set me in the middle of a valley; it was full of bones. He led me back and forth among them, and I saw a great many bones on the floor of the valley, bones that were very dry. He asked me, "Son of man, can these bones live?"

I said, "O Sovereign Lord, you alone know."

Then he said to me, "Prophesy to these bones and say to them, 'Dry bones, hear the word of the Lord!

This is what the Sovereign Lord says to these bones: I will make breath enter you, and you will come to life. I will attach tendons to you and make flesh come upon you and cover you with skin; I will put breath in you, and you will come to life. Then you will know that I am the Lord.'"

So I prophesied as I was commanded. And as I was prophesying, there was a noise, a rattling sound, and the bones came together, bone to bone. I looked, and tendons and flesh appeared on them and skin covered them, but there was no breath in them.

Then he said to me, "Prophesy to the breath; prophesy, son of man, and say to it, 'This is what the Sovereign Lord says: Come from the four winds, O breath, and breathe into these slain, that they may live.'" So I prophesied as he commanded me, and breath entered them; they came to life and stood up on their feet—a vast army.

Then he said to me: "Son of man, these bones are the whole house of Israel. They say, 'Our bones are dried up and our hope is gone; we are cut off.' Therefore prophesy and say to them: 'This is what the Sovereign Lord says: O my people, I am going to open your graves and bring you up from them; I will bring you back to the land of Israel. Then you, my people, will know that I am the Lord, when I open your graves and bring you up from them. I will put my Spirit in you and you will live, and I will settle you in your own land. Then you will know that I the Lord have spoken, and I have done it, declares the Lord.'" (Ezekiel 37:1-10)

Prayer: Gracious Lord, breathe your Spirit into me as I read your Word to your people. Let the words come alive in me by your power, that your people will know you are the Lord, that they may truly live. And even as you use me and my voice, let us all know that you the Lord have spoken, and you have done it to the glory of your holy name. Amen.

**Reading Scripture Aloud**. Consider the many things that happen inside our heads when we read Scripture silently to ourselves. Thoughts come to life. Feelings emerge. Stories take on the flesh and blood of their characters, the settings appear in vivid color, the action moves along with varied pacing and pauses and changes of scene. In our imagination. All of it.

Now we're going to stand before other people and read God's Word aloud. And somehow, by grace, what happens in our imagination as we read silently has to happen in public. This means we need to know the material well, internalize it, so the thoughts we speak are clear, the emotions true to life, and the stories alive. I think I've already shown my hand sufficiently that you know I think it's a blessing for you and me to read Scripture to others. But if it's really to be a blessing *to them*, we need to prepare with care and intelligence so our reading isn't a slapdash affair. Here's what Paul Scherer wrote about the matter in his book *For We Have This Treasure*[1]:

> Let Scripture always be read with care and intelligence, and never without a previous studied reading, lest [people] see for themselves that the words are going in at our eyes and coming out at our mouth without ever passing through our mind. *Understandest thou what thou readest?* asked Philip of the eunuch (Acts 8:30 A.V.). Then give your lips to it. Read it so that others may understand it. Read it ... like a [person] who is listening; not as one who knows the psalm but as one who knows the shepherd!

That's terrific advice! And everyone who's given the ministry of reading Scripture would be so wise to take it to heart. Another great statement is by William Tyndale, the English reformer and translator, who wrote in his *Prologue to Romans* (1534) these words about reading God's Word:

> The more it is chewed, the pleasanter it is, and the more groundedly it is searched, the preciouser things are found in it.

Impression and Expression. So, in my public reading of Scripture, I need to "chew up" as much of God's pleasant, precious Word as I possibly can. So I can communicate thoughts and feelings as faithfully and accurately as I can. What I take in (the *impression* I receive) ought to equal what I speak (my *expression*). If the expression is <u>less</u> than my impression, I inadequately share my thoughts and feelings. If expression is <u>greater</u> than impression, I'm overdoing it. This can be a pretty tricky line to walk. What I'm striving for eventually is a *match* between what I think I'm doing and what my hearers are hearing. We tend, as a rule, to hold back. Especially when it comes to reading Scripture. We don't want to overdo it. We don't want to come across as theatrical or hammy. But the result is, we often *underdo* it—all the way from insufficient voice and diction to underplayed drama and understated thoughts. I'm probably going to go overboard a little (or a lot, to my mind) in order to get the hang of things.

More of us tend to *understate* than to go overboard. Thank goodness! Nevertheless, it's frustrating to hear an intelligent reading that just lacks *fire* (passion, zip, oomph—whatever you want to call it). Try to "take the lid off" and "let it out" whenever it has that closed-in feeling. It takes a little courage. It takes a lot of trust in the Lord that you're not going to do something outrageous to the Word. Now, if you'll trust *me*, I want you to try something: Get a tape recorder, turn it on, and read your passage. And *overdo* it! Yes, do what in your mind will seem overdone, "unnatural" to you, "foreign" to your personality, and all that.

And then play the tape back. Listen as objectively as you can, as if you were hearing someone *else*, and not yourself. As you listen critically, let yourself judge what you hear: "Now that sounds *really* overdone!" "Hey, that sounds pretty good!" "Wow, I thought I was really being wild there, but it doesn't *sound* like it—I could really even do *more* with it!" And so forth. What you want to do is develop for yourself a *listener's sense* of what's happening as you read. And chances are good—*really really good*—that in the process you'll think you're "off the wall" when you first try it. But do try it. And start to develop that critical ear that says "More!" or "Hold back!" or "Hmm, that sounds OK!" That tape recorder will let you know what works and what doesn't. A friend sitting in the back row will let you know. And I have a hunch the Lord will let you know. Just ask.

When I read *first-person* material, it should have a <u>first-time</u> quality, as if I myself am speaking the words <u>now</u>, for the first time, on behalf of the author or character whose words I'm speaking. When I'm reading *third-person* narrative material, it should also have a <u>now</u> quality, as if the story as I'm <u>observing</u> it were being "replayed" in the theatre of my mind. And, even though I know it very well, the story should "surprise" me as it unfolds in my mind's eye.

In my initial approach to a passage I need to ask questions about the **logical content**. For example: What's the historic context of the writing? What's the context of the particular passage? What is the main theme of the passage? Do I understand all the words, and can I pronounce them accurately? Are there any problems of phrasing and emphasis I need to deal with? And then there are issues of **emotional content**: What's the character of the individuals described and quoted? What are their mental, emotional and physical states? What are their objectives? What are the relationships among the individuals? What's the atmosphere of the scenes and situations described in the passage?

<u>*Different Kinds of Passages*</u>. Also, it's helpful if I can see that there are different *kinds* of material I'm reading. We've already been talking about the different kinds of passages. Let's name them. Some can be called **vital** (e.g. story passages) some **mental** (like Paul's letters) and some **empathic** (such as the psalms). Not every passage fits neatly into one category or the other, and often the categories overlap within a single passage, but there are within each kind of passage enough differences that I ought to know how they're going to affect my public reading.

For convenience, I've drawn up a chart that spells out some of the basic differences. I think all the items are pretty self-explanatory. Let me give you an example of one kind of difference. Look at the comments on emphasis. Suppose I'm reading the story of Belshazzar's Feast (Daniel 5). I'll want all kinds of energy and enthusiasm as I depict the story from the beginning:

"***Belshazzar the king*** made a *GREAT FEAST* to a *THOUSAND of his lords....*"

I can't use that same "style" when I'm reading Galatians 6:

"***Brothers****, if SOMEONE* is caught in a *SIN*, you who are *spiritual* should *RESTORE* him...."

or Psalm 8:

"O *Lord*, our *Lord*, how *EXCELLENT* is thy name in *ALL* the *earth....*"

I'd probably come across as if I were selling snake oil or giving God a good old pep talk: "Yea, rah, Almighty God!!!" Reading the Galatians passage, I'll want to provide emphases largely through inflection (let the capitalized words denote words on which I'll put a lift of pitch, or rising inflection, a fairly gentle emphasis as opposed to a thud):

"Brothers, IF someone is caught in a SIN, you who are SPIRITUAL should RESTORE him...."

That doesn't work with:

"BELSHAZZAR the KING made a GREAT FEAST to a THOUSAND of his LORDS...."

or with:

"O LORD, our LORD, how EXCELLENT is thy name in ALL the earth...."

In the first instance, it sounds as if I'm talking rationally *about* the story, rather than being in any way involved *in* the story. And in the latter, it sounds as if I'm passing on information to God: "I say, old fellow, did you realize how very excellent your name really *is*?" Finally, the quiet extension of vowel and consonant sounds (I've underlined them here) that expresses the prayerful feeling of

"O Lord, our Lord, how excellent is thy name in all the earth...."

would sound silly on

"Brothers, if someone is caught in a sin...."

or on

"Belshazzar the king made a great feast...."

It would make these passages sound sleepy rather than letting them come across as thoughtful counsel or an exciting story. (Or as if Count Dracula were reading the passages.)

Think and work through some passages you think might fit these "categories" and you'll see how they apply. Remember, not every passage will neatly "fit" one of these slots, and there'll be a lot of overlapping. This is just to try to help distinguish among the kinds of things you're reading.

CHARACTERISTICS OF VITAL, MENTAL, EMPATHIC MATERIALS

VITAL	MENTAL	EMPATHIC
Vitality dominant: a slice of life appealing to life.	Thoughts dominant: appeal is from mind to mind.	Empathy dominant: appeal is from heart to heart.
Action moves the telling.	Ideas move the telling.	Images move the telling.
Narration + characterization: Revealing action + characters. *Internalize the story:* _see it > say it._	Sharing of thoughts: Revealing discovery of ideas. *Internalize the thoughts:* _think it > say it._	Sharing of feelings: Revealing feeling depth. *Internalize images / feelings:* _feel it > say it._
Direct eye for narration, indirect for characterization. [Character is "in scene"]	Direct eye: focused. Thoughts are spoken directly to listeners.	Indirect eye: internal focus. Thoughts to self (contemplation) or to God.
Internalize character's thoughts and feelings (vs. impersonation).	Internalize clear thought patterns; progression of ideas; phrasing and emphasis.	Internalize depth of feeling; recall as your own feeling ("faked feeling" = schmaltz).
Emphasis = energy of story (movement & vitality; not necessarily volume, hurry or excitement) *Action moves the delivery.*	Emphasis = inflection (rising & falling pitch highlights what's important, "downstresses" all the rest) *Thought flow moves delivery.*	Emphasis = extended sound (extended vowels & consonants sounded in response to depth of feeling) *Feeling moves the delivery.*
Pauses shape story into sequences; give reader & listener time to get with action as it happens.	Pauses shape progression of thoughts; give reader & listener time to get inside the thoughts.	Pauses enable empathy; give reader & listener time to respond on a level that captures the feelings.

[1]*Paul Sherer. For We Have This Treasure. Grand Rapids: Baker Book House, 1944, pp. 140-141.*

Explore the Word

Seek the Lord while he may be found; call on him while he is near. Let the wicked forsake his way and the evil man his thoughts. Let him turn to the Lord and he will have mercy on him, and to our God, for he will freely pardon. "For my thoughts are not your thoughts, neither are your ways my ways," declares the Lord. "As the heavens are higher than the earth, so are my ways higher than your ways and my thoughts than your thoughts. As the rain and the snow come down from heaven, and do not return to it without watering the earth and making it bud and flourish, so that it yields seed for the sower and bread for the eater, so is my word that goes out from my mouth: It will not return to me empty, but will accomplish what I desire and achieve the purpose for which I sent it." (Isaiah 55:6-11)

Prayer: Lord, what a vast world I explore when I delve into your world. It is a world touched by your gracious hand. A world of people singing, dancing, weeping, laughing, praying, living under the banner of your grace. As I explore your Word, make me wide-eyed with the wonder of all I'm going to discover. Let me soar with eagles' wings as your Word inspires me, inspirits me. As your Word goes out from your mouth to accomplish your desires and purposes, grant that that same Word from my mouth may bring you great glory and praise. Amen.

I'm sure you heard in communicants' class, or Sunday School, or somewhere, that the Bible isn't just a book. It's a whole library. Sixty-six books. History, letters, songs, and all.

Well, I'd like to have you think your *voice* isn't just one voice. It's a whole *orchestra*. Strings, brass, percussion, woodwinds, and all.

And one of the things that's fun to explore is the relationship between the *sounds* our bodies can make and the *sense* we're trying to communicate when we speak. I want to experiment and explore with you now some of the vocal dynamics we have at our use. Most of the time I think of **pitch, rate and volume** as the three variables we can play with. And it's helpful to look at each idea we want to express and judge its particular texture or weight or color: Is this a bright high-pitched idea or a darker low one? Is this one brisk or meandering? How about this—gentle and light or heavy and booming. In any kind of vocal performance it's fun to look at ideas as if they were part of a musical score. Of course on the score you'd have all the dynamics marked. The pitches would be obvious, as notes on the staffs, there would be *pp* or *ff* markings to tell you to be quiet or loud, and *allegro* and *andante* and *rallentando* to cue you in on tempo. All of these dynamics are there when the word is spoken rather than sung. They're just hidden. Not marked. You have to discover them for yourself. And what a wonderful world of discovery lies ahead!

Let's spend some time looking at a broader spectrum of vocal dynamics. We'll experiment a bit with all the following:

- ◆ voice quality
- ◆ pitch and inflection
- ◆ stress and volume
- ◆ rate and pauses
- ◆ progression and movement

◆ _Voice Quality_. Think of all the things you can do with your <u>voice quality</u>. You can make it harsh or breathy, strident, throaty, nasally twangy or denasally thuddy. And when you think about marrying _sounds_ and _sense_ the prospects can really be exciting. Or they can be disastrous. You decide. I'll vote for exciting.

Most of us don't have the dimmest idea of how our voices really sound to other people. We may have heard ourselves on tape at one time, but if you're like I am you didn't like what you heard and vowed never to do that again. So we go through life sounding like what _we_ always sound like depending on the shapes and spaces of our physiognomies and probably never think twice about it. It's just a habit thing. Speech is precisely that: _habit_. And we live in a super-polite society where nobody ever goes around saying things like "Gee, you have a strident nasal voice!" or "Go blow your nose and maybe you'll sound better!" And so our habits frolic unbeknown to us but excruciatingly beknown to others. And now a commercial for tape recorders: a tape recorder can reveal the real you to you. It can let you know how you sound to other people. And if you're going to be doing any kind of public speaking, a tape recorder can be a valuable helpmeet in giving you honest feedback, once you're brave enough to ask for it.

Which brings me back to talking about being exciting speakers or disastrous ones. Having voices with all the hues of the rainbow or sounding black-and-white. Look at some examples of places where you want to wed sound and sense. I'm not going to give biblical citations for all these verses, but trust me, they're in the Bible. Here's a sentence you might get to read some day:

And the Philistine said, "I defy the ranks of Israel this day; give me a man, that we may fight together."

If you've been using (remember, I said speech is _habit_— and habits can be altered) a small, breathy voice most of your life and you go ahead and use that particular habit on this particular verse, you're going to sound very funny. Or your Philistine is going to sound funny. But you'll get the blame. A thin breathy voice will make Goliath sound like Superwimp. And he's going to fight by hitting with his purse. Okay, if that's the way you want it. But _my_ Goliath is at least as ominous as the big guy in *Jack and the Beanstalk*, so I'm going to use my killer giant voice. It's not the voice *I* use all the time, either, but I'm sure I can find it somewhere. And *you* can come up with such a voice too. Haven't you ever told jokes and used different pitches, volumes, voice qualities, to make your characters lively?

The minute we start talking about integrating sound and sense here, we're moving into the realm of *imagination*. You and I had an imagination once, when we were children. And then people started trying to educate the imagination out of us so we'd get serious and see the cold, cruel world as it really is. But you remember what Jesus said? "Unless you become like a little child you can't enter the kingdom of heaven." Do you suppose he meant we ought to try to redeem the childlikeness that embraces the imagination? Anyway, you and I need to use our imaginations the minute we start trying to read and do it well. The key word for you and me is *image*. We need *image*-ination to do the job at hand. I'll throw in another key word: *visualization*. As you read the words of Goliath, for example, if you capture an image of this giant, if you visualize him, if you can now visualize *yourself* as him as you speak his words, you've got it!! In the Genesis 1 passage, visualize the emptiness, the darkness. In the psalm, visualize yourself singing to the Lord. Or walking hand in hand with God as your shepherd. Visualize. Visualize. Visualize. And you're bound to get it right. Someone said that a good speaker is one who can recreate the image in her mind in the mind's eye of her listener. Try it out.

One thing we're going to have to face here. That is, sometimes we'll read things that aren't true to *our* nature. Like the above giant voice. I don't usually talk that way. At least not to my friends. And—confess it—people who go to seminary and become pastors and go to church a lot are nice people. They take nice pills every morning. And they act nice. And sound nice. And then when they have to sound like giants they beat their breasts and say, "I just can't! I *can't*!" But you truly can. Try taking that verse up above again. Give it as much full sound as you can muster. And do just one thing with it: *overdo the consonant sounds*. Spit them out. You're never going to be fierce and gianty, but you can blast those consonant sounds. Try this:

And the *P*hilis*t*ine *s*aid, "I *d*e*f*y the ranks of Israel this *d*ay; give me a *m*an, that we may *fight* together."

Play around with the idea. Notice I'm not suggesting hitting *all* the consonant sounds. You don't want Goliath to sound like Robbie the Robot. I don't think you do. Anyway, here you've been playing around a little with, say, the brass and percussion sections of your orchestra.

Don't use brass and percussion on these verses:

In the beginning, God created the heavens and the earth. The earth was without form and void, and darkness was upon the face of the deep.

Don't you think maybe strings and woodwinds would work better? Try a nice legato approach. Gently extend some of the vowel sounds. They're sounds you can sing with, and can contribute a musical quality to your speech. And there are some consonant sounds you can sing too. Try "Mary Had a Little Lamb" using these sounds: **m n ng z l**. (Don't try this with **r**—it's an unpleasant sound. Your choir director would kill you if you sang "P*r*aise the Lo*rr*d." It should sound nice and southern: "Praise the Lawd." I'm serious!) In any case, try sustaining some of the vowel and consonant sounds in these verses, and you'll see how well they contribute to the sense you're trying to get across. (Once again, don't extend *every* extendable sound, or you'll sound strange.)

You could do the same thing, nicely, with the **ng** sounds in this verse:

> Sing to the Lord a new song!

And even though I sing second bass, I'd probably go up into a comfortably high register with these words, because the higher sound is brighter and happier and the lower sound works better with dark and somber ideas.

You don't want to sound too bright-eyed and bushy-tailed on

> The Lord is my shepherd, I shall not want.

Sure, it's a happy thought, but it's less a "gee whillikers!" kind of happy than a "being in the presence of God is the most wonderful thing there is" kind of comfortable, blessed happy.

Here's another one to experiment with:

> God thunders wondrously with his voice; he does great things which we cannot comprehend.

♦ *Pitch and Inflection*. Add to all this some of the things you can do with <u>pitch and inflection</u>. Pitch can do wonderful things with images and moods. Think musically. Is this image, this idea, a happy, bright, cheery one? Try some of the higher notes in your range. Is the image dark, somber, morose? Go for the lower tones. Be careful that the image and the pitch don't clash. If you say "Rejoice in the Lord always. I will say it again: Rejoice!" (Philippians 4:4) or "This is the day the Lord has made; let us rejoice and be glad in it" (Psalm 118:24) with your deepest *basso profundo* growl, you're more likely to frighten us than elate us. Too high a twitter on "O Lord, you have searched me and you know me" (Psalm 139:1) will convey all the solemnity of "Ooh, that tickles!" Or "How long, O Lord? Will you forget me forever?" (Psalm 13:1) will sound more like impatience than lamentation. Whatever pitch you choose, be sure it matches the thought. And make it comfortably within your range. If you go too high or too low you're likely to strain the voice. Also if you go too high, people will wonder if you've been inhaling helium. Just kidding.

In the middle of Psalm 27, you have a phenomenal shift of moods—from "whoopee" to "I'm down so low I'm reaching up to touch bottom." These are the verses (6b and 7):

> I will sing and make melody to the Lord.
>
> Hear, O Lord, when I cry aloud, be gracious to me and answer me!

Try your upper register for the first line and a lower, darker sound on the second. You could probably cut back a bit on the volume, too, on the second line.

Inflection is movement of pitch from one level to another. Generally, a *rising* inflection (/) will convey questioning or uncertainty ("Are you /really/?") and a *falling* inflection (\) will suggest finality ("Yes, I \am\!") There can be also *circumflex* inflections, which will either rise and fall (/\) or fall and rise (\/). We use the first ("/Oh\, I /see\!"), when we're suspicious or sarcastic. And we use the fall-rise inflection ("You did \what/?") when we're surprised or doubtful. Just as pitch should match the thought, so also our inflections should match. Sometimes they don't. Did you ever notice how sometimes when people introduce themselves they get caught up in a bunch of rising inflections: ("My name is /Jamie/ and I'm from /Chicago/ and I'm /married/ ....") and it sounds as if they're asking for permission? And we've already dealt with the problem of *teacups* (falling inflection pattern—see the chapter on *DOs and DON'Ts*).

A fairly quiet tone and sustained sounds (rather than a lot of bouncy inflection) would work best on Psalm 8, where the psalmist is meditating and reflecting:

> O Lord, our Lord, how excellent is thy name in all the earth; who hast set thy glory above the heavens.

When you're speaking the voice of God, be cautious about using much inflection (if any). For example, God speaking to Abraham (Genesis 22:11):

> But the angel of the Lord called to him from heaven;, and said, "Abraham, Abraham!"

What do you do with that "Abraham, Abraham!"? Well, if you use a rising inflection on the last part, it sounds very human ("Abra/HAM, Abra/HAM... come in for supper!") If you use a falling inflection ("ABRA\ham, ABRA\ham... stop hitting your sister!") it sounds just as odd. I'd opt for a non-inflected extended sound (something like "AABRAHAMM, AABRAHAMM!") just as long as you can keep it from sounding spooky. I like to read God's words with a kind of steadiness and calmness—revealing how steady God always is, God's constancy in the face of our vacillation.

Again, it helps to experiment. Your inflection can say things you may not want to say. How does Paul on the road to Damascus say these words: "Who are you, Lord?" Here are some options:

WHO are you, Lord?

Who ARE you, Lord?

> Who are YOU, Lord?
>
> Who are you, LORD?

Depending upon what you think Paul's frame of mind is at that moment, you'd probably go for the second choice, since it sounds more mystified and less hostile or simple-minded.

A simple inflection can nicely bring out something that's merely *suggested* by the words. For example:

> Belshazzar, whiles he tasted the wine, commanded to bring the golden and silver vessels....

could be easily rewritten this way:

> Belshazzar, whiles he tasted the wine, commanded, "Bring the golden and silver vessels...."

and Belshazzar's direct quote (indirectly expressed in the original) comes to life. But since I don't want to sit down and rewrite my Scripture lesson, I might just put a lift of inflection beginning on the word "bring," like this:

> Belshazzar, whiles he tasted the wine, commanded to /BRING THE GOLDEN AND SILVER VESSELS....

and I've added that direct-quote dimension to that particular line.

♦ ***Stress and Volume***. A lot of the time when we think about <u>stress and volume</u>, we think of *more*—loud pedal, thump and yell. A preacher wrote in the margin of a page of his sermon manuscript: "Point is weak—shout like fury!" I was told that, anyway. And it wasn't me. Although, you know, a lot of people do write notes to themselves. One time when I was pastor in a church in Indiana, the pastor emeritus had preached on Sunday. During the week I wandered into the sanctuary, and there was his sermon manuscript still on the pulpit, all marked up with every kind of dynamic you can think of. Maybe that's why he was such a good preacher. He took seriously the idea that ideas had their own peculiar weight and texture and he marked everything so he'd be sure not to get it wrong. Now don't tell me you'll depend on the Holy Spirit to do that for you at the time. You might find it's not such a bad idea to ask the Holy Spirit for a hand during the week so you can be prepared come Sunday morning. Well, I don't want to wander too far away from just talking about stress and volume, except to say that sometimes you want *less* instead of more.

Compare the following texts:

> Goliath stood and shouted to the ranks of Israel, "Why have you come down to me?"
>
> O Lord, thou hast searched me and known me!
>
> And when the king of Israel read the letter, he rent his clothes and said, "Am I God, to kill and to make alive...?"

The first one (1 Samuel 17:8) obviously wants lots of stress and as much volume as you can get away with without blasting the troops out of the pews. Remember, this is that big Goliath. And don't forget to hit the consonant sounds here too. Now the second one (Psalm 139) could fool you, if you were really not too bright, because you'd see the exclamation point at the end and think, "Oh, boy, here's my chance to yell at God!" But it's really a quiet, soft-pedal thought, and the exclamation point at the end just suggests intensity of feeling. The third text, from the story of Naaman the leper (2 Kings 5) is the reaction of the King of Israel to a letter from the King of Syria asking him to cure Naaman. He's really angry (enough to tear up his clothes), so don't take your "nice" pill the morning you read this. Also, don't wimp the narrative line and then suddenly burst forth on "Am I God..." You want the narrative to crescendo into the dialogue (the narrator's empathy with what the character is saying). And besides, if you go from very soft to very loud you're very likely to scare someone. It happened to me once! This woman was reading (it wasn't this same passage, but a similar one—I've forgotten), and she had this little, tiny narrative voice and then decided to be real dramatic like the whole Battle of Gettysburg, and it sounded like:

And when the king of Israel read the letter, he rent his clothes and said, **"Am I God, to kill and to make alive...?"**

Promise you won't do that!

Finally, you don't want to overlook changes of stress and volume for mood shifts. In the story of Belshazzar's Feast, the party's going on and everyone is hooting and hollering, and the text says:

They drank wine, and praised the gods of gold and of silver, of brass, of iron, of wood, and of stone.

Now you'd better believe that with all that drinking and praising going on there was a lot of noise. But then something happened! (Long pause for dramatic effect.) Suddenly this *hand* comes and writes on the wall, and everybody sees it, and it's scary. So after that pause (during which, of course, you yourself see the hand!) you cut back in volume and give it your best Twilight Zone shot. (I'm kidding!) But you do want a really big contrast here for the mood shift.

♦ *Rate and Pauses*. Now we come to a category that can make the difference between a so-so reading and a really great reading. A cardinal rule you should memorize is this: *ignore the punctuation*. Yes, you heard right: _IGNORE THE PUNCTUATION!!_ Remember what I said about imaging? About visualization? This is what should determine your rate and your use of pauses. Not the commas. Not even sometimes the heavier stuff like semicolons and periods. Move with the image. Try this text, from 1 Kings 18, where God zaps Elijah's offering with fire:

Then the fire of the Lord fell, and consumed the burnt offering, and the wood, and the stones, and the dust, and licked up the water that was in the trench.

If you observe all those commas, you have a very leisurely tongue of flame coming down and tasting the burnt offering—then sipping tea—then the wood—then more tea—then the stones, and so forth. It didn't happen like that! It was like *Shazam!!!* Try it, taking all the punctuation out. Get a good breath, and read it like this:

Then the fire of the Lord fell and consumed the burnt offering and the wood and the stones and the dust and licked up the water that was in the trench.

And as you're saying it you're watching that sucker nuke things and you're thinking, "Yea, rah, go GOD!"

Take a look at these verses from John 9:

> As he said this, he spat on the ground and made clay of the spittle and anointed the man's eyes with the clay. ... So he went and washed and came back seeing.

That's exactly the way it appears, with virtually no commas or other punctuation to suggest pacing or pauses. But if you read the first line nonstop you create a very humorous sort of slapstick image in your listener's mind's eye: *spit-stir-splat!* It couldn't be any funnier with a cream pie! And then: *boing-zingg-blap!* he zooms off and washes and comes back seeing. Like a scene from a silent movie. But when you ignore the (lack of) punctuation, when you *look* at the scene, when you *visualize* what's happening, you get a really different picture:

> As he said this, he spat on the ground *[spits, gets down and kneels in the dirt, swirls together the spittle and the dust with his finger]* and made clay of the spittle *[now stands up, clay in one hand, daubs man's eyes]* and anointed the man's eyes with the clay. ... So he went *[there he goes, watch him, now he reaches into the fountain and cups water in his hands and splashes the water onto his face]* and washed and came back *[here he comes, getting closer, and when he gets close enough, you can tell: he's not blind any more!!!]* seeing.

You see, all that's going on and it's not even mentioned in the *words* describing the scene. You've got to be tuned in to more than just the words. You've got to *see* the whole picture, and then you can tell what you see to others—with just the right kind of movement and pauses to let things happen. Didn't I tell you this was the fun part?

Another example to sell everyone on the value of pauses. This is from Psalm 8:

> When I consider thy heavens, the work of thy fingers, the moon and the stars, which thou hast ordained; what is man, that thou art mindful of him?

All right, comma lovers, here's your chance to shine. But even if you observe the pauses, slow down the rate, or you'll be listing heavens, fingers, moon, stars, like items on a grocery list. Again, *image* the scene: here's the psalmist lying out on a grassy knoll (I used to think a knoll was like a knish) on a warm summer evening looking up into the skies and contemplating the human condition and the existential relationship between the divine and the mundane. You're not likely to do that riding through town on a moped. So give yourself (the psalmist) the time and the leisure to let it happen.

> When I consider thy heavens . . . the work of thy fingers . . . the moon . . . and the stars, which thou hast ordained . . . . . . what is man . . . that thou art mindful of him?

One more, and this is probably my favorite, from Luke 22—one of the most powerful, poignant moments in Scripture:

But Peter said, "Man, I do not know what you are saying." And immediately, while he was still speaking, the cock crowed. And the Lord turned and looked at Peter. And Peter remembered the word of the Lord, how he had said to him, "Before the cock crows today, you will deny me three times." And he went out and wept bitterly.

Look at this scene as if you were going to film it as part of a movie. We're going to mark where the camera shots move in transition from one image to another, like this:

{-1-}But Peter said, "Man, I do not know what you are saying."

{-2-}And immediately, while he was still speaking, the cock crowed.

{-3-} And the Lord turned and looked at Peter.

{-4-} And Peter remembered the word of the Lord, how he had said to him, "Before the cock crows today, you will deny me three times."

{-5-}And he went out

{-6-}and wept

{-7-} bitterly.

Here's what's happening: (1) focus on Peter stating his denial, (2) pan shot takes in darkness of the night, we hear the cock crowing, (3) close up of Jesus turning, looking towards Peter, (4) closeup of Peter's eyes, voice-over with Jesus' words, (5) Peter rushing out of the courtyard, (6) closeup of burning tears streaming down Peter's face, (7) zoom in on Peter's face, to black.

You could comfortably take a slow count of three at each of those scene shifts, probably even longer toward the end of the passage, and those pauses would not be too long. I know, pauses can be uncomfortable—a pause of three seconds can make you feel like you're standing stark naked in front of your audience for three *minutes*. But if your concentration is really involved in the scene you're describing or the thought you're thinking, a pause won't really seem all that long. Once again, checking with a tape recorder to see how it sounds would be helpful. Do your pauses by the numbers if you need to, to get comfortable with them. But it's much better if you visualize intensely, and if you're caught up in the scene your listeners will be too. Just be careful not to go home for lunch during any of your pauses.

♦ *Progression and Movement*. Everything you read is going to have some kind of progression and movement. Nothing, whether the passage is a story, a thought, or a meditation, is just going to sit there and look at you. So you don't want to just sit there and look at it. Watch it move. Watch it progress. And then tell us what you're seeing as you see it. Here are a couple of examples from the Abraham and Isaac story (Genesis 22):

(a) So Abraham rose early in the morning, saddled his ass, and took two of his young men with him, and his son Isaac. ... So they went both of them together.

This (a) is the immediate response Abraham makes to God's command to sacrifice his son. Certainly, mood is important in interpreting these lines. Man of faith Abraham is saying, "Yes, Lord." Loving father Abraham is saying, *"No,* Lord, how can I?" That tension—if you can see it and *feel* it on Abraham's behalf—will tell you how these words should move. The air is heavy with imminent horror. Don't let us see Abraham and Isaac springing out of bed and heading off for a picnic.

> (b) Abraham built an altar there, and laid the wood in order, and bound Isaac his son, and laid him on the altar, upon the wood. Then Abraham put forth his hand, and took the knife to slay his son. But the angel of the Lord called to him from heaven, and said, "Abraham, Abraham!"

In (b), the tension mounts almost like stairsteps. The altar. Then the wood. Then the binding. Then laying Isaac on the altar. Then the hand reaches for the knife. The knife is lifted high into the air above Isaac's body. And *then .... THE ANGEL APPEARS!!!!!* Feel it. See it. And you've got it. You should be sharing in the terror going through Abraham's mind, Isaac's mind, your listeners' minds. Hearing Abraham's heart beat louder and louder. Feeling the sweat mixed with tears streaming down his face. Then all the tension breaks and the cavalry appear!!!

There's another kind of tension going on in the story of Belshazzar's Feast. After the hand comes and writes on the wall, Belshazzar turns to the wise men of Babylon, and says:

> Whosoever shall read this writing, and show me the interpretation thereof, shall be clothed with scarlet, and have a chain of gold about his neck, and shall be the third ruler in the kingdom.

Here the tension arises from the mystery and potential danger connected with *the writing*. So you imagine you're one of those wise men, and Belshazzar offers you a red robe. What's your reaction? Something like "No way, Jose!" So Belshazzar ups the ante: a gold chain. Is he kidding? Do an analysis of God's handwriting for a golden chain? Up the ante goes again, this time to the maximum: a *third of the kingdom*. Participate in the progression and tension in that scene, and you'll certainly get it right.

One more example. This from the Naaman story. The lines from the text read as follows:

> So he went, taking with him ten talents of silver, six thousand shekels of gold, and ten festal garments. ...\
> So Naaman came with his horses and chariots, and halted at the door of Elisha's house.

The important thing here is to know how much talents and shekels are worth. In this case, the whole caboodle is worth about $80,000—*eighty thousand dollars*! Now you're not going to interrupt the reading and say, "By the way, folks, all that's worth $80,000!" But by the *way* you say it, presuming you can get your eyes to bug out a little and look a little awed (not *odd*), you can communicate that he took a little bit more than a toothbrush and a change of underwear. And then he went with *all his money and all his horses and all his chariots, because he was a really important person* to see the prophet Elisha. Keep in mind how important tone of voice and facial expression can be in communicating values. Incredibly important!

Here's What's New and Important: Emphasis Matters

Now an angel of the Lord said to Philip, "Go south to the road—the desert road—that goes down from Jerusalem to Gaza." So he started out, and on his way he met an Ethiopian eunuch, an important official in charge of all the treasury of Candace, queen of the Ethiopians. This man had gone to Jerusalem to worship, and on his way home was reading the book of Isaiah the prophet. The Spirit told Philip, "Go to that chariot and stay near it."

Then Philip ran up to the chariot and heard the man reading Isaiah the prophet. "Do you understand what you are reading?" Philip asked.

"How can I," he said, "unless someone explains it to me?" So he invited Philip to come up and sit with him.

The eunuch was reading this passage of Scripture:

"He was led like a sheep to the slaughter, and as a lamb before the shearer is silent, so he did not open his mouth.

In his humiliation he was deprived of justice. Who can speak of his descendants? For his life was taken from the earth."

The eunuch asked Philip, "Tell me, please, who is the prophet talking about, himself or someone else?" Then Philip began with that very passage of Scripture and told him the good news about Jesus.

As they traveled along the road, they came to some water and the eunuch said, "Look, here is water. Why shouldn't I be baptized?" And he gave orders to stop the chariot. Then both Philip and the eunuch went down into the water and Philip baptized him. When they came up out of the water, the Spirit of the Lord suddenly took Philip away, and the eunuch did not see him again, but went on his way rejoicing. (Acts 8:26-39)

Prayer: Lord, guide me by your Spirit in whatever ministry you give me. I thank you for the ministry of reading your Word for others to hear. May each of us be moved by your Spirit to surrender ourselves to Christ, that our lives may be filled by the joy and peace He alone can give. In his strong name I pray. Amen.

A really good reader of Scripture will not put a congregation to sleep. That's an obvious statement. But it could apply to my reading if I wasn't aware of how it sounded. Some people make their reading *sound* <u>read</u>. Everything's dispassionate. Bland. Characters sound like they're reading their lines from a script for the first time. Every word gets the same emphasis, as if every word were equally important. The result sounds something like this:

Bel|shaz|zar|the|king|made|a|great|feast|to|a|thou|sand|of|his|lords|and|drank|wine|be|fore|the|thou|sand.

It's all very *straight-line* sounding, a little bit like words in print on a page—everything about the same size with little spaces between words. And it's all very monotonous and very boring. It's not at all the way we *talk*, if we were speaking the same words as *our own* ideas, *our own* stories. When we speak, we naturally use peaks and valleys to highlight what's important and to "throw away" what isn't important. The result is something like this:

Bel**shaz**zar ᴛʜᴇ **king** ᴍᴀᴅᴇ ᴀ **great feast** ᴛᴏ ᴀ **thou**sand ᴏꜰ ʜɪs **lords** ᴀɴᴅ drank **wine** before the thousand.

When we read silently to ourselves, of course, what's important stands out in our minds and we don't have any trouble knowing where the peaks and valleys are. When we read *aloud*, we need to translate that internal mental enlarging of what's important into some sort of vocal emphasis, so our listeners will be able to discern as they hear the words exactly *what*, among this spate of words, is really important. Probably the reason some of us sound like

Bel|shaz|zar|the|king|made|a|great|feast|to|a|thou|sand|of|his|lords|and|drank|wine|be|fore|the|thou|sand

is that we're afraid of "overdoing it," but the result is often that it's *so underdone* there's no life to it. Here, again, is where a tape recorder or a good honest friend can help us decide just how far we should go when we're trying vocally to let the ideas come to life.

<u>*What to Emphasize*</u>. We've already talked a little about how different kinds of material (vital, mental or empathic) take different kinds of emphases (stress, inflection, extension). Let's get at the matter of *what* should be emphasized and a little bit more about *how* to do it.

David, a student from Ireland, once asked me, "Are you aware that there's a great deal of con<u>*trah*</u>versy over the word *'**con**troversy'*?" Different emphases within a single word are not generally an issue.[1] But changing the emphasis from one word to another can radically alter the significance of what's being said. Take for example the sentence

I am going to church today.

In and of itself it makes good sense, states the fact that I'm going to church. But what if I place the emphasis on the first word, like this:

I am going to church today.

I've shaded the meaning to suggest that *I'm* going to church no matter who else does. Or how about

I ***am*** going to church today.

Suggests that someone has said I'd better *not* if I know what's good for me, but I'm going to be defiant and go anyway. So there. (Feisty little devil!) Or you could emphasize

I am ***going*** to church today.

But I'm not going to do anything while I'm there. You can get me there but you can't **make me** worship—or something like that. Then you could say

I am going ***to*** church today.

Sounds like you might not be coming back, doesn't it? Or

I am going to ***church*** today.

Not to the mall, for goodness' sake! Or, finally,

I am going to church ***today***.

But don't bug me about next week.

What's New? What's Important?

Let's set up some ground rules about what kinds of things we want to emphasize, and then get at some examples. A pretty solid rule-of-thumb for emphasizing would be to consider simply WHAT'S NEW / WHAT'S IMPORTANT? Let's unpack that a bit.

(1) First of all, we'll want to emphasize *idea carriers, & not unimportant words.* Much of the time these will be the nouns, but not always. Certainly the initial presentation of a *main idea or theme* will deserve emphasis, or practically any *character* in a story passage, as well as *locations.* Sometimes, especially in a story passage, the verbs will be emphasized, setting forth the action taking place. Sometimes, we'll stress adjectives when what's important is describing, comparing, contrasting or classifying. Now and then you'll stress a pronoun or an adverb. Very rarely (I'd say "never" but all rules can be broken or bent up a bit) emphasize conjunctions (such as "and" and "but"), or articles ("the" or "a"), or prepositions. More on that later. So, in descending order, look to nouns, verbs, adjectives, pronouns, adverbs, conjunctions, articles & prepositions in that order in terms of what's likely to deserve the emphasis. Your last items will rarely get emphasized.

(2) *The new idea or the contrasting idea* will be emphasized, rather than something that's already been named. As a rule, words like pronouns are "old" ideas, because they refer to something or someone already mentioned. (Again, you're looking for words that carry ideas, describe important action, or express newness or contrast.)

(3) *Conditional or causal relationships* will be brought out. Look for "if ... then" statements (conditional) and "because ... therefore" constructions (causal). Sometimes these are not terribly obvious but simply implied.

Another general rule would be: Don't stress anything you could leave out without changing the meaning.

It just occurred to me how important the phrase "when you come to think about it" is. I started to formulate a thought like that, and then realized that *"thinking about it"* is what it's all about! So much of the time things are read with stupid phrasing and emphasis because we just aren't *thinking* about what we're saying when we *read*, the way we think about what we're saying when we *talk* to people. That's why it's so important to think of our reading as being a matter of sharing thoughts, telling stories, "talking" with others rather than just *reading something*. End of that sermon. Look at some of the things we do so easily when we're not thinking very much about what we're doing or when we do things out of habit.

As a Rule: Don't Stress Prepositions. In ecclesiastical circles we seem to be very fond of *prepositions*. Listen to any congregation reciting a responsive reading or even a unison prayer, and you're likely to hear them pounce upon every preposition that comes along the pike. Does it make sense? No. But once you get into a habit, it's hard to break, isn't it? How often have you heard this blessing:

> The Lord make his face to shine upon you, and be gracious unto you; the Lord lift up his countenance upon you, and give you peace.

read with every one of the prepositions stressed? Like this:

> The Lord make his face to shine *upon* you, and be gracious *unto* you; the Lord lift up his countenance *upon* you, and give you peace.

Doesn't it make sense to anyone to stress more important words than prepositions? Like:

> The Lord make his face to *shine* upon you, and be *gracious* unto you; the Lord lift up his *countenance* upon you, and give you *peace*.

Wouldn't you rather be blessed by God's shining face, God's grace and God's countenance than by a handful of prepositions?

People have asked me why I supposed we had this love affair with prepositions. And I'll tell you what I told them: I don't know.[2] *But my hunch* is it's because they're "heavier" than the prepositions we *normally* use and since they're in the Bible we figure they're important, so we jump on them. Invariably you'll hear someone read a phrase like "The hand of the Lord was upon me" (Ezekiel 37:1) or "The Spirit of the Lord is upon me" (Luke 4:18) with the stress on the preposition:

> The hand of the Lord was *upon* me
> The Spirit of the Lord is *upon* me

which just plain doesn't make sense. The weight of those phrases is in "the hand of the Lord" or "the Spirit of the Lord," isn't it? We wouldn't say

> The hand of the Lord was *on* me
> The Spirit of the Lord is *on* me

unless we were responding to someone's question as to whether the hand or the Spirit was *on* us or *off* us. So let's make it:

> The *hand of the Lord* was upon me
> The *Spirit of the Lord* is upon me

Normally, we probably wouldn't use "upon" or "unto"—two-syllable words—to begin with. We tend to go with the one-syllable words "on" and "to" instead. Normally, we'd probably say something like "shine on you," "be gracious to you," and "lift up his countenance on you" if we were going to say those things to someone. We wouldn't likely say "Mother, he's got his shoes upon the table again!" or "She gave that book unto me." So when we see the "upon" and "unto" we figure they're more serious and deserve more respect, I guess. If you can figure out otherwise, please let me know.

Another place where stressed prepositions don't make sense is here, in Psalm 27.

> When evildoers assail me, uttering slanders against me, my adversaries and foes they will stumble and fall. Though a host encamp against me, I will not be afraid. Though war arise against me, yet I will be confident.

Most of the time, when you hear it read you hear "against" emphasized each of three times. Granted, the idea of "againstness" is more important here than the words "upon" and "unto" usually are. But look at the marvelous progression of ideas: (1) they're slandering me, (2) things are getting worse and they're setting up camp out there, and (3) look out, here come the spears and arrows! And even in the face of all that, I'm going to be confident in my God! Isn't that great? And you miss that if you stress each "against". Look at it both ways:

> When evildoers assail me, uttering slanders *against* me, my adversaries and foes they will stumble and fall. Though a host encamp *against* me, I will not be afraid. Though war arise *against* me, yet I will be confident.

> When evildoers assail me, uttering *slanders* against me, my adversaries and foes they will stumble and fall. Though a host *encamp* against me, I will not be afraid. Though *war* arise against me, yet I will be confident.

You decide which one makes more sense.

<u>As Opposed to What?</u> When you emphasize a word, you suggest that it's important in relation to something else or, often, instead of something else. Take, for example, a simple statement: "I'm with you." If I say, *"I'm with you,"* I'm suggesting that even if *no one else* is with you, by golly, *I* am. If I say "I'm *with* you," I'm suggesting that I'm not *against* you. If I say, "I'm with *you*," I may be suggesting that I'm not with *them.*

What then are my listeners to think when they hear (for example) Blind Bartimaeus (Mark 10:47) say, "Jesus, Son of David, have mercy *on* me!" (I just heard it read this way.) Is he suggesting that Jesus shouldn't take mercy *off* me?

In the book of Ruth (chapter 1 verse 16, KJV) Ruth says: "Intreat me not to leave thee, or to return from following after thee...." At least nine out of ten readers read "following *after* thee." Is that what she's saying? "Don't ask me to stop following *after* you. It's okay, though, if you ask me to stop following *before* you." Of course not. You could leave out the word "after" altogether. So why stress it?

Jesus tells his disciples (Mark 11:2, KJV), "Go your way into the village over against you: and as soon as ye be entered into it, ye shall find a colt tied ...." And we hear "the village over *against* you" as though it were an enemy outpost instead of some friendly folks and "as soon as ye be entered *into* it" as though it were somehow possible to enter *out of* it. It simply means "that village over there." And of course the word "into" could be eliminated altogether—so why stress it?

We come into God's presence and "humbly confess our sins *before* thee"—because we shouldn't confess them *"behind* thee"? We ask God to "have mercy *upon* us" rather than having mercy *"under* us"? Is God the "power that worketh *in* us" instead of *on top of us* or the "power that *worketh* in us"? When we ask God to "renew a right spirit *within* us" is it because God would be likely to "renew a right spirit *outside of* us?"

Likewise, when Paul is waiting for Silas and Timothy at Athens, we're told (Acts 17:16, RSV) "his spirit was provoked within him when he saw that the city was full of idols." The majority of readers tell us that "his spirit was provoked *within* him"—assuring us that his spirit was not doing some sort of out-of-body trip somewhere, perhaps basking in the sun on the Côte d'Azur. Where *else*, for goodness' sake, would Paul's spirit be? And isn't the important information that his spirit was *provoked* within him? He was ticked off. And you should be too when you hear people stressing prepositions that shouldn't be stressed.

Which is more important: That Jesus took on flesh and dwelt *among* us (instead of out in the suburbs), or that he *dwelt* among us? The "among" is important, certainly. But isn't it more significant that he *took up residence and lived in our midst*?

Does it ever happen to you that once you get "tuned in" to something (like a particular pronunciation problem, or a particular anomaly like *stressing prepositions where it doesn't make sense*) all of a sudden you begin hearing it *everywhere*? I've begun to notice on radio broadcasts how announcers will more often than not say things like:

> "Thank you for listening *to* us . . . ."
> "You'll be hearing *from* us right away . . . ."
> "We'll have more news *for* you . . . ."
> Doesn't it make a lot more sense to say:
> "Thank you for *listening* to us . . . ."
> "You'll be *hearing* from us right away . . . ."
> "We'll have *more news* for you . . . ."
> . . . or is it just me???

No "Things". Then there's the word "thing" (or "thang" if you're from the South). There's a lot of "thing"s in the Bible, but take Mary's statement in Luke 1 as an example:

> He has filled the hungry with good things....

What you hear most of the time is this:

> He has filled the hungry with good *things*....

Who among us would like a *thing* for a snack? I've got a plate of them sitting out in the kitchen in case you're interested. No takers? Well, then, how about a *good* thing? See, now I'm fighting off the takers! The word "thing" is invariably nowhere when it comes to importance. It's the adjective alongside it that gets the honors. Consider how we treat words like *some*thing, *no*thing, *any*thing, *every*thing. A few more examples to look at—you decide which makes the better sense. Here's one from Psalm 8:

> Thou hast put all things under his feet.

Which reads better:

> Thou hast put all *things* under his feet

or:

> Thou hast put *all* things under his feet?

And from Psalm 27:

> One thing have I asked of the Lord . . . .

Should it read "One *thing* have I asked . . ." or *"One* thing have I asked . . . "*? Which makes the better sense?

Nouns? Sometimes. Some people think if there's a noun in the sentence it should be stressed. I guess that's what they think, because I've heard the following sentence several times:

> And for fear of him the guards trembled and became like dead *men*.

Leading the listener logically to ponder: What were they previously? Dead horses? Dead dogs? I think it's somewhat obvious they'd been men all along, don't you imagine? Maybe the important idea here is they became like "dead," whereas previously they'd been like "alive."

Another spot where the noun's not the star is in the Belshazzar story. Daniel the prophet has just told King Belshazzar that his father, Nebuchadnezzar, had not been a very humble sort of fellow, and now he says to the son:

> And thou his son, O Belshazzar, hast not humbled thine *heart*.

The emphasis on "heart," as you may guess, is wrong. What it implies is "Thou hast humbled thy liver, thy kidneys and thy pancreas, but thou hastn't humbled thine *heart*." If that really makes sense to you, then go for it. But what I think Daniel really has in mind is "Thou hast not humbled *thine* heart either!"

Verbs? Sometimes. And then, there are those who think all *verbs*—because they're action words—get the emphasis. So, in the Naaman story, you have Elisha the man of God saying to the King of Israel:

> "Why have you *rent* your clothes?"

I am not making this up. I have heard this rendition many times. The implied next question is, of course, "Why didn't you *buy* them?" or something equally brilliant. I have a suspicion what Elisha is really trying to convey is

> "*Why* have you rent your clothes?"

because he goes on to suggest the king didn't really *need* to fret, he could have shipped Naaman off to "see me" instead.

Set the Stage. At the beginning of practically every reading, you'll want to emphasize a lot of things simply because they're new and we want to capture our listeners' attention as to what the passage is about. With a story passage, the process of visualizing or imaging is also important here, both for us and for our listeners. At the beginning of a Scripture reading, consider that your listeners' mind is a **blank canvas.** As if you were setting bits of scenery, setting, characters, etc., down upon a blank stage—or as if you were putting into position the expository elements of the story onto a flannel board—then you carefully limn the elements of *setting, character* and *situation*. Once these are in place, the story begins to unfold itself, moving according to its *own* pacing (moving the reader according to that pacing!), as if the picture had suddenly come to life.

Think of John 2 (the miracle at Cana) as an example. First of all you put into place **wedding, Cana, Mary, Jesus, disciples, empty water jar,** etc.—all the essential components of the story. Then the story starts to move. Mary turns to Jesus and says, "Look, the wine's all gone." Jesus answers her. She talks to the stewards, tells them to do what Jesus says. Right at this point, the action stops. Here, in verse 6, we notice a corner of the canvas still blank. So we bring the story to a halt to paint in the "six stone jars" standing there empty. Now the action takes up again. Jesus refers to the empty jars, tells the stewards to fill them with water. And so on through to the end of the story. Any time you bring in a new character, a new element in the situation, a new important detail in the setting, you want to set it off as if you'd marked it with your yellow highlighter. *How* you set it off will vary: through volume, lengthened sound, slower rate, pauses, or inflection.

Present the Characters. Don't presume that when people in the congregation read the citation for a Scripture passage they'll know what it's all about. For sure, most of them will have no clue. Therefore, in a story passage, be especially careful about introducing each character. Think of a stage play where this character or that steps onstage for the first time and is applauded by the audience. Give your characters that same kind of recognition. Don't let them "sneak" onstage or enter into the story as if they'd been there all along. Take, for example, the story of Belshazzar's Feast. In the bulletin we'll read that the Old Testament Lesson is from Daniel, chapter 5. You're probably the only person who will know what that passage is all about. So introduce us, carefully, to each character. Your opening line is:

> Belshazzar the king made a great feast to a thousand of his lords . . . .

Don't presume we've met Belshazzar before. You're presenting him as though you were saying, "Ladies and gentlemen, meet *Belshazzar, the King*, [ta-da!] who is the main character in this story." That's not what you're really going to say, of course. But to accomplish that purpose you might (1) extend the sounds in the three words "Belshazzar the king" (as though you had highlighted them with a fluorescent yellow marker and were now vocally doing the same thing), and (2) put a small pause after "Belshazzar the king" (remember that pauses are very effective as means of emphasis) to set off the presentation of this character. Something like this:

> *BELSHAZZAR the KING* ‖ made a great feast . . . .

A little farther on in the story you'd do something similar with these verses (without the fanfare, however, because these are pretty minor characters):

> The king cried aloud to bring in the **astrologers**, the **Chaldeans**, and the **soothsayers** . . . .

Soon after this, the queen mother appears:

> Now the *QUEEN*, by reason of words of the king and his lords, came into the banquet house . . . .

She, of course, gets to be presented in capital letters because she's a key figure in the drama, and besides she's Belshazzar's mother and you should always respect someone's mother. She's the one who mentions the man who had "light and understanding and excellent wisdom" in the days when Belshazzar's father Nebuchadnezzar was alive—that being Daniel, whom she sets up but doesn't name. And then, finally, comes Daniel onstage and we do meet him by name:

> Then was *DANIEL* brought in before the king.

And with that we've finally met the entire cast of characters.

Don't Leave Us in the Dark. There are a couple of other situations in reading Scripture publicly that we need to mention here. They don't have to do with emphasis, as such, but they are matters of clarification which deal with characters in story passages. Remember, when you're reading silently to yourself you have the opportunity to read back and discover the context in which an event takes place and who all the characters are. As listeners, we don't have that information at hand.

Supply the Missing Person(s). Frequently a pericope will begin with a pronoun, not identifying the person or persons being referred to. There are many spots in the New Testament dealing with some event involving Jesus, which begin without mentioning his name. Look, for example, at the passage beginning with Luke 4:31:

> [31]*He* went down to Capernaum, a city in Galilee, and was teaching *them* on the sabbath. [32]They were astounded at his teaching, because he spoke with authority. [33]In the synagogue there was a man who had the spirit of an unclean demon, and he cried out with a loud voice,[34]"Let us alone! What have you to do with us, Jesus of Nazareth? Have you come to destroy us? I know who you are, the Holy One of God." (Luke 4:31-34, NRSV [italics mine])

In verse 34, the "man with the spirit" identifies the main character (the "he" at the beginning of verse 31) as "Jesus of Nazareth." But the rest of us didn't know that right away, did we? Most of us, probably, assumed that the word "he" referred to Jesus. But suppose some poor souls in our congregation didn't have an inkling who "he" was. They would be sitting there scratching their heads, totally lost, until we finally got to verse 34. So why not be kind to all and *supply the missing person*, and begin like this:

> *Jesus* went down to Capernaum, a city in Galilee, and was teaching *the people* on the sabbath.

We've changed the "he" to "Jesus" and the "them" to "the people." Why change "them"? For clarity's sake. In this instance, it was simply an unnamed amorphous mass of people (and not a specific group like his disciples or the Pharisees). Letting us know that Jesus was teaching "the people" rather than some mysterious "them" will keep someone among our listeners from assuming Jesus was talking to something other than people.

Here's another example, from Mark 10:46:

> *They* came to Jericho. As *he and his* disciples and a large crowd were leaving Jericho ....

As a Scripture reader, I want to guide my listeners through the story or the thoughts (or whatever the content) as carefully as possible—trying to insure that they're with me and what I'm saying. If I leave "open doors" in the form of pronouns without naming the characters, I'm inviting my listeners to go off on a tangent of imagination of their own. It's like saying, "OK, I'm not going to tell you who this story is about, so you can 'fill in the blanks' and create your own story." So I may be sitting there filling in what's not been specified:

> *The Harlem Globetrotters* came to Jericho. As *Warren Beatty* and *Mahatma Gandhi's* disciples and a large crowd were leaving Jericho ....

You may think it's obvious that your listeners will be able to discern who you're talking about even if you don't tell them. Don't presume that. Could it be that we lose some unchurched who come into our midst as seekers because we presume they know what our message is? Can we presume they know our language? You need to decide that. The issue is not whether or not I should "edit" as I'm reading Scripture. The issue is *clarity and understanding*. Woe unto me if I change the message or the intent of the message to serve my own purposes or to be "helpful" to my listeners. But maybe double-woe if I blithely give voice to the Word without at the same time caring if people understand clearly what that Word is all about.

Another passage, this one from Acts, chapter 17 (NRSV), illustrates the same principle. This time, however, our listeners could guess from now until the next of never and probably not figure out who Paul was waiting for. Here's the way this pericope begins:

> While Paul was waiting for *them* [italics mine again] in Athens, he was deeply distressed . . . .

Do *you* know who Paul was waiting for? Probably not, unless you had been reading the earlier verses of the chapter. Then you'd know that Silas and Timothy had not yet come into the scene. I think the most considerate thing we could do for our readers is to inform them by *substituting the missing persons* for the pronoun:

> While Paul was waiting for *Silas and Timothy* in Athens, he was deeply distressed . . . .

And it's done. Obviously, you could accomplish the same thing by saying something in an introduction to the passage ("In this passage, Paul is waiting for Silas and Timothy, etc. . . ."). But in terms of economy of words and for the sake of simplicity, the substitution of names for the pronoun does the job well.

Sort Out the Characters. There are some stories in which pronouns are used instead of names, to the point where confusion may well reign as one tries to sort out who's doing what to whom? One such passage that immediately comes to mind is from Genesis 32, where Jacob wrestles with the angel. The passage (Genesis 32:22-29, RSV) reads like this [italics throughout are mine]:

> The same night *he* arose and took his two wives, his two maids, and his eleven children, and crossed the ford of the Jabbok. He took them and sent them across the stream, and likewise everything that he had. And Jacob was left alone; and a man wrestled with him until the breaking of the day. When the man saw that he did not prevail against Jacob, he touched the hollow of *his* thigh; and Jacob's thigh was put out of joint as *he* wrestled with *him*. Then *he* said, "Let me go;, for the day is breaking." But Jacob said, "I will not let you go, unless you bless me." And *he* said to *him*, "What is your name?" And he said, "Jacob." Then *he* said, "Your name shall no more be called Jacob, but Israel, for you have striven with God and with men, and have prevailed." Then Jacob asked him, "Tell me, I pray, your name?" But *he* said, "Why is it that you ask my name?" And there *he* blessed *him*.

Now, if I'm really very familiar with the story, I can probably sort out for myself what's happening. But just look at all those italicized pronouns! Again, if I'm reading it silently to myself,

I can take the time to figure out who is acting, who is speaking, and what's going on. But it really would be kinder to my listeners to provide them now and then with some sort of clue as to who's who. Something like this would be in order:

> The same night *Jacob* arose and took his two wives, his two maids, and his eleven children, and crossed the ford of the Jabbok. He took them and sent them across the stream, and likewise everything that he had. And Jacob was left alone; and a man wrestled with him until the breaking of the day. When the man saw that he did not prevail against Jacob, he touched the hollow of *[Jacob's]* thigh; and Jacob's thigh was put out of joint as *the man* wrestled with *him*. Then *the man* said, "Let me go, for the day is breaking." But Jacob said, "I will not let you go, unless you bless me." And *the man* said to *him*, "What is your name?" And he said, "Jacob." Then *the man* said, "Your name shall no more be called Jacob, but Israel, for you have striven with God and with men, and have prevailed." Then Jacob asked him, "Tell me, I pray, your name." But *he* said, "Why is it that you ask my name?" And there *the man* blessed *him*. (Or: And there *he* blessed *Jacob*.)

At the end of the story of Elisha and the Shunammite woman, there's similar confusion of identities in the climactic scene where Elisha goes into the room where the dead child is lying. This passage (2 Kings 4:32-36) reads:

> When Elisha came into the house, he saw the child lying dead on his bed. So he went in and shut the door upon the two of them, and prayed to the Lord. Then he went up and lay upon the child, putting *his* mouth upon *his* mouth, *his* eyes upon *his* eyes, and *his* hands upon *his* hands; and as *he* stretched himself upon *him*, the flesh of the child became warm. Then *he* got up again, and walked once to and fro in the house, and went up, and stretched himself upon *him*; the child sneezed seven times, and the child opened his eyes. Then *he* summoned Gehazi and said, "Call this Shunammite." So he called her. And when she came to him, he said, "Take up your son."

Italics, again, are mine. A few other pronouns could *possibly* be italicized to avoid total confusion, but I suspect things would be a lot clearer just by making a few changes like this:

> When Elisha came into the house, he saw the child lying dead on his bed. So he went in and shut the door upon the two of them, and prayed to the Lord. Then he went up and lay upon the child, putting *his* mouth upon *the child's* mouth, *his* eyes upon *the child's* eyes, and *his* hands upon *the child's* hands; and as *he* stretched himself upon *the child*, the flesh of the child became warm. Then *Elisha* got up again, and walked once to and fro in the house, and went up, and stretched himself upon *the child*; the child sneezed seven times, and the child opened his eyes. Then *Elisha* summoned Gehazi and said, "Call this Shunammite." So he called her. And when she came to him, he said, "Take up your son."

You might change things a bit differently, but some changes are helpful, I think.

The question invariably arises, when one makes these sorts of "adjustments" in the oral reading of Scripture: "Is it okay to 'edit' the Bible that way?" I suppose you'll have to answer that for yourself. It's not as though you were *changing the meaning* of the passage or *being untrue to the intent* of the passage. If you did that, we'd probably all agree that you shouldn't. But just as different groups of scholars, over the years, have come up with different translations of Scripture—each hoping to provide the clearest, most faithful translation—I think this kind of "editing" is both justified and appropriate.

Be Surprised! *Another important thing to keep in mind when wondering what to emphasize is the surprise factor. In the Cana story, YOU DON'T KNOW when Jesus tells the servants to fill the jars with water that they're going to be turned into wine!!! And you're as surprised as the chief steward when he tastes the* __water__ *- (yes, you too think it's still water) and discovers it's been turned into* **WINE!!!**

There are lots of places like this in Scripture where we ought to be surprised. For example, the scene (Matthew 14) where the disciples are out in the boat and Jesus comes to them "walking towards them on the sea." Now I haven't seen that done very many times, so when I read that, I'm going to emphasize it with about a hundred exclamation points because I think it's pretty surprising. I've heard it read as if it happened every day. Have I been missing out on something? Maybe if we're surprised as the story unfolds before us as if for the first time, our listeners will also be surprised and maybe even amazed at the miraculous power of God to act in Jesus Christ!!!

Reading "Lists." What about lists of things, or statements that parallel one another, like some of Paul's lists ("neither death nor life") or Ruth's "where you go I will go"? In general, I'd suggest *varying* them as much as you can without sounding as if you're trying to be terribly inventive or contrived. For example, the Ruth passage (1:16-17) is often read this way:

> Where *you* go *I* will go, and where *you* stay *I* will stay. *Your* people will be *my* people and *your* God *my* God. Where *you* die *I* will die....

The problem with this is (1) it takes on a singsong quality, and (2) it's terribly predictable (read "boring"). Wouldn't it be better to do something like

> Where *you* go *I* will go, and where you *stay* I will *stay*. Your *people* will be *my* people and your *God* my God. Where you *die I* will die....

Two more things, and then a few exercises.

One: certain words just plead to be emphasized by virtue of their very nature. For instance:

> *all   whole   full   always*

cry out to have the /l/ sound extended. Which is more convincing?

> He's got the whole world in his hands

or

> He's got the *wh**o**le* **wor**ld in his hands?

(Be careful, of course, not to overdo it.)

Two: don't emphasize with your head. It looks funny. Besides you might get whiplash.

SOME SIMPLE EXERCISES IN EMPHASIS

1. Peace I leave with you; my peace I give to you. I do not give to you as the world gives. *[John 14:27]*
   Take it phrase by phrase. Major idea in the first phrase is peace, *with possibly a minor emphasis on* leave. *In the second phrase, the only really new idea is* my. *And in the last phrase the contrast is between what* I *give and the* world *gives, with the new concept being* world. *Upshot will be something like this:*

   > *Peace* I *leave* with you; *my* peace I give to you. *I* do not give to you as the *world* gives.

2. For where your treasure is, there your heart will be also. *[Luke 12:34]*
   Major idea in the first phrase is treasure, *with possibly a minor emphasis on* where. *In the second phrase, the new idea is* heart, *with a minor emphasis for contrast on* there ... also. *Logical result: something like this:*

   > For where your *treasure* is, *there* your *heart* will be *also*.

3. If the LORD is God, follow him; but if Baal, then follow him. *[1 Kings 18:21]*
   This one's a bit tricky. It looks as if it's a simple contrast between following God or following Baal. And that's part of it. To emphasize it that way would make it: If the *LORD* is God, follow *him*; but if *Baal*, then follow *him*. *The result* sounds *a little monotonous, but the real problem is, that's the wrong meaning. Elijah's telling the people to stop hobbling back and forth between two "opinions"—two gods. What he's saying is:* If the *LORD* is God, *follow* him.... *In other words, stop equivocating. Then he goes on to add:* but if *Baal*, then follow *him*. *He sets up the command to follow, then makes the contrast.*

   > If the *LORD* is *God*, *follow* him; but if *Baal*, then follow *him*.

4. Everyone then who hears these words of mine and acts on them will be like a wise man who built his house on rock.... And everyone who hears these words of mine and does not act on them will be like a foolish man who built his house on sand. *[Matthew 7:24,26]*
   Lots and lots of new stuff in the first sentence: everyone hearing words of mine *and* acting on them *(major emphases on hearing words and acting) is like a* wise man *who* built his house *on* rock. *But in the second sentence, not much at all is new, except:* not, foolish, his *and* sand—*all matters of contrast. Most people fail to see the need for emphasis on* his, *but it's in contrast to the first man:*

> *Everyone* then who *hears* these _words_ of _mine_ and _acts_ on them will be like a _wise_ man who built his _house_ on _rock_.... And everyone who hears these words of mine and does _not_ act on them will be like a _foolish_ man who built _his_ house on _sand_.

5. If anyone is overtaken in a transgression, you who have received the Spirit should restore such a one in a spirit of gentleness. Take care that you yourselves are not tempted. Bear one another's burdens, and in this way you will fulfill the law of Christ. *[Galatians 6:1-2]*

*This is fairly simple: an **If ... then** clause, a contrast between the sinner and the saints, and a cause and effect statement—with a number of more minor emphases along the way:*

> _If_ anyone is _overtaken_ in a _transgression_, you who have received the _Spirit_ should _restore_ such a one in a spirit of _gentleness_. Take care that _you yourselves_ are not tempted. _Bear_ one another's burdens, and in this way you will _fulfill_ the law of Christ.

6. Now I know in part, then I shall understand fully, even as I have been fully understood. *[1 Corinthians 13:12b]*

*A neat jamboree of contrasts: **now** and **then**, **in part** and **fully**, **understanding** and **being understood***

> _Now_ I know _in part_, _then_ I shall understand _fully_, even as I have **been** fully understood.

7. Then Elijah said to all the people, "Come near to me"; and all the people came near to him. *[1 Kings 18:30]*

A good, simple cause and effect statement—he said "come," and they came:

> Then Elijah said to all the people, _"Come near_ to me"; and all the people _came_ near to him.

Incidentally, if you're reading from the King James Version, take note regarding the significance of those italicized words. The italics *do not* mean you should emphasize these words (as in the words "do not" in this sentence). They indicate words not found in the original Greek, which have been added to make better sense when read in English. For example (from Luke 1:28):

> "And the angel came in unto her, and said, Hail, *thou that art* highly favored, the Lord is with thee: blessed *art* thou among women."

In the original Greek it would read something like:

> "And the angel came in unto her, and said, Hail, highly favored, the Lord with thee: blessed thou among women."

A summary of matters relating to emphasis:

♦ Emphasize *idea carriers, & not unimportant words*. In descending order, the following are likely to deserve emphasis: nouns, verbs, adjectives, pronouns, adverbs, conjunctions, articles & prepositions. Give special attention to the initial presentation of *main idea or theme, characters, locations*.

♦ Be especially careful not to pounce on *prepositions*.

♦ Emphasize *the new idea or contrasting idea*, rather than something already named.

♦ Emphasize *conditional* ("if ... then") *or causal* ("because ... therefore") *relationships*.

♦ *Don't stress anything you could leave out without changing the meaning.*

---

[1] *I did learn of one instance where a misplaced inflection in Swedish can be, shall we say, "devastating." I think the whole phrase goes like this: "i Gud Faders, Sons och Heliga Andens namn." If you leave the inflection level on the word "andens," you're praying "in the name of God the Father, Son, and Holy Ghost." If you let the inflection fall on "andens," you're praying "in the name of God the Father, Son, and Holy Duck."*

[2] *One of the delights of sharing my working manuscript with former students (among others) is the added insight they provide. Steve Shaffer suggests that our penchant for punching prepositions comes "because we learn them in huge lists in grade school, punching them for emphasis while drilling—ex.: 'The squirrel went over the log, through the log, around the log, under the log.'" In addition, Steve offered the following: "Two things that always help me train orally are 1) slowing down until I get that idea of what is being said, and 2) repeating phrases over and over until I'm in the groove and master the rhythm." Helpful insights.*

Putting It All Together: Phrasing Matters

...in the church I would rather speak five intelligible words to instruct others than ten thousand words in a tongue. (1 Corinthians 14:19)
Deal with your servant according to your love and teach me your decrees.
I am your servant; give me discernment that I may understand your statutes.
The unfolding of your words gives light; it gives understanding.... (Psalm 119:124-125, 130)

Prayer: Lord, how utterly gracious you are that you trust me to speak your Word of life. Teach my head and my heart as I prepare to read. Let me learn so I can be intelligible, and what I teach let me be taught. Let me first understand as fully as possible what your message is, and then let me speak so that message will be fully understood. Let me be enlightened by what I read, that my reading may bring the light of life to those who hear. And let it all be to your glory. In the name of Jesus my Lord and Savior I pray. Amen.

Where to Pause. One of the trickiest things to work out, sometimes, when reading aloud, is the matter of phrasing. Let me repeat what I said earlier: as a general rule, ignore punctuation in favor of moving with the image or the idea. In other words, you don't want to pause at every comma or other punctuation mark. The question then arises, Where *do* you put your pauses? You use pauses to combine words into meaningful phrases, making sure you put together things that belong together. And you coordinate pauses with breathing, making sure you don't have a phrase so lengthy that you'd have a hard time getting through it on a single breath. (I use double lines [||] to indicate a break or pause for phrasing. For a very small pause, I'd use only a single line [|].)

It pays to look carefully (or maybe I should say "listen carefully") at what you're going to read aloud. Misplaced pauses can misconstrue meaning. Look at this example, from Acts 5:30:

The God of our fathers raised Jesus whom you killed by hanging him on a tree.

You and I know very well what that means: Peter is saying, "God raised Jesus. You killed him, remember, crucified him on that tree?" And that's perfectly clear if you phrase it this way:

The God of our fathers raised Jesus || whom you killed by hanging him on a tree.

But you might be reading along, thinking about something else, and decide that "Jesus whom you killed" certainly is a group of words that go together all right, and so you read:

The God of our fathers raised Jesus whom you killed || by hanging him on a tree.

Even if you have only a tiny little pause there, you've got some kind of heavenly marionette being raised up instead of what really happened. See what does and doesn't make sense? When you read aloud, you really have to be careful to get it together. The right way.

What Goes With What? I recently heard the story of the Good Samaritan read in chapel. In this passage, Jesus answers the lawyer's question, "What must I do to inherit eternal life?" with another question, "What is written in the law? What do you read there?" And the answer, as written, is this (Luke 10:27, NRSV):

> "You shall love the Lord your God with all your heart, and with all your soul, and with all your strength, and with all your mind; and your neighbor as yourself."

Had the reader observed the punctuation, we would have heard that we should love (1) *God* (with totality of heart, soul, and strength) and (2) *our neighbor* (as much as we love ourselves). But the reader's phrasing made the statement come out like this:

> "You shall love the Lord your God with all your heart, and with all your soul, and with all your strength, and with all your mind, and your neighbor ‖ as yourself."

Now we were told to love *God* (with totality of heart and soul and strength and mind and our neighbor) as much as we love *ourselves*. I don't think that's what Jesus had in mind.

And what about our recitation of the Lord's Prayer? Look at it first the way it's punctuated:

> Our Father, who art in heaven; Hallowed be Thy name. Thy kingdom come. Thy will be done; On earth as it is in heaven. Give us this day our daily bread. And forgive us our debts; As we forgive our debtors. And lead us not into temptation; But deliver us from evil; For Thine is the kingdom, and the power, and the glory, for ever. Amen.

Not very many of us *read* this prayer and make note of the punctuation. We've memorized it. And like so many things memorized it can come out pretty much devoid of meaning and especially feeling. Where congregations think about what they're saying, one often hears phrases put together that actually belong together, like:

> Thy will be done On earth as it is in heaven

eliminating a pause at the semicolon in order to say "May your will be done on earth just as it's done in heaven." Thoughtful congregations usually do the same with

> And forgive us our debts As we forgive our debtors

linking the two thought units: "You forgive us as we forgive our debtors." But what happens to the sense of things when we get down to the ending:

> For Thine is the kingdom, and the power, and the glory, for ever.

I don't think I've ever heard a congregation that didn't recite it like this:

> For Thine is the kingdom | and the power | and the glory for ever.

Do we make sense when we say it this way? Or do we do it just out of habit? This phrasing says, in essence: "Yours is the kingdom, and the power, and the *eternal glory*," since we've placed the "for ever" into a phrase with "glory" and *only* "glory". What about God's kingdom and power?

Are they merely evanescent while God's glory alone is eternal? If that's what you *mean*, then okay. But if God's kingdom and God's power and God's glory are *all three* in the "world without end" category, then we ought to change the way we phrase the words. What if we took away the commas (and pauses) after "kingdom" and "power" and shifted the pause so it occurs after "glory," and in fact made it a good healthy pause? It would come out like this:

> For Thine is the kingdom and the power and the glory || for ever.

Now all three—kingdom and power and glory—are eternal, sempiternal, everlasting, unending! Isn't that what we *really* mean? Furthermore, since a pause is one means of emphasizing what we're saying, that pause before "for ever" gives the end of the prayer a much more affirming ring ("for ever!! Amen!!") than letting things peter out with "and the glory forever. Amen." I really like those traditions which put "kingdom and power and glory" together and then end with "for ever and ever." But since other traditions (including my own) don't include that final "and ever" couldn't we at least learn to phrase things so they make sense? I realize that if we're ever convinced we *ought* to say the Lord's Prayer in ways that make sense we're going to have to teach our congregations how to do it. But that's not really such a formidable job, is it? To begin with, we as worship leader (the one who's leading us in the recitation of the Lord's Prayer) could on our own simply stop dead with a big pause between "glory" and "for ever." Granted, for a few weeks we'd be saying "for ever" and "Amen" after everyone else has finished. But maybe after a while we'd gain a cult following of "Pausers" and then turn a whole congregation around. Or something could be said in a printed or spoken announcement or even in a sermon about making sense when we speak. I think God would be happy that we realized the "foreverness" of His kingdom and power—as well as His glory!

Punctuation. Often, the punctuation is not only <u>not</u> helpful, but it's downright *in the way* of making sense. Consider this example from the Belshazzar story:

> There is a man in thy kingdom, in whom is the spirit of the holy gods; and in the days of thy father light and understanding and wisdom, like the wisdom of the gods, was found in him.

Grammatically, of course, the punctuation's right on target. And when you read it silently to yourself it will make sense to you. But if you observe the commas as pause indicators when you read *aloud*, it messes up the meaning altogether. First of all, if you stop at the comma after the word "kingdom," you've given an incomplete idea. *There is a man in thy kingdom.* Big deal! There's a lot of men in thy kingdom. The *whole idea* is: there's a man in your kingdom who has the spirit of the gods. So you need to read right through that comma. Next, you need a pause after "father" even though there's no punctuation to indicate a break. "When your father was alive, this man...." Finally, look at the phrase "like the wisdom of the gods," set off in print by two commas. What does it modify? Light and understanding and wisdom? Or just wisdom? It's the latter, of course. What it's saying is simply "godlike wisdom" was found in him. So put a break after "understanding" and none after "wisdom," and you've got it right. The result, then, is this:

> There is a man in thy kingdom in whom is the spirit of the holy gods ||
> and in the days of thy father || light and understanding ||
> and wisdom like the wisdom of the gods | was found in him.

I suggested a little break after "gods" since you might need it for breathing. For sense, it doesn't really matter.

Every once in a while, you run into a sentence that's both long and un-punctuated. Such a sentence demonstrates the principle that you can't let your phrasing be guided by punctuation. For example, this sentence appears in a book by Aldous Huxley:

> It is from the more or less obscure intuition of the oneness that is the ground and principle of all
> multiplicity that philosophy takes its source.[1]

Reading silently to myself, I'll take the time to "unscrew the inscrutable" nature of this statement and put in a few pauses to make sense—even though there are no punctuation marks to help me out. It's saying something about the intuition of some kind of oneness. And from that intuition-of-oneness philosophy emerges. If that's the case, I'll probably package "that is the ground and principle of all multiplicity" together because it tells me what kind of oneness I'm dealing with. That takes some time to do when I'm figuring out a statement as I read to myself. But that's okay, because I have the leisure to be able to take the time to do that. But if I'm reading this sentence to an audience I'm in a bit of a bind. First of all, I can't just stop and say "Now you take a moment to sort all that out and then I'll go on." And second, it would be presumptuous and probably arrogant of me to lay a sentence like that on my audience and *expect* them to decipher it on the spot. And third, unless I have really great breath control, I'm likely to be hard put to get through that sentence on a single breath. So I will need and want to phrase the statement with a few well-placed pauses. And I'll probably want to make those pauses big enough that I can catch a breath and my listeners can catch my train of thought before it chugs off without them. The result might be something like this:

> It is from the more or less obscure intuition of the oneness || that is the ground and principle of
> all multiplicity || that philosophy takes its source.

Or we may run into a passage that's punctuated perfectly well (given that punctuation serves the eye of the reader) but that punctuation doesn't help when the passage is *read aloud*. Look, for example, at this sequence from the Gospel of John (John 8:4-9, NRSV). In its printed form it looks like this:

> [The scribes and the Pharisees said to Jesus], "Teacher, this woman was caught in the very act of
> committing adultery. Now in the law Moses commanded us to stone such women. Now what do
> you say?" They said this to test him, so that they might have some charge to bring against him.
> Jesus bent down and wrote with his finger on the ground. When they kept on questioning him, he
> straightened up and said to them. "Let anyone among you who is without sin be the first to throw

a stone at her." And once again he bent down and wrote on the ground. When they heard it, they went away, one by one, beginning with the elders; and Jesus was left alone with the woman standing before him.

This is a marvelous passage to read. It defies being read "straight" through without the drama in it coming to life. First of all there's the skulduggery of the scribes and Pharisees, trying to trap Jesus by getting him to go against Moses' command in the law. Short of twisting one's black mustache like Simon Legree going "Heh, heh, heh!" the reader ought to try to let their scheming come through. If we read their three lines straight through, we miss that element of "Let's get Jesus" that's there as a subtext to their statements. There are any number of ways their lines could be broken up. Here's one example:

"Teacher || this woman | was caught in the very act | of committing | adultery ||| Now in the law | Moses || commanded us | to stone | such women. Now what do | you | say?"

The next line, "They said this to test him, so that they might have some charge to bring against him," is almost like a stage-direction "aside" telling the narrator how to read their lines, and given to the narrator to "clue in" the audience. In the line that follows, let the phrasing match the movements—in other words, let Jesus move purposefully here and without any rush:

Jesus bent down || and wrote | with his finger | on the ground.

Again, the pacing of the action moves the pacing of the reading and the placement of pauses:

When they kept on questioning him | he straightened up || and said to them | "Let anyone among you | who is without sin || be the first | to throw a stone at her." And once again he bent down ||and wrote | on the ground.

The punctuation in the rest of the passage is close to being helpful to our phrasing. But the movement of the passage—the hesitation with which everyone moves—should help our placement of pauses. Watch what's happening. Look at their eyes. One of them is looking towards another. "Will *he* do it?" Eyes dart back and forth. Finally one man drops his stone. He turns quietly, hoping not to be noticed. He shuffles away from the circle standing there. Another man looks around. Now his glance falls down to the dirt in front of him. His stone lands there, and he too turns and walks off. *Play with the tension of this scene.* They don't all hear Jesus, and say, "OK, that's it! You win!" and all turn at once and skip away. Jesus has called their bluff. Jesus has beaten them at their game. As you see them slowly move away, tell us about it:

When they heard it || they went away || one | by one || beginning | with the elders ||| and Jesus | was left alone | with the woman | standing before him.

Look again at the contrast between the punctuation and the pauses built in for phrasing. We've ignored most of the punctuation and built in our own pauses. Remember that punctuation guides the reader's eyes (when reading silently) and that phrasing serves the hearers' ears (when reading aloud). And remember that we're moving with the image and not with the punctuation. Look again at the passage from John 9 (cf. *Explore the Word - rate and pauses*). Build in phrasing pauses as needed, or things can happen too fast, too all-at-once, like a silent movie.

Leave the commas in, and a fast moving action can get bogged down. As in this portion from the Belshazzar story (Daniel 5, KJV), where a drunken king calls for the sacred vessels from the temple:

> that the king, and his princes, his wives and his concubines might drink therein.

Observe all the commas, and you give us a grocery list:

> that the king,
> and his princes,
> his wives
> and his concubines
> might drink therein.

(I know, I added a few "stops" where there were no commas, but once you start the "list" that's the way it usually gets read.) Take the commas out, and the party begins:

> that the king and his princes his wives and his concubines might drink therein.

And you can almost hear them shouting, "All right!!! Let's all drink from those gold and silver goblets! Right on!!" And then the revelry continues:

> They drank wine, and praised the gods of gold, and of silver, of brass, of iron, of wood, and of stone.

Again, leave the commas in and you have a shopping list:

> They drank wine
> and praised the gods of gold
> and of silver
> of brass
> of iron
> of wood
> and of stone.

And a loaf of bread, a pound of hamburger and a dozen eggs. And that's not very true to life. Here, your best bet is to ignore the commas altogether, catch a good breath, and sail through the statement nonstop, letting the revelers have their fling:

> They drank wine and praised the gods of gold and of silver of brass of iron of wood and of stone.

We change or modify or obliterate the punctuation because we're trying in speaking to create a moving image in our listeners' minds' eyes. To accomplish this, we've begun the process of *looking through words* as we're reading those words and *visualizing* the image that we're trying to communicate. This process of visualization is wonderfully helpful when we're trying to give voice to the written word.

Phrasing and Visualization. Here's something you're going to hear and laugh about (once you've thought about it) over and over at Christmas time—from Luke 2:

> And they went with haste, and found Mary and Joseph, and the babe lying in a manger.

If you did read this the way it's punctuated, it'd be all right. They found Mary and Joseph. And over on the other side of the room was the baby Jesus in the manger. And if you *visualized* it that way it would work for you. But how many times have you heard it read thus:

> And they went with haste || and found Mary and Joseph and the babe || lying in a manger.

or even:

> And they went with haste || and found Mary || and Joseph || and the babe || lying in a manger.

Either way, you've got mighty crowded housing conditions. Keep in mind the absolute importance of *visualization*. It's not likely you're going to visualize all three lying in a manger. So if you visualize them occupying different spaces let that spacing come through in your phrasing:

> And they went with haste, and found Mary and Joseph|← *[on one side of the room; and on the other side:]* →|and the babe lying in a manger.

A bit earlier in Luke 2 you're confronted with this Gordian knot of a sentence:

> And Joseph also went up from Galilee, out of the city of Nazareth, into Judea, unto the city of David, which is called Bethlehem; (because he was of the house and lineage of David;) to be taxed with Mary his espoused wife, being great with child.

Please, for your listeners' sake, erase all those commas and put in your own phrase markings. Break the passage down into its logical structure: *Joseph went from point A to point B (for this reason) for a particular purpose and accompanied by his pregnant wife.* In other words:

Joseph went from point A:	And Joseph also went up from Galilee, out of the city of Nazareth ||
to point B:	into Judea, unto the city of David, which is called Bethlehem ||
(for this reason):	(because he was of the house and lineage of David) ||
for a particular purpose:	to be taxed ||
along with his pregnant wife:	with Mary his espoused wife, being great with child.

Remember, he wasn't taxed with Mary (at least not noticeably so this time, though she may have taxed his patience on other occasions). This time he was taxed with money. And get it straight in your head and in ours which one of them was pregnant.

Connecting Words and Phrases. Here's another matter. How do you read the following texts?

> (a) And suddenly there was with the angel a multitude of the heavenly host praising God and saying, "Glory to God in the highest and on earth peace among those with whom he is pleased!"
>
> (b) And when the king of Israel read the letter, he rent his clothes and said, "Am I God, to kill and to make alive, that this man sends word to me to cure a man of his leprosy? Only consider and see how he is seeking a quarrel with me."

The problem at hand is the *connecting phrase or word* in each case. In (a) it's the words "and saying" and in (b) the words "and said." Most readers will look at the fact that there's no comma after the first "God" in (a) or after "clothes" in (b) and that there *is* a comma after "saying" (a) and "said" (b) and they'll pause with the comma. This would make good sense if (a) read "praising God and *dancing*" and (b) read "rent his clothes and *swore a blue streak*"—in other

Getting the WORD Across—97
Putting It All Together: Phrasing Matters

words, did *two* things. But the heavenly host was doing only one thing: "praising." And the king of Israel did only one thing: "rent." So doesn't it make more sense to put the pauses elsewhere? Try reading it this way:

    (a) And suddenly there was with the angel a multitude of the heavenly host || praising God ||
    and saying *[no pause]* "Glory to God in the highest ...."
    (b) And when the king of Israel read the letter || he rent his clothes ||
    and said *[no pause]* "Am I God ...?"

I sometimes wonder if the habit of pausing after a construction like "and saying" is so ingrained because of the influence of Handel's *Messiah*. The soprano sings: "praising God, and saying"—then there's a gap while everyone turns the page and waits for the downbeat from the conductor, and then the choir comes in: "Glory to God, glory to God in the highest...." (Sorry to lay that on you, George Frideric. It was just a thought.)

While we're at it, take another look at what the heavenly host said:

    "Glory to God in the highest and on earth peace among those with whom he is pleased!"

Does it not make sense that the most important word in that proclamation is the promise of "peace"? If so, does it make sense to phrase it the way it's punctuated—i.e. with no pauses except maybe for a quick gasp after "highest" for the shallow breathers among us? Read that way, the long-expected Jesus, the promise that the world would one day have a Prince of Peace, is treated as sort of a "throwaway." Why not a healthy pause before and after the word "peace" to set it off? Let the promised "peace" be heralded like the gem it is in that setting, like this:

    And suddenly there was with the angel | a multitude of the heavenly host || praising God || and saying,
    "Glory to God in the highest | and on earth ||| peace ||| among those with whom he is pleased!"

As a general rule, any <u>connective</u> such as *saying* or *and said* should go with what is being said *<u>with no pause between the connective and the words spoken.</u>*
For instance: *[one action]* He opened his mouth and taught them | |PAUSE| |
        [next action] saying, "Blessed are the poor in spirit...."
               [NO PAUSE BETWEEN <u>saying</u> and "Blessed]
- or - *[one action]* They...went out to meet him | |PAUSE| |
        [next action] shouting, "Hosanna! Blessed is the one...!"
               [NO PAUSE BETWEEN <u>shouting</u> and "Hosanna!]
- or - *[one action]* ...a multitude of the heavenly host, praising God | |PAUSE| |
        [next action] and saying, "Glory to God in the highest heaven...."
               [NO PAUSE BETWEEN <u>and saying</u> and "Glory]
- or - *[one action]* ...and he came to her | |PAUSE| |
        [next action] and said, "Greetings, favored one!"
               [NO PAUSE BETWEEN <u>and said</u> and "Greetings]

**Make the Best Sense**. Sometimes when and where you pause for phrasing can be moot. But it's important to think ahead and try to make sure you're making the best sense. A couple of spots where a little pause is needed in order not to be confusing might be noted. Here's one from the book of Ruth (1:16):

> Entreat me not to leave you or to return from following you ....

To make sense, you need a little pause after "not"—"Don't ask me to ...."

> Entreat me not ‖ to leave you or to return from following you ....

Another spot occurs in the Joseph story (Genesis 37:23):

> ...they stripped him of his robe, the long robe with sleeves that he wore ....

It just doesn't sound right to hear "with sleeves that he wore," does it? It sounds as if he had a robe but wore only the sleeves. I'd put a small pause after "sleeves" in order to make it _sound_ right.

> ...they stripped him of his robe ‖ the long robe with sleeves | that he wore ....

A similar "that _sounds_ odd" feeling comes from the passage about Jesus and the woman taken in adultery (John 8:8):

> And once more he bent down and wrote with his finger on the ground.

That presents an odd picture. I'd put a small break after "wrote" and another after "finger" in order to sort out for my listeners what's happening.

> And once more he bent down and wrote | with his finger | on the ground.

Or you could take away the pause after "wrote":

> And once more he bent down and wrote with his finger | on the ground.

In 1 Corinthians 13, Paul writes:

> So faith, hope, love abide, these three; but the greatest of these is love.

"Love abide" doesn't work. Please put a break after "love." In fact, there's so much that's important in this statement, I'd break it up like this:

> So faith | hope | love | abide ‖ these three ‖ but the greatest of these is love.

In 1 Kings 18:30 this appears:

> And he repaired the altar of the Lord that had been thrown down.

Just so we fully understand _what_ (instead of _who_) had been thrown down, we really need a small break after "Lord."

> And he repaired the altar of the Lord | that had been thrown down.

Finally, just for the fun of it, I'll share two examples that made me chuckle when I heard them.

One was in the reading of Luke 11:14:

> [Jesus] was casting out a demon that was dumb.

The reader put a pause, along with a falling inflection, after "demon." The result *sounded like*:

> Jesus was casting out a demon. That was dumb.

The other was in a sermon, rather than in a reading. The sentence was "Jesus Christ, says the New Testament, died for you." It was phrased with the punctuation (pauses where the commas were), which was okay. But unfortunately there was no change of inflection, so the listener *heard*: "Jesus Christ says the New Testament died for you." I couldn't find anything about that in my theology books. That was a sentence, by the way, virtually crying out, *"Rewrite!!!"*

Don't you hope God has a really good sense of humor?

---

[1]Aldous Huxley. *The Perennial Philosophy.* New York: Harper & Row, Publishers, 1970, p. 5.

Internalizing

The boy Samuel ministered before the Lord under Eli. In those days the word of the Lord was rare; there were not many visions.

One night Eli, whose eyes were becoming so weak that he could barely see, was lying down in his usual place. The lamp of God had not yet gone out, and Samuel was lying down in the temple of the Lord, where the ark of God was. Then the Lord called Samuel.

Samuel answered, "Here I am." And he ran to Eli and said, "Here I am; you called me."

But Eli said, "I did not call; go back and lie down" So he went and lay down.

Again the Lord called, "Samuel!" And Samuel got up and went to Eli and said, "Here I am; you called me."

"My son," Eli said, "I did not call; go back and lie down."

Now Samuel did not yet know the Lord: The word of the Lord had not yet been revealed to him.

The Lord called Samuel a third time, and Samuel got up and went to Eli and said, "Here I am; you called me."

Then Eli realized that the Lord was calling the boy. So Eli told Samuel, "Go and lie down, and if he calls you, say, 'Speak, Lord, for your servant is listening.'" So Samuel went and lay down in his place.

The Lord came and stood there, calling as at the other times, "Samuel! Samuel!"

Then Samuel said, "Speak, for your servant is listening."

Prayer: Lord, I thank you that you enter into our world and speak to us. I pray that your Word, as I study it and read it, will fully enter into my world and speak to me. Help me, Lord, to listen to what you have to say. Help me to know that it's not my message but yours. But at the same time help me to internalize your message as fully as possible that through my words, my thoughts, and my life your grace and your blessing will flow from me into the lives of others. I pray in the name of my Savior and Lord, Jesus Christ. Amen.

Visualization. After Princeton Seminary's commencement service a few years ago, a former student approached me with a mile-wide smile and a big hug, and said, "I just want to thank you for teaching me one of the most valuable things I've ever learned!"

Not being terribly accustomed to such effusive badinage, I stammered something back at him along with a puzzled expression on my face that caused him to go on.

"You taught me how important it is to *visualize* in order to internalize what I was reading. And it's helped me not just in my Scripture reading but also in my preaching and just general empathy towards people—towards life in general."

That young man went on to get his Ph.D. in speech communication. Which is totally beside the point of this story. The point is: it's very helpful (important, crucial) to internalize whatever you're going to communicate through the process of visualization. Again, it's a matter of giving your *imagination* over to the Lord to be a sanctified part of your ministry.

Now what am I talking about? You may remember, in the chapter on *phrasing (Putting It All Together: Phrasing Matters)*, the problem in Luke chapter 2 with the statement:

> And they went with haste, and found Mary and Joseph, and the babe lying in a manger.

It's so easy to misread it, putting pauses in places they don't belong and winding up with all three of them in the manger. But if you visualize the scene you're telling about, there's no way you're going to see all three of them lying there. Not unless you have a strange sort of imagination. So that visualizing *tells* you to read:

> And they went with haste,
> and found Mary and Joseph| ←*HERE; now look OVER THERE* → |and the babe lying in a manger.

A good principle to keep in mind: *See* it, then tell us what you see.

A few other examples of the process of visualization and internalization might be helpful.

In Character. A young woman brought in Genesis 22:1-14 to read in conference. The reading was pretty good, but after a semester of working on breathing and keeping the throat free, the voice was very tight and thin. (This often happens. When you're concentrating so hard on trying to interpret the passage well, you lose touch with the voice and diction work you've been doing. It's not easy to integrate the two. At least it doesn't happen overnight, or at the end of one semester as was the case here. But it's important to keep working on both aspects: voice production and diction *and* interpretative skills. Just pray for grace that eventually things will come together. And they will. Trust me. Or better still, trust God.) When she had finished, I suggested she read the passage again in first-person, *as Abraham*. The passage as written (NRSV) begins like this:

> After these things God tested Abraham. He said to him, "Abraham!" And he said, "Here I am."
> He said, "Take your son, your only son Isaac, whom you love, and go to the land of Moriah, and
> offer him there as a burnt offering on one of the mountains that I shall show you." So Abraham
> rose early in the morning, saddled his donkey, and took two of his young men with him, and his
> son Isaac; he cut the wood for the burnt offering, and set out and went to the place in the distance
> that God had shown him. On the third day Abraham looked up and saw the place far away.

Converted to first-person, it reads like this:

After these things God tested me. He said to me, "Abraham!" And I said, "Here I am." He said, "Take your son, your only son Isaac, whom you love, and go to the land of Moriah, and offer him there as a burnt offering on one of the mountains that I shall show you." So I rose early in the morning, saddled my donkey, and took two of my young men with me, and my son Isaac; he cut the wood for the burnt offering, and set out and went to the place in the distance that God had shown me. On the third day I looked up and saw the place far away.

She read the passage "as Abraham," and then re-read it as it was originally written. The result was incredible. Not only did the story itself take on a richer sense of compassion for this faithful father who loved both the Lord and his son, the promised one. But the voice! It was supported, it was full, it was totally free from tension! Why? Because the reader had stepped outside of her own persona and taken on the persona of Abraham, and that enabled her to relax into the character—free from her own vocal tension!

I am absolutely convinced: once you have "become" a character in a passage you're reading, you can never read the passage again without real empathy, real involvement, real entry into the life of the passage.

> Ecstasy. Several years ago, I met a man who was interested in knowing what and how I taught, since I had told him that even though I was a teacher of speech communication I didn't teach people how to write and make speeches. One of the things I told him about was this process of internalization. When I finished, he turned to me with a straight face and said, "Oh, you teach ecstasy!!" My tacit reply was something like, "Yeah, sure!" And then he went on. "Ecstasy means getting outside of your own skin, standing outside of yourself. You know, 'ἐκστάσις'— ἐκ-: *out*, and στάσις: *stand*. You teach people to stand *outside* of themselves and *in* the story, *in* the character, *in* the thoughts!" And you know, he was right. I'd never thought of using the word *ecstasy*, but this man was right on target. And when you come to think of it, doesn't the whole idea of getting into character, getting into the scene, getting into the thought jibe perfectly with our faith? Consider such thoughts as these: "For to me to live is Christ...." (Phil. 1:21), "I have been crucified with Christ; it is no longer I who live, but Christ who lives in me...." (Gal. 2:20), "For you have died, and your life is hid with Christ in God." (Col. 3:3), and even "He must increase, but I must decrease." (John 3:30). Isn't that *real* "ecstasy"? Think about that!

On another occasion, I was working with a student on a reading of Ephesians 6:10-20. Again, the reading was very well done, but it lacked passion. And I think Paul is pretty passionate in his ideas in this passage. I said, "Doug, the problem is that it sounds like a Scripture reading." And it did. Very nicely read. Very polite. Very Presbyterian. So I suggested, "Give yourself a different *image*. You are no longer a person standing in front of a congregation reading the New Testament. You are an officer addressing his troops before the big battle—or a coach pepping up his team before the big game—whatever, but *you are not 'reading Scripture'*!" So he read the passage again. And whoa! Wow! There was *passion*. There was urgency about the spiritual battle at hand. I don't know if it was just the different self-image that did the trick or not. When we watched the videotape of the "before" and "after" readings, we were both astonished at the dramatic difference between them. And we both had the feeling that Someone else was present and at work in that classroom! Don't ever tell me God doesn't do miracles!

Image It. Another little "miracle" took place once when a woman student was working with me on Psalm 139. Her reading was good. But it was bland. It was un*believ*able. I mean, you couldn't believe she was experiencing all the things she was saying to God in that wonderful psalm. A big part of the problem was that she wasn't giving herself any pause time to take in the images and thoughts and feelings she was trying to express. Once again, we tried imaging. The psalm (NRSV) begins like this:

> O Lord, you have searched me and known me.
> You know when I sit down and when I rise up;
> you discern my thoughts from far away.
> You search out my path and my lying down,
> and are acquainted with all my ways.
> Even before a word is on my tongue,
> O Lord, you know it completely.
> You hem me in, behind and before,
> and lay your hand upon me.
> Such knowledge is too wonderful for me;
> it is so high that I cannot attain it.

Our session went something like the following. "Okay, before you say 'O Lord, you have searched me and known me,' *visualize* yourself being sought out by the eye of God. Then say it. See yourself sitting down—*and being seen by God*. Standing up—*and being seen by God*. Thinking thoughts in a little cartoon balloon *that God is looking at*. Seeing God seeing you walking along the path. Then lying down. And seeing and knowing *everything you do and are*. Again, see a word beginning to form on your tongue—*and the Lord already knows it!* See God fencing you in. Behind and before. See God laying a hand on you. See a big rainbow labeled: 'GOD'S KNOWLEDGE' that's absolutely splendiferous and millions of miles beyond your reach." And so forth. When she at last read the passage, it was marvelously believable. She had taken the time and gone through the words into the substance of what the psalmist was trying to communicate about his experience with the Lord.

> You've got to go beyond the words—through the words, underneath the words—into the reality the words are giving expression to. Or else it's not real. No matter how strong your faith is. No matter how much you believe in the words you're speaking. If you're not <u>experiencing</u> the reality as you give voice to it, no one who hears you is likely to know how much you believe it.

Self-image as a reader. I mentioned above a little about self-image as the reader of Scripture. And it's important to mention that here, because it too challenges and deploys the imagination. If you're reading a *story* passage, who you are, where you are and what you're doing as a reader *works* for you as a self-image. You are the presenter, standing before the audience, relating the story. Same goes for reading a *mental* passage (e.g. the thoughts of Paul). Again, you are the presenter, before the audience, sharing these thoughts. But if you're reading a psalm, you're not presenting thoughts directly to an audience. In a sense, you are now not a presenter at all (okay, you *are* presenting it in public, but bear with me), but you're a meditator, a pray-er, a contemplator, doing what you're doing *vis à vis* <u>God</u>, with an audience looking on and listening in. You are not addressing your audience when you say "O Lord, you have searched me and known me." Or "O Lord, our Lord, how excellent is thy name in all the earth." You're addressing *God*, and your audience is *overhearing* what you're doing. So in a sense your *real* image or *real* physical presence (speaker + audience + text) is *contradictory* to the message you're speaking. Therefore, in order to participate in the reality of what you're saying, you may find it useful to create for yourself a *helping image*.

Suppose you're reading Psalm 8. Let your imagination replace your real self-image with this alternative one. You are not standing at a lectern reading Scripture. Instead, you are the psalmist (or you, doing what the psalmist may have been doing) out at night on a grassy hillock, lying on your back, looking up into the sky. Thoughts race through your head, "Wow, Lord! Just look at these heavens of yours! How awesome and grand and magnificent they are, revealing your sovereign grandeur. Look at that moon! Those stars! There must be billions of them. So many. So far away. Such greatness!! And look at me. I'm so small. So infinitesimally tiny. So insignificant. Like a little ant. And yet, Lord, *you* created me! *You* have crowned me with glory and honor. *You* have called *me* to care for this wonderful earth of yours!" And that's going on in your imagination as you read (this time from the KJV):

> When I consider thy heavens, the work of thy fingers, the moon and the stars, which thou hast ordained; What is man, that thou art mindful of him? and the son of man, that thou visitest him?

For thou hast made him a little lower than the angels, and hast crowned him with glory and honor. Thou madest him to have dominion over the works of thy hands; thou has put all things under his feet....

Or take, as another example, the *Magnificat* (Luke 1:46-55, KJV). Mary is speaking these words:

> My soul doth magnify the Lord,
> And my spirit hath rejoiced in God my Saviour.
> For he hath regarded the low estate of his handmaiden:
> for, behold, from henceforth all generations shall call me blessed.
> For he that is mighty hath done to me great things; and holy is his name.
> And his mercy is on them that fear him from generation to generation.
> He hath shewed strength with his arm;
> he hath scattered the proud in the imagination of their hearts.
> He hath put down the mighty from their seats, and exalted them of low degree.
> He hath filled the hungry with good things; and the rich he hath sent empty away.
> He hath holpen his servant Israel, in remembrance of his mercy;
> As he spake to our fathers, to Abraham, and to his seed for ever.

Now you, the reader, are saying these words on behalf of Mary—if you will, *in character* as Mary. You can't possibly image Mary as standing up at a lectern of some sort before the Kiwanis Club or an audience at Chautauqua, saying, "Good afternoon, ladies and gentlemen. My soul doth magnify the Lord." So your real image as you stand there reading is preposterously antithetical to the Mary-image you're presenting. So *imagine* Mary. Is she kneeling? Sitting? Head bowed? Whatever, that's your *helping image*. Or provide an image of *yourself* saying these words of Mary's as a devotional act of your own[1]. Are you doing this in some posture of prayer? In your study? Whatever that image is, that can be your helping image. The important thing to remember is: both the imagery of the *content* of your material and your own *self-image* as the communicator must work together somewhere within the realm of internalization - visualization - imagination if your communication is going to be more than just the reciting of words.

I mentioned above that your self-image as one reading a mental passage (e.g. the thoughts of Paul) is compatible with the message and its content. But as you prepare to read the passage, and even as you read it publicly, what if you were to imagine yourself as Paul, addressing the Corinthians, the Philippians, Timothy, etc.? It might help you get outside of your own head. It might also make you a little more passionate sharing Paul's thoughts as though you were he and not a Scripture reader twenty centuries removed from the situation Paul is addressing. Try it! It couldn't hurt. And it might even help.

Group Study of a Passage. Both speech communication classes and narrative preaching classes have found beneficial the following sequence of approaches to a story passage. The same procedures can be done by individuals in preparing a passage. The purpose is to stretch the imagination to the maximum.

1. _READ_ your Scripture text to others in your group.
2. _Paraphrasing_ (i.e. in your own words), _RE-TELL_ the story to your group.
3. Tell the story from the perspective of the _MAIN CHARACTER_ in the story.
4. Tell the story from the perspective of _ANY OTHER CHARACTER_ in the story _(real or imagined)_.
5. Now _YOU_ are the _ORIGINAL STORYTELLER_, telling the story as you experience its unfolding. Entering into the _sensory world_ of the story, respond to the _following questions_ which members of your group will be asking you:
    - _What do you see?_
    - _What do you hear?_
    - _What do you taste?_
    - _What do you smell?_
    - _What do you feel?_
(Responses must be _concrete_ and not abstract. For example, you cannot _see_ or _hear_ "joy"—but you _can_ see "a broad smile" and hear "laughter".)
6. Assume the identity of _ANY CHARACTER_ in the story. Members of your group are to interview you _as that character_. You must maintain your identity as that character, even if the group distracts you or laughs, and you must respond to all questions _in character_.

Beyond Words. Remember, as we read the Word of God, we need to go _beyond words_. Through them. Beneath them into another kind of reality. Words on a page _represent_ a reality: an event, a thought, a feeling. The words themselves are not the reality. If anything, they're realities embalmed in ink on paper. The event took place, the thought occurred, the feeling arose—_then_ came the words to relate these realities. As people who read Scripture aloud, it's as important for us to energize and utilize our imaginations as anything else we bring to that ministry. The process of internalization enables us to step through the wardrobe of words and enter into the real world touched by the hand of God. When we enter that world and that world indwells us, then it comes to life through us in our reading. That fully happens only when we surrender ourselves and our ministry to God, asking God to sanctify our imaginations so the original life of the material we read will come back into us—become incarnate in our imaginations—so that as we read it it may come to life through us as the living Word of God for our listeners and for us.

----

[1]*Let me suggest that* any *passage you read will become more alive if you spend time in prayer with it. This is particularly true of the psalms and other devotional material. If their very nature is devotional, how can we presume to read them to others without having experienced them as devotional ourselves?*

PART TWO

The
INSTRUMENT
Comes Alive

What Happens When We Speak?

For you created my inmost being;
   you knit me together in my mother's womb.
I praise you because I am fearfully and wonderfully made;
   your works are wonderful,
   I know that full well. (Psalm 139:13-14)

Prayer: O Lord, my Creator, I thank you for my life, for every breath I take, every word and every thought that reminds me of you. I know that you have created me, wonderfully, because you are a wonderful God. Forgive me for taking so many of your gifts for granted, including my very life. Even as you have redeemed me through the blood of Jesus Christ your Son, so redeem my everyday thoughts, my everyday awareness, that I may see your touch in all of my life. Help me to understand myself better that I may better serve and glorify you, for the sake of your blessed Son. Amen.

Where did you learn to speak? That's a rather tricky question to try to answer. In a real sense, you and I learned to speak from people who never learned to speak from people who never learned to speak, and so on. It just happened. Just like the habit of eating and sleeping and breathing and bathing and all sorts of other things we never learned to do but just *do*, speech is a habit. We just got into particular habits of speaking and probably weren't (a) aware of what those habits were or (b) told by others that we ought to change or do something about our speech habits. The exception to (b), of course, would be the kind of extra help we might have received to work on a lisp, a faulty [l] or [r] sound, or correction for some sort of speech pathology. But, basically, speech is *habit*. And habits bear certain qualities.

Speech is habit.

First of all, these habits may be annoying to others. If I were in the habit of taking off my shoes and playing with my toes, you might find that offensive. But I wouldn't know that unless you told me. Then I would know and then I could do something about it. And you probably would tell me. You might take me aside and gently say, "You know, it really is rather distracting to see you playing with your toes during our conversation." And I would understand and quit playing with my toes. Suppose the situation were the same with my speech habit. I may have a voice that annoys you—one you find offensive. But I wouldn't know that unless you told me. And here's where the comparison between the *playing with toes habit* and the *voice like fingernails on the blackboard habit* would probably end. Because you probably *wouldn't* take me aside and gently say, "You know, your voice is terribly annoying." Because you're too polite. And the rest of society is too polite. So I go through life with a disgusting voice and am never aware of it. Oh, I may not like the sound of my voice if I hear it on a tape recorder, but that's true of most of us. I can't stand to hear myself on tape. There may not be anything wrong with my voice, but it just doesn't sound to me when I hear it played back like it sounds to me when I'm speaking. And even if there were something bothersome about the sound of my voice as I hear it played back, I probably wouldn't know what to do about it. So the habit could persist.

Second, those habits can be changed. You told me I shouldn't play with my toes, so I stopped. And even though you're not going to say anything critical about my voice, I can learn what my voice habits are and I can change them. "Polite" people won't say anything. After all, to criticize someone's voice is such a personal matter—voice is so directly associated with my persona—that others will just let me go on being annoying and not say anything. But there are "impolite" people who can tell me lots about my voice. People who teach speech. People who love you and care about you so much they'll dare to say, "Y'know, your voice is *{fill in the blank}*...," and then you can work on the habit you want to modify or get rid of. So, please consider me to be one who loves you and cares so much about you that I want you to have the best, clearest, most pleasant voice that *you* can possibly have when you open your mouth to praise the Lord.

The Speech Habits

(This is a simplified overview. So please, if you have a master's degree in speech pathology or whatever, don't come and tell me, "You failed to mention the effect of the flagellating hymenoptera on the suppurated physostegia!" Because I'm not going to mention it on purpose.)

Simplified overview: There are four things that take place whenever we speak. Four parts of us that function: a **motor**, a set of **vibrators**, some **resonators**, and some **articulators**.

If you asked the person on the street "What is the ***motor*** you use for speaking?" they'd probably think it was the stupidest question they ever heard. (Well, I'm being honest. It's a rhetorical question that has little practical value to practically anyone.) But if you *did* ask people a question like that, they'd probably give you answers like "the mouth," or "the throat," or some location in the vicinity of the neck and shoulders. And those answers would seem pretty logical, since we associate speech with the mouth and neck area. But not only are those answers wrong, they're *extremely* wrong and totally far afield when it comes to locating the motor for speech. Regardless of someone calling you "motor mouth," the mouth is not the motor, nor is anything in the neck/throat area the motor for voice.

The motor is the *diaphragm*. The diaphragm is a muscular structure at the base of the rib cage. It's shaped like an upside-down bowl. When we *inhale*, the "bowl" flattens down as the lungs fill with air, and at the same time the abdominal area *expands*. When we *exhale*, the bowl reverts to its upside-downness shape and pushes the air out of the lungs, and at the same time the abdominal area *contracts*. This happens automatically when we breath. It's something we do twenty-four hours a day. Nonstop basic habit. A lot more will be said about developing this kind of breathing for speaking, in the chapter on Breathing. Our objective is to harness this involuntary function to provide breath support for speaking (just as one would do for singing or playing a wind insturment).

Without altering your breathing, observe now the way the body expands on the inhaled breath and contracts on the exhale. It all takes place around your waistline and in the area below your solar plexus. As we'll see, developing this kind of breathing for speech is crucial for maintaining a healthy and strong voice. As you read the chapter on Breathing, it's important to perform the exercises, rather than just reading about them. You'll probably want to go back and re-read this material several times, since it is so fundamental to a good speaking voice.

Next, the *vibrators*. Speech is called an *overlaid* function—meaning it piggybacks on another function, which is breathing. We speak on an exhaled breath, then inhale, then speak some more on more exhaled breath. What's different is, people don't usually *hear* our breathing (unless we snore in church) but they do hear our speaking. They hear our speech because the exhaled breath passes over a set of *vibrators* and causes them to make noise. Those vibrators are the *vocal folds* or *vocal bands*. The popular name for them is "vocal cords," but I don't like to use that term because (1) people usually misspell and write "vocal chords," and (2) "cord" suggests something tough and resilient like you use to tie up packages to send off at Christmas, and the vocal folds are anything but tough and resilient.

The vocal folds are delicate folds of flesh situated in the *larynx*. They lie beside one another and they run from front to back in the larynx. The larynx is what's commonly called the "Adam's apple," that thing that goes *"goink"* when you swallow hard (well, mine does) and moves when you speak. (And it's <u>not</u> your "*lar*-nicks"!)

Adam's apple. It does, sort of, have something to do with Adam. That something is: he was a man. Men usually have more noticeable Adam's apples than women, and this is not a sexist remark. Something happens to the male vocal folds at puberty that creates the more prominent "lump": the vocal bands thicken and lengthen, resulting in a lower voice. If you play a guitar, you'll notice that the lower, bass-producing strings are the longer, thicker ones. Or open up the top of a piano and you'll see the same thing. So men wind up with longer, thicker vocal bands that have nowhere to go because they're "caged in" in the throat, and therefore they protrude. Remember, this is not scientific, it's "simplified." But it's true.

You could say the vocal bands are a little like the reeds in an oboe, which also lie side by side, something like this: || and vibrate when you breathe (blow) against them to play the instrument. You probably did this as a child, with a blade of grass between the knuckles of your thumbs that you could blow on and produce a kind of squawky sound. Same principle. The vocal bands gently come together and vibrate and produce a pure and pleasant sound. If you've ever been in an orchestra, or heard someone practice who is learning to play a reed instrument, you'll know that if your technique is wrong you're going to hear a squawk. The same, in a sense, can happen with the human voice—a matter we'll attend to momentarily.

Here are a few things you can do to "Get To Know Your Larynx!":
§ You can place your fingers on your larynx (gently, or you'll hurt yourself) and gently *whisper* an "Ah" sound. Then add *voice* (phonate) on the "Ah" sound. Go back and forth between the whispered and the voiced sound, and you'll feel the movement and vibration in the vocal bands. Only when the vocal bands are in vibration do you produce an audible sound. (Remember that when we talk about final consonant sounds.)
§ Again, with the fingers lightly placed against the larynx, produce the [s] sound, a *voiceless* consonant sound. Now change it to a [z] sound, a *voiced* consonant sound. Same means of production, but one sound is called "voiceless," the other "voiced," depending upon whether or not there is vibration in the larynx.
§ You can hold your nose and beat against your larynx with the index-finger side of your hand and make a sound something like a jaw's-harp, but it sounds pretty silly and has nothing to do with what we're talking about here.

On to the _resonators_. The pure vibrated sound produced by the vocal bands is immediately reinforced or re-*sound*-ed (re-*son*-ated) by the rest of the mass of our bodies. In a sense, the whole body, like the body of a piano, re-sounds with the voice. And focusing upon different areas of the body can produce different vocal sounds (e.g., *head* tones, *chest* tones). We're going to deal with three areas in which resonance can be modified or controlled: the **oral** cavity (mouth), the **nasal** passages, and the **chest** area—**oral**, **nasal**, and **chest** resonance.

There is _oral resonance_ on all _vowel sounds_. _Nasal resonance_ occurs on three sounds only, the [m], the [n], and the [ŋ][1] sounds. _Chest resonance_ is found on three sounds: the [z], the [ʒ] (as in "televi*s*ion") and the [v] sounds.

To demonstrate or explore the notion of resonance, try the following:

§ _Oral resonance_: (1) Open the mouth wide and flip your cheek (on the outside) with your middle finger. You'll hear a kind of hollow thumping noise just from the striking of the cheek with the finger. Continue flipping, and gradually close the opening of the mouth, and the sound disappears. Production of that sound depends upon the _open oral cavity_. (Please note: This is my first commercial for "opening your mouth.") (2) Again open wide and produce an "Ah" sound. It should be a nice rich (resonant) sound. Continue producing that sound as you close up the mouth space. What happens? The richness goes, the sound becomes, literally, _flat_, and it generally takes on a nasal quality. That's another commercial for opening the mouth. The resulting sound is richer, fuller, projects better, and is much more pleasant than the flat sound resulting from talking like you have lockjaw. (Be observant. Next time you hear someone with a kind of flat, whiny, nasal, thin voice, look. You'll probably see someone who isn't opening the mouth much at all. Cause and effect: flat mouth space = flat voice.)

§ _Nasal resonance_: Produce an [m] sound. Now hold your nose and try it. Produce an [n] sound. Now hold your nose and try it. Produce an [ŋ] sound. Now hold your nose and try it. I rest my case. You can't produce any of these three sounds without unobstructed nasal passages. Without the resulting nasal resonance, the [m] sounds like a [b], the [n] sounds like a [d], and the [ŋ] sounds like a [g].

§ _Chest resonance_: Place a hand on your upper chest and produce, in turn, the following sounds: [z], [ʒ], [v]. You'll feel the vibration in the chest as you make these sounds. That's chest resonance. Now keep the hand there and produce: [s], [ʃ], [f]. No vibration. No resonance. The [s], [ʃ], and [f] sounds are the voiceless (non-resonant) counterparts of the [z], [ʒ], and [v] sounds. The latter, like all other resonant sounds, contribute to the richness and carrying power of the speaking voice.

And now for the **_articulators_**. These are the agents that take the vibrated, resonated sounds and convert them into intelligible (and presumably intelligent) speech. The three agents (tongue, lips, and velum) act sometimes against or upon themselves and sometimes against or upon other parts of the mouth. First of all, let's explore.

Place your tongue tip right behind your upper teeth, and you'll find a ridge. That's called the *gum ridge* or *alveolar ridge*. The tongue does a lot of work there, as we'll see in a moment. Keep the tongue moving backwards, and it goes up against a hard surface. That's your *hard palate*. Now keep the tongue going back even farther, and it goes up again and becomes soft, and if you keep going you gag (this is the tongue movement you do when you have peanut butter stuck to the roof of your mouth). This is your *velum* or *soft palate*. This whole area is the work space for the active speech agents.

The most active of the speech agents is the ***tongue***. It touches the alveolus to produce [t], [d], [n], [s], [z], [ts], [dz], and [l] sounds. It moves to the front of the hard palate for the [ʃ], [ʒ], [tʃ], [dʒ], [j] and [r] sounds. It goes between the teeth to produce the [θ] and [ð] sounds. And the back of the tongue contacts the velum for the [k], [g], and [ng] sounds.

The next most active agents are the ***lips***. They come together to produce the [p] and [b] and [m] sounds. The lower lip contacts the upper teeth for the [f] and [v] sounds. And the lips round and glide to produce the [ʍ] and [w] sounds.

Least "active," although it acts and is acted upon at the same time, is the ***velum***. The tongue back and velum together produce the [k], [g], and [ŋ] sounds.

The only consonant sound unaccounted for is the [h] sound, and that is produced simply by the passage of air over the *glottis*, the space between the relaxed vocal folds. More about consonant sounds in a later chapter.

<u>In summary</u>: All these things are happening whenever we open our mouths to speak. The diaphragm is pumping out exhaled air, the vocal folds are vibrating, the resonators are doing their job, and the articulators are shaping it all into speech.. There's a lot going on. And a lot that can go wrong. In other words, a lot of things we do habitually that can be "bad habits" which we may want to change or alter—for the sake of a pleasant voice, or for the sake of a healthy voice. More about this in the next chapter!

---

[1]*This chapter introduces some of the symbols of the International Phonetic Alphabet.*

What ELSE Happens When We Speak?

...An angel of the Lord appeared to [Zechariah], standing at the right side of the altar of incense. When Zechariah saw him, he was startled and was gripped with fear. But the angel said to him: "Do not be afraid, Zechariah; your prayer has been heard. Your wife Elizabeth will bear you a son, and you are to give him the name John. He will be a joy and delight to you, and many will rejoice because of his birth, for he will be great in the sight of the Lord."... Zechariah asked the angel, "How can I be sure of this? I am an old man and my wife is well along in years." The angel answered, "I am Gabriel. I stand in the presence of God, and I have been sent to speak to you and to tell you this good news. And now you will be silent and not able to speak until the day this happens, because you did not believe my words, which will come true at their proper time."

When it was time for Elizabeth to have her baby, she gave birth to a son. Her neighbors and relatives heard that the Lord had shown her great mercy, and they shared her joy. On the eighth day they came to circumcise the child, and they were going to name him after his father Zechariah, but his mother spoke up and said, "No! He is to be called John." They said to her, "There is no one among your relatives who has that name." Then they made signs to his father, to find out what he would like to name the child. He asked for a writing tablet, and to everyone's astonishment he wrote, "His name is John." Immediately his mouth was opened and his tongue was loosed, and he began to speak, praising God. The neighbors were all filled with awe, and throughout the hill country of Judea people were talking about all these things. Everyone who heard this wondered about it, asking, "What then is this child going to be?" For the Lord's hand was with him. (Luke 1:11-14, 18-20, 57-66)

Prayer: Lord, it's true we often don't appreciate what we have until we lose it. You've given me a voice that I take for granted until something happens to it. Help me to understand a little better how best to use that voice to sing and shout and speak praises to your Holy Name, for Jesus' sake. Amen.

In the last chapter, we went through the many things that function whenever we speak. We talked of the **motor** (the diaphragm), the **vibrators** (vocal bands or folds), the **resonators** (mouth for *oral resonance*, nasal passages for *nasal resonance*, chest for *chest resonance*) and the **articulators** (tongue, lips and velum). It's logical that the more moving parts there are to a machine the more things there are to go wrong. And that's exactly the case when it comes to speaking. We do a lot of things by habit that get in our way. First, we need to become aware of what our speech habits are, and then we need to get rid of or modify the ones that don't serve us (or the Lord) very well. Let's go back through the motor / vibrators / resonators / articulators list again, pointing out some of the things we do that don't work very well for us.

The Motor. First of all, and for my money the most important, many of us bypass the **motor** (the diaphragm) and try to use another part of the body to function as motive force for voice. They go (more or less) directly to the region where the *vibrators* are. When one breathes naturally, letting the diaphragm do its bit and developing the abdominal muscles for support for the voice, the upper body is relatively stable. But sometimes nerves get in the way, or a bad habit has replaced the natural breathing process, and we resort to very shallow breathing. You could call it "cheap" breathing, because it's shallow and is used up very quickly. But in terms of its effect upon the vocal mechanism, it's really a rather "expensive" kind of breathing. For one thing, because it's shallow and quickly used up, it's *tiring* because you wind up nearly panting to gain the breath you need for speaking. For another thing, because it localizes the speech activity in the shoulders and neck area, it's detrimental to anyone who needs to use the voice for public speaking. It contributes to one's overall tension, and adds noticeable tension to the voice.

> Tension. Tension is natural. You can't avoid it. But you can learn how to control it rather than letting it control you. If your breathing is shallow to begin with, that tension is going to hit you in the throat just as if someone had tied a string around your neck. Stand tall and as relaxed as you can, and then *on purpose* tense your *gluteus maximus* muscles. That tension will work for you. Tension in your neck and throat will always work against you. Remember that.

If you've been engaging in some activity and are short of breath, notice how you take quick breaths which cause the chest to heave and the shoulders to rise. If you have the chance to see yourself on videotape, it's fairly easy to notice that shoulder rising movement—especially if you're wearing a shirt or blouse with horizontal stripes. If there's any one speech habit you want to change, this should be it. Get rid of the shallow, upper chest breathing, and learn to "use your belt" for a supported voice.

The Vibrators. If I'm bypassing the powerful motor (diaphragmatic breathing with abdominal muscular control) I should be using for speech, some other motor is going to have to do the work. So I wind up with tension in the throat area. There are a number of manifestations of this tension, and they all ought to be a kind of red flag whenever we become aware of them.

Tight Throat. First of all there's the *general* tension of a tight throat. All of the energy for speaking is generated from this area of the body. Often you can notice the straining neck muscles, a "giveaway" for the source of the strained sound. Sometimes the head will be tilted back a bit, which will nearly always create a tight sound. (Try this: Prolong an "AH" sound. Slowly tilt the head back and then forward, back and forward as you continue to produce the sound. You'll notice that the sound is full and free when the head moves forward and the front of the neck is relaxed. The sound becomes tight and strained when the head goes back and the front of the neck is tensed.) Realizing that the act of public speaking can be tension-producing, and realizing that tension often will strike us in the neck and shoulder area, one would be wise to do some kind of warm-up with relaxation exercises before speaking. Most important: recognize the tension, and then learn ways of letting it go. Think of the throat as an open passageway for the sound to flow through, not as a motor for grinding out the sound. And continue to focus upon support from the abdominal muscles. Relax the throat and let the sound rise easily with a tug from the abdomen. Go into a yawn, and feel the muscles relax; then let out a nice easy soft "AH" sound with no constriction in the throat. Breathe out a nice gentle sigh, "HAHH", letting it float from your body as if it were coming out of the top of your head.

Glottal shock is another kind of tension to try to avoid. I may not be tight-throated all the time, but may tense within certain phonetic contexts, such as _on words beginning with vowel sounds_. _Glottal shock_ is a term describing that sort of sharp, staccato, cough-like click with which I produce a word beginning with a vowel sound. The cause is too much tension in the closure of the vocal bands, causing them to be blasted apart by breath pressure in this particular phonetic setting (words beginning with vowel sounds). You will often hear someone use a glottal attack for _e_mphasis. (Imagine a cough-like blast initiating the "e" sound in the word "emphasis.") Take a sentence like this one:

Ollie and Edith are overactive easterners.

If there's glottal shock involved, you'll hear that little "cough" (on all the underlined sounds):

_O_llie _a_nd _E_dith _a_re _o_veractive _e_asterners.

Try it. It's very easy to produce that little bit of tension. Just "cough" a bit on each of those highlighted sounds. (Ironically, many people who use a great deal of glottal shock are simply very conscientious about their enunciation, and this kind of "sharp" delineation of the sounds of each word is the result.) To correct this tension, try to let the sounds in a phrase flow together, as if the phrase were one uninterrupted vocal unit rather than a string of individual words. Let it flow together as in an unbroken musical line—the ending sound of one word flowing into the beginning sound of the next word, and so on. Like this:

Olli_e [y] and Edith are [r]_ overacti_ve [v]_ easterners.

In some phonetic contexts there will be a _y_-connective (e.g.: I_y_am = I am, we_y_are = we are) or a _w_-connective (to_w_all = to all, who_w_is = who is). If the vowel sound is at the beginning of a word or phrase, try relaxing the vocal bands with a tiny [h] sound. The word "Ollie" in the above sentence would be produced something like " Ollie," with the [h] so tiny no one would hear it. Or you can begin the word by consciously initiating the sound with an inward tug of the abdominal muscles, drawing the tension away from the glottal area. Or simply consciously relax the jaw as much as you can and let the word come out free from tension. It pays to experiment—again recognizing the tension and then recognizing when it's not there. Try these pairs of words. Notice the freedom from tension on those words beginning with the [h] sound, and try to match that freedom on the words beginning with vowel sounds.

hear . . . ear	high . . . eye	hail . . . ail	had . . . add
head . . . Ed	hairy . . . airy	hallow . . . aloe	ham . . . am
hand . . . and	hasp . . . asp	hitch . . . itch	hike . . . Ike
hone . . . own	heart . . . art	hedge . . . edge	hod . . . odd

Or try some of the following sentences. Remember (a) free the initial vowel sound with a tiny [h], (b) *link* end sounds of words with beginning sounds of the next word, and (c) use the *y-* or *w*-connective when applicable—like this: 'I wonder_if_I _y_ am_able to _w_ eat_anything_at_all.

Ask Edward if Annie ate our oranges.
Adam actually entered the arena.
If I were to emphasize, I'd italicize the entire entry.
Every evening, Alice asks me for some egg rolls.
Take it easy, or you won't have any energy at all.

A word about glottal shock. It's not a big thing. OK, it's a nuisance-y bit of tension in the throat, so what? Let me suggest a couple of "what"s: First of all, it's tension and you don't need tension and it's not going to do you any good. And if it's stacked up on top of a lot of other tension, it could do you some harm. We'll get to that. Second, it's somewhat of an aesthetic matter, and you may think aesthetic matters don't matter that much. But it *is* going to get in the way of your communication. Suppose you're preaching or reading a passage about some of the wonderfully comforting aspects of living under the grace of a loving God. And you punctuate that message with the perpetual "ack-ack-ack" of glottal shock. Now, I may not be sitting there, thinking, "Gee, she's using a lot of glottal shock, and that's pretty antithetical to her message," because I probably won't know *glottal shock* from Adam. But that "ack-ack-ack" is going to get through to me—albeit perhaps subliminally—as sure as a scratch on an old phonograph record, or static on a short-wave broadcast, or the jackhammer outside my office window. You don't need it, and the rest of us don't need it. So isn't it worth getting rid of it? *People may react more to how you sound than to what you say. If you sound tense, we're likely to think you are uptight regardless of all the kind and gentle and peaceful words you're giving us.*

Try some of these sentences. Go easy (as easy as possible) on the glottal attacks:

> The eternal God is your refuge, and underneath are the everlasting arms.
> The Lord is the everlasting God, the Creator of the ends of the earth.
> Love the Lord your God with all your heart and with all your soul and with all your mind.
> I have been crucified with Christ and I no longer live, but Christ lives in me.
> God, who is rich in mercy, made us alive with Christ even when we were dead in transgressions.
> To him who is able to do immeasurably more than all we ask or imagine, according to his power
>   that is at work in us, to him be glory in the church and in Christ Jesus throughout all
>   generations, for ever and ever! Amen.
> I thank my God every time I remember you.
> In all my prayers for all of you, I always pray with joy because of your partnership in the
>   gospel....
> If you have any encouragement from being united with Christ, if any comfort from his love, if
>   any fellowship with the Spirit, if any tenderness and compassion, then make my joy
>   complete ....
> Rejoice in the Lord always. Do not be anxious about anything, but in everything, ... present your
> requests to God.
> And the peace of God, which transcends all understanding, will guard your hearts and your
>   minds in Christ Jesus.
> He is the image of the invisible God, the firstborn over all creation.
> For by him all things were created: things in heaven and on earth, visible and invisible....
> He is before all things and in him all things hold together.

Glottal Fry is a kind of cousin of glottal shock, in that it's a sort of sustained glottal rumble. Imagine you're sound asleep and someone comes and rouses you, and says, "It's time to get up!" and you groan, right from the throat, "Ohhhh, let me sleeeeep!" No breath support at all under it, just a phrase ground out from the throat itself. Apocryphally it is written that some time ago speech pathologists thought this sounded remarkably like bacon frying in a frying pan. Hence the name glottal fry. You'll hear it from a person who's slouched down in his chair, not giving the body a chance to support the voice. Or from the man who slumps over the lectern, and says, "I'd just like to say a few words about . . . " which you can't really hear because they haven't escaped from his throat. Or from the person who tries to get through too much on a single breath and winds up grinding out the last bit way down in the throat. Like glottal shock, you don't need it.

Back placement, etc. I'll touch here upon another vocal problem that we'll look at more closely later. This used to be something quite common to men, but lately I've noticed even women falling into the habit. It's a kind of grab bag of vocal tricks that includes _back placement_ (placement of sound in the back of the throat), _too-low pitch_, and what I call the _"cloud cover"_ over the voice. Many men, when their voices change at last after twelve years or so of captivity to sopranodom, fall in love with the deep voice and *sit on it* (figuratively, of course). They seek the deepest pitch they can muster and center the voice there. ("Don't I sound macho???") Problem is, they wind up with something of a growl. There is a correlation between pitch and the placement of sound. The lower the pitch, the more likely the placement will be back in the back of the mouth or down in the pharyngeal region. Admittedly, it sounds better to *my* ears to have the voice back there, because it's being reinforced as I speak by spaces and bones and cartilages back there inside my own head, which make it sound quite rich and gorgeous to me. But it's so locked in to the back of my physiognomy that it's not going anywhere. I'm not being very Christian with this kind of voice. I'm keeping it all for myself. ("I love my voice!"). But if my listeners are going to hear what I have to say, I need to bring it up in pitch and in placement—forward, out of the throat, out of the back of the mouth, into focus—aimed towards my *listeners'* ears. In other words, I need to give it away rather than keeping it for myself. We'll talk about this more when we deal with getting the voice into focus. Let's just say now that it contributes to the overall tension in the speaking voice and like the rest of the stuff I don't need, I don't need this. *A word of caution: using your voice at the bottom of your pitch range and with inadequate air can lead to hoarseness and losing your voice. If this happens, your therapy will* <u>*begin*</u> *with learning diaphragmatic breathing and finding and using your natural pitch and voice that are not forced.*

Pitch Breaks deserve a mention here. These are the "cracks" in (usually) the male voice, often heard when the voice is changing at puberty. The sound is a kind of crackly "yodel" as the pitch suddenly goes from lower to higher. When these occur in the mature voice, they are possibly the result of speaking in a pitch too low. Try simply speaking on a higher pitch level as a means of preventing the problem.

<u>**What Can Go Wrong?**</u> We noted above that the vocal folds vibrate gently to produce voice on the exhaled breath. Paired something like this: || (they actually run from front to back within the larynx), they vibrate without strain unless subjected to undue tension. If we're not using the right motor for voice (the diaphragm with abdominal muscular control) there is going to be undue tension—either the tension of a generally tight constricted voice, or the tension of glottal shock or glottal fry, or the tension caused by a voice pitched too low and strained in the process. If the vocal folds are subjected over a period of time to extreme tension, a number of problems may result. (As a rule, these are problems faced not by "your average layperson," but by people who use their voices a great deal—especially in professions such as teaching, singing, preaching, acting—professions where the voice is placed under greater than usual demand.)

Vocal Nodules. Think of the effect using a hand tool has on the surfaces of the skin. If I'm raking leaves in the fall (especially without gloves) I'm likely to get blisters. If not blisters, then calluses.

Playing banjo or guitar, I expected I'd get calluses (in this case helpful to me) from the pressure of the fingers on the left hand holding down the strings to chord. If I'm wearing shoes that persistently rub against some part of my foot, again I can expect calluses. It's the tension of some external pressure against the hand, the fingers, the foot, that causes scar tissue to build up wherever that tension exists. Something of the same sort may occur on the vocal bands if they are subject to persistent tension. Scar tissue can build up on the bands. I may wind up with *vocal nodules* or *vocal nodes*, callus-like "bumps" on the vocal folds. When this happens, the vocal bands will now be unable to come together to produce the pure vibrated tone, because they are kept apart by these "bumps." As a result, the voice will have a somewhat husky, hoarse quality. I'll go to a doctor, and she'll tell me not to use my voice—sometimes for a period of six months or so—in the hopes that these nodules will disappear on their own. In the meantime, I'll be unable to preach or read or do any kind of public speaking, presuming I obey the doctor's orders. (I know of one man, a fellow student during my student years in seminary, who got by by using a microphone and the speaker system on his tape recorder. He whispered into the mike and was able to make himself heard. The effect, however, was not entirely pleasant!)

Here is a rough sketch of what the vocal bands might look like with nodules on them. It's admittedly a *very* rough sketch. Think of it as the equivalent of something drawn with a marker on the board.[1]

If I'm lucky, the offending nodes will, on their own, disappear. If not, I may need to have them surgically removed. The result will be raw tissue where the nodules once were, and again I'll be unable to use my voice until all this heals over—a lapse of perhaps another six months for recuperation. Not a pleasant prospect for my ministry.

Vocal Ulcers. There's a possibility that, where the tension occurs on the vocal bands, the tissue may ulcerate rather than building up scar tissue. Again, imagine my ungloved hands after a long stint of raking leaves. Or some other area where chafing rubs the skin raw. The tissue wears away. Now imagine that happening with the vocal folds. Raw tissue, vocal folds unable to come together cleanly, a hoarse, husky sound, and more medical treatment. Once again, I'll be restricted in the use of my voice until healing takes place.

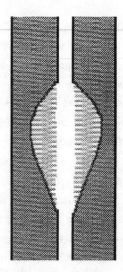

Another rough sketch—a suggestion of how the vocal bands might look if they became ulcerated.

These pathologies may sound like extreme situations, but they are not uncommon. Over the years, I've worked with a number of students (and students' spouses who teach) who have developed some such problem. The first approach one takes to healing something like vocal nodes or vocal ulcers is *to train the person to breathe using the diaphragm with abdominal muscular control—the ultimate answer to avoiding wear and tear on the vocal bands.*

Worst Possible Scenario. The most dire outcome of abuse of the vocal bands would be a pathology so severe that it would require surgery to remove the larynx—a *laryngectomy.* When this takes place, one has no "vibrating system" of one's own. One is therefore required to use a vibrating mechanism held to the throat to produce the vibrated sound, which is then resonated and articulated into speech. Or one may drink humongous quantities of carbonated beverages and then articulate a *belch.* Again, not at all a pleasant prospect.

Now, am I trying to scare you? You bet. I don't want you to abuse the perfectly good, absolutely wonderful vocal mechanism God has given you. If you learn how to use it properly, it should last you for the next hundred years or so. But if you mistreat it, it could wind up being very unhappy. Consider this my most urgent supplication for learning how to breathe correctly. Master the right kind of breathing at the onset of your ministry, and you'll be a very happy camper!

Other Things That Can Get Messed Up. Let's skip over, for now, some of the problems with regard to the areas of *Resonance* and *Articulation.* These can be covered in separate chapters, and are in no way as considerable as the problems that can arise in terms of phonation. The purpose of this chapter has been, primarily, to encourage all of us in whatever ministry we have, to take the time and effort to "tune the instrument" so it can be used efficiently and effectively in our serving.

---

[1] *Once again: these descriptions of vocal nodes or ulcers and the representations of them are not intended to be scientific or anatomically correct. For our purposes, they really don't need to be. Books on anatomy deal with these kinds of pathologies in greater scientific detail.*

Warming Up the Instrument: Exercises for Relaxation, Breath Control and Easy Phonation

Command and teach these things. Don't let anyone look down on you because you are young, but set an example for the believers in speech, in life, in love, in faith and in purity. Until I come, devote yourself to the public reading of Scripture, to preaching and to teaching. Do not neglect your gift, which was given you through a prophetic message when the body of elders laid their hands on you. Be diligent in these matters; give yourself wholly to them, so that everyone may see your progress. (1 Timothy 4:11-15)

Prayer: Precious gracious Lord, I thank you for the gifts you have given me, of life itself, and breath and a voice to speak of your grace and to sing your praises and to glorify your Holy Name. Help me to use these gifts in ministry to those you've called me to serve. Even now as I seek to "tune the instrument" that is my body, my breath, my voice, I would leave the real job of "tuning" in your hands. Melt me, mold me, fill me, use me, for the sake of your precious Son, Jesus Christ. Amen.

Why Warm Up? I used to walk six blocks to school every day. When I was eight years old, I took piano lessons from Mrs. Johnson down at 54th and Carrollton. That took me an extra two blocks every Tuesday when I went to her house. I loved taking piano lessons. And I certainly didn't mind the walk, because Freddy Hoffnung lived right next door to the Johnsons and we could walk together. But come November, or sometimes even in October—and certainly throughout the rest of the winter months—I had to add a little something to my half-hour of performing for Mrs. Johnson. I had to warm up my hands. No matter how many pairs of gloves or mittens I wore, by the time I'd gone eight blocks my hands were cold and stiff. So Mrs. Johnson would spend the first few minutes of our lesson in polite conversation while I sat on my hands. That warmed them up a little. "Now we play the scales," she would say. And we played scales. Major and minor. I'd be playing in the middle of the keyboard and she'd play an octave or so higher. "Next the Hanon and the Czerny," she'd then say. So for about five minutes (it seemed more like half an hour) we would do some Hanon and Czerny. And by then I'd be warmed up. Temperature-wise and limber-wise. "Now we do the Tchaikovsky." And finally I could go ahead and play Tchaikovsky or Debussy. But without that warm-up, Debussy's *La Mer* would be a disaster—Tchaikovsky's *Waltz of the Flowers* nothing but a faded bouquet. If you've ever played any kind of instrument, or any kind of sport for that matter, you know what I'm talking about.

> "Now we play the scales . . . Next the Hanon and the Czerny," . . . By then I'd be warmed up. "Now we do the Tchaikovsky." . . . Without that warm-up . . . a disaster. If you've ever played any kind of instrument, or any kind of sport for that matter, you know what I'm talking about. . . . A good choir director takes the warm-up period very seriously. . . . I'm convinced that it's crucial!

If you have ever sung in a choir, you know that a good choir director takes the warm-up period very seriously. Many choir directors begin their rehearsals lining up people for back rubs. I begin every one of my classes that way. Because I'm convinced that it's crucial to get the body relaxed and as free from tension as possible before trying to perform—whether that performance is singing or speaking in public. Realize that muscular tension will be reflected in the voice. For that reason, we ought to try to relax the whole body—especially the shoulders, neck and head.

You will find the kind of warming-up that works best for you. Let me suggest a sampling of exercises and "routines" that have been helpful over the years. Remember, they're not going to do you a particle of good if you just *read* about them. Get up and *do them!* Nor will it do you much good to do them once and then forget about them. A good musician will often practice at least five hours a day. You probably won't have time for that. But you can develop an awareness of what you're aiming for and then practice a little bit each day.

Scripture and Prayer. Okay, you're going to tell me this doesn't sound much like aerobic exercise. And it's not. But whatever you're setting out to do, especially if it's the task of reading God's Word or leading worship, it's a good idea to turn the matter over to God before you start. A brief time of devotion will help you get your perspectives and priorities in order. I've said before that a certain amount of tension is going to follow you just as surely as goodness and mercy into the chancel. So why not give that up to the Lord who can handle it better than you can, and pray that you can use a little bit of tension creatively and relax a little more surely because you know the Lord's got a hand in things.

Back rubs. My fondest desire would be to see a class of a hundred and fifty students begin their introductory course in Church History with back rubs! We've done it in nearly every choir I've been in, and it's a great way to start things off a little less tense than you were when you came in. Yes, they do have a bit of a socialization value, but that's not the main purpose of doing back rubs. The main aim is to get rid of the tension that generally strikes us right in the shoulder, upper back and neck area.

> I remember spending the 1969-70 academic year in a self-administered crash course in Swedish. I'd be stationed at my desk, with a text at my right hand, a dictionary at my left, and a pad of paper with a well-erased and scribbled-over translation in front of me. I worked at this every free hour of every day. And every evening I'd be stiff and sore. Always in the neck and shoulders. That tension just localized itself right there. I think the tension we experience during the day hits most of us the same way. For that reason we try to "erase" some of the knots that build up in that shoulder-neck area. Call it one of the benefits of being in a choir or a speech class: you'd pay well for it if you engaged the services of a chiropractor or a masseur. Here it's free!

Spend two or three minutes of warm-up time doing back rubs. This should be easy if you're in a choir or a classroom. If you're in the vestry or the pastor's office with others leading in worship, try it there. The "traditional" massage with the thumbs doing most of the work is effective. But the most effective action of all is one I learned from my teaching assistant Doug. Use the middle knuckles of each hand in an outward-to-inward kneading motion—just like kneading bread. Then switch to an inward-to-outward motion. It really takes those kinks away! And don't forget the "pummeling" with the outsides of the hands. That's more fun if you sound out an "AH" which becomes "AH~~~~~~" as you're being thwacked. (Seriously, this helps you associate the process of relaxation with the production of voice.)

EXERCISES FOR RELAXATION

1. Recognizing and Relieving Tension. Dress comfortably, keeping clothing as loose and free from constriction as possible. Lie down on the floor on your back. (You can also do this lying on a bed, but the floor is not likely to sag under your weight.)
    - Begin by imaging the most peaceful relaxed moment and setting you can recall.

- Starting with the *toes*, tightly tense, then relax the muscles. Feel the tension and then its absence.
- Slowly proceed as above, up the entire body: Tense, then relax, the muscles of the *feet*, *calves, thighs,* and *buttocks*. Then the *fingers, hands* and *arms*. Next the *abdomen, chest, shoulders, neck* and each of the *facial muscles* in turn: the *jaw, lips, cheeks, eyes, temples, forehead.*
- As you relax the body, feel it to be weightless.
- Rest for a few moments, enjoying the freedom from tension.
- Repeat, same as above. But instead of tensing and relaxing the muscles, _tell_ each part of your body to relax.
- The final sensation should be one of nearly floating in space, rather than being "plastered" against the floor or bed.

(This exercise is a wonderful way to relax at night just before falling off to sleep. We spend so much of our lives with our bodies dictating what we should be doing. This one gives us the upper hand: *we're* telling our *bodies* what to do.)

In the following exercises for shoulders and neck, try to keep the jaw relaxed (the "take a bite of apple" sensation talked about in the chapter on resonance should help) and the throat open. It also really helps if you keep the mouth slightly open, although it does tend to give you the appearance of the village idiot. Try it when no one else is around.

2. *Relaxing the Shoulders.*

(a) "Hug your ears" with your shoulders. Hold it for a moment, then relax. Repeat as often as you find it helpful.

(b) Make big circles with your shoulders. First rotate them clockwise (up, forward, down, back) and then counterclockwise (up, back, down, forward). Feel as if you're giving yourself a back rub.

3. *"Neckxercises".*

(a) Gently circle the head clockwise (down, left, up, right), repeating *slowly* half a dozen times or so. Then repeat, circling counterclockwise (down, right, up, left). Take care to do this slowly and carefully.

(b) Gently turn the head as far as possible to the right, with a little stretch. (You can *gently* encourage the stretch with your hands. Hold the back of the neck with your left hand; with the heel of your right hand nudge the head into a slightly greater range of motion. Don't overdo. Don't hurt yourself!) Then repeat, turning the head to the left. Be careful not to strain as you stretch easily in each direction.

4. Rag Doll. (Some of the men from my classes instituted this as "the" pre-game warm-up at the beginning of the football season. At the end of the spring semester, they bestowed upon me the Order of the Rag Doll. He's hanging up on my bulletin board right now!)

- Stand with your legs comfortably apart, your body well balanced.

- As if you were a marionette with the strings released, drop forward from your waist so that your head hangs limp and your arms dangle as close to the ground as possible. Bend the knees a little and keep the legs relaxed. Feel as if the tension were flowing out of your fingertips.

- Now, as if strings attached to your head and upper body were pulling you up, come up *slowly*, keeping arms, head and especially shoulders relaxed. Repeat several times.

At the end of this exercise, as you stand erect, be sure to avoid any semblance of a military "at attention" stance. Maintain the almost lightheaded feeling of floating upwards, relaxing towards the ceiling. Follow this exercise with the following stretches.

5. Stretch.

(a) Rise up on your toes, gently stretching the body upwards, then relax back down on your heels. *As you come down, leave your head as high as when you were stretching.* Again, think of relaxing toward the ceiling. Repeat several times. (You really can add to your height this way. As we plod through our day, we tend to pack the body down, tamping it into a tight little scrunch. Try this exercise in front of a mirror. Establish a spot where your eye level is. When you've finished the exercise you'll find your eye level has risen at least as much as an inch. I don't think this contradicts what Jesus said about not being able to add a single cubit to one's height. After all, isn't a cubit about 18-21 inches? Don't expect this exercise to do *that*!)

(b) "Climbing a ladder": Reach up with your right hand, then your left, repeating and reaching higher each time. (Use your imagination. If you don't like the idea of climbing a ladder, "reach for something up on a high shelf.") Repeat several times. At the finish, shake off the tension, and relax (upwards, *always*).

6. *Resistance Exercises.*

(a) *Iron Butterfly.* With the right hand, make a little butterfly that flits easily and gently through the air. (I know this sounds weird, but it does work!) Then imagine the butterfly suddenly becomes iron or lead or whatever—very heavy. Let the hand drop in a relaxed free fall. *Don't throw the hand down. Let it fall from the change in weight and texture.* Repeat with a left hand butterfly. Then try both hands.

(b) *Swimming in Jello.* Relax forward at the waist, as if you were waist-deep in a swimming pool. Bring one arm at a time up from behind, over your head, forward and down, as if you were swimming through Jello (your favorite flavor). Feel the gentle resistance.

(c) *Many Sweaters.* You've just come inside from play time. Mom says, "Let me help you off with your sweater." And so you gently flop forward at the waist as Mom tugs the sweater off first from the waist up, then over the head, then off of each arm in turn. Let Mom provide the tension. You just relax and let it happen to you. Whoops! There's another sweater under the first one. Repeat. And *another* under that. And so on until you're down to your skivvies (figuratively speaking, *bien sur*).

EXERCISES FOR BREATH CONTROL

1. *Alternate Nostril Breathing.*
- Sit (or lie) comfortably, with your left hand on your abdomen, just below the rib cage.
- Placing your right index finger on the bridge of your nose, gently block the left nostril with your middle finger. Inhale *slowly, to a count of 1,* through your right nostril. As you inhale, feel the stomach wall *expand.*
- Blocking both nostrils (again, gently) with the thumb and middle finger, hold the breath *for a slow count of 4.*
- Releasing the middle finger, exhale slowly through the left nostril *to a slow count of 2,* feeling the stomach wall *contract* on the exhale. As the final air is expelled, sharply pull the abdomen in towards the rib cage as far as possible.
- Repeat, inhaling through the left nostril *slowly, to a count of 1.* Hold the breath *for a slow count of 4.* Exhale through the right nostril *to a slow count of 2.*
- Repeat, adding to the count on each repetition, keeping the ratio the same (1/4/2), e.g.: 2/8/4 - 3/12/6 - 4/16/8 - 5/20/10. Go as far as you can comfortably control the intake and

exhalation of breath.

One may also do this exercise to a count of 8/8/8: inhale to a count of 8, hold for a count of 8, then exhale to a count of 8. This exercise helps develop diaphragmatic breathing, clears the sinuses, and is extremely relaxing.

> One good way to relate these breathing exercises to phonation is to release the exhaled air on a whisper-count (instead of silently counting to yourself.) You can also release the exhaled breath on a hissing sound [sss], which helps control the breath rather than letting it escape all at once with a "whoosh" like a balloon let go to fly around the room. What you're working for in all these exercises is control of the exhaled breath.

2. Deep Breathing—Expand Your Capacity.
- Sit tall, relaxed upward.
- Inhale, feeling your stomach *expand*, and hold the breath *for a slow count of 3*. Do not tense your throat to hold your breath. Let the stomach muscles do the job.
- Inhale *again* (on top of the first breath), holding the breath *for a slow count of 10*. You will be expanding the costal and dorsal areas with this second breath.)
- Exhale slowly, *for a slow count of 10*. (This is the crucial step: controlling the exhaled breath.)
- Repeat this exercise five times.

3. Soaring.
- Do this exercise in one motion—no pause between steps *a* and *b*.
- *a.* Stand relaxed and tall. As you *inhale*, slowly bring your arms forward to eye level and then out to the sides. Prolong this movement and the inhale *for a slow count of 15*.
- *b. Exhaling*, bring your arms slowly down to your sides *on a slow count of 10*.
- Repeat the entire exercise three times. Be sure to keep your chest high, body tall but relaxed. This exercise helps control breathing, slowing down the breathing cycle. It also improves posture, and lifts the chest.

4. "Walk the Talk" Exercise.
- Walking slowly and steadily, inhale as you count to yourself *a slow count of 5*.
- Continue walking and exhale as you count aloud, softly: "1 - 2 - 3 - 4 - 5."

- Continue until you're comfortable with this count, then increase the inhale to *a slow count of 6*, and the audible count to: "1 - 2 - 3 - 4 - 5 - 6."
- Keep going, increasing the inhale-count and the exhale-count by one (or more) as the controlled breathing becomes easy for you.
- *Variations: (1) Exhale on a hissing sound [sss], counting silently to yourself. (2) Exhale on an easy humming sound, counting silently to yourself.*

5. Use the "Belt"—Not the Chest.

Here are several exercises designed to help keep the chest elevated and encourage diaphragmatic breathing with abdominal muscular control. Practice them first as simple breathing and breath-expansion exercises, then use them in some easy phonation exercises (e.g.: "HA-HA-HA-HA-HA" with gentle tugs from the abdomen).

- *Standing*. Interlace fingers of both hands and lift your hands high above your head. *Inhale*, letting the breathing action expand the abdominal area. In this position, your upper chest should not lift or heave at all on the inhale; keep it relaxed, and focus on the "belt." As you *exhale*, be careful not to lower the hands *or the chest*. You may find it helpful on the exhale to exert a gentle lifting movement of the hands and chest as a counter to the tendency to lower the chest.

- *Sitting*. Sitting tall and comfortably, reach down and grasp the sides of the chair seat. (Or, reach down and grasp the back rung of the chair.) Pull upwards as if you were trying to lift the chair and yourself off the floor. Maintain the upward pull, immobilizing the chest. As you *inhale*, let the abdominal area expand, being careful not to lift the chest at all. As you *exhale*, do not relax the upward pulling movement and do not lower the chest—let the abdominal wall contract instead.

- *Lifting*. Stand in front of a lectern (or a bookcase or bookshelf approximately as high as your waist level). Grasp the underside of the lectern or shelf and lift. If it's a lightweight lectern, place a foot on the base to keep it from actually lifting. Sustain the lifting movement, keeping the upper chest stabilized. *Inhale*, expanding the abdominal area, and being careful not to let the chest rise. *Exhale*, maintaining the lifting motion, keeping the chest high and contracting the abdominal wall.

- *Chest Stretch*. Stand about four feet from the wall, facing the wall. Let yourself fall forward with your arms outstretched and hands against the wall. Push against the wall until you feel the stretch in the backs of your legs. In this position, the upper body is now immobilized. *Inhale*, feeling the inhaled breath automatically expand the abdominal area. Gravity helps. Observe the inhale-expand/exhale-contract movement of the abdomen.

EXERCISES FOR EASY PHONATION

1. Energize Diaphragm and Diction—Increase Control.

- Whisper-count *with athletic diction—no tension in the throat*:

 1 // 1-2 // 1-2-3 // 1-2-3-4 // 1-2-3-4-5 // etc.

Add by ones to a count of ten, then by fives to as high as possible on a single breath. Add a count of five each week. You are striving to stretch the breath control. Count slowly, and don't fudge. Keep the diction as "athletic" as possible (think isometrics). "Overdo" the action of the lips and the tongue.

- Do the count, same as above, but with the teeth together (as if you'd been to the dentist and your jaws were now wired together). Feel the extra energy in the lips and the tongue tip. Do on a whisper or aloud. Now imagine the wires have been removed. Repeat the counting, opening the oral cavity nice and wide, *keeping the focus of energy in the lips and the tongue tip.*

2. Coordinate Phonation with Breathing.

- Gently place a hand on your abdomen, and observe what happens when you are relaxed and breathing *naturally*. The abdomen expands on an inhale, contracts on an exhale, and the upper chest remains immobile. This is all *involuntary* movement.
- In the *natural rhythm of breathing*, slowly and easily:
 - Whisper "HA" (repeat several times, *always on an exhale in your natural breathing rhythm*).
 - Phonate softly on an "AH" (again repeating several times on a natural exhale).
 - Gradually on subsequent exhaled breaths, enlarge the sound to a strong "AH" *initiated by the abdominal muscles. There should be no tension whatsoever in the throat.*

3. Keep the Throat Free, Phonation Easy.

These exercises are helpful in keeping the entire throat and buccal cavity open and free. There are essentially two ways of opening the mouth. One is to *drop the jaw*, which is to be discouraged because it tends to constrict the lower jaw and laryngeal area resulting in a throaty placement and a throaty sound. The other is to *lift the palate as if you were taking a bite of apple*. Try it, and you'll see how naturally and easily you perform this lifting action. **This is the approach to take with the following exercises. Do not "drop the jaw"; lift the palate instead.**

- *Yawn*: sound and prolong an easy "AH" keeping the palate lifted. Repeat, coordinating the yawn and the "AH" with deep diaphragmatic breathing.
- *Forward yawn*: Interlace the fingers of both hands and stretch arms, hands and upper

body forward. Yawn and produce an "AH," aiming the sound against the back of your hands. Feel the *focus of sound* on the **hard palate**.

- *Backward yawn*: Interlace fingers of both hands behind the back of your neck. Yawn, and aim an "AH" against the ceiling. Feel the *focus of sound* on the **lifted soft palate**.

- *Sing/AH*: Begin with the word "sing," lifting the palate as you prolong the /ng/ sound, then open into an easy "AH" sound ("sing/AH"). This can be done as a simple vocalise, singing up the scale on four notes and opening into an "AH" on the fifth, then singing back down to the original note: *[do-re-mi-fa-SOL-fa-mi-re-do]*; or on an arpeggio up an octave, opening to the "ah" on the octave and then singing down the entire scale: *[do-me-sol-DO-ti-la-sol-fa-mi-re-do]*.

4. Yawn Relaxercise

With the mouth closed, go into a yawn, inhaling lavishly (with expansion at the abdominal area, of course). Then exhale on a very soft, very gentle "mmmm" and feel the throat relaxed and open. This is a great way to relax the voice just before speaking. You can even do it while you're sitting up in the chancel waiting to do whatever you'll be doing next. (It's not nearly so noticeable as doing, say, the Rag Doll Exercise up in the chancel. Although the latter could lead to some new kind of liturgical dance group. Who knows?)

5. Get All Shook Up

Shaking parts of the body, or the whole body itself, is one way to relax the muscles (especially the ones in the shoulder and throat area) and to let the body breathe the way it naturally wants to breathe. Try these exercises, first, simply to feel the relaxation and easy breathing they encourage, then add some easy sounds such as "HO-HO-HO-HO-HO."

- *Shaking Maracas*: Holding an imaginary maraca in each hand, shake first with the right hand, then the left, then both together. Add some easy voicing or a happy tune. Notice how relaxed the whole body is and how free the throat is.

- *Shake a Leg*: As if you were doing the "Hokey-Pokey," shake the right leg first, then the left leg, adding some easy sounds as you feel the body and throat relaxed. (You can *try* shaking both legs at the same time, but it doesn't seem to work too well.)

- *Run In Place*: Just do a nice easy jog in place, adding some "HO"s or a series of easy open sounds ("HEY, HEE, HI, HO, HOO"). This is wonderfully freeing to the voice. I once saw Roger Daltrey doing this *during* a <u>Who</u> concert. It's probably not a good idea to do this while you're leading worship.

ABDOMINAL AWARENESS

When you're trying to learn a new "habit" or unlearn an old one, you're going through a period of extreme self-consciousness, awareness, possibly a sensation that breathing or producing voice or speaking *this new way* "feels strange." That's good. That means you're changing and growing. When you're *unaware, unselfconscious,* you're probably sinking back into the old habits and there's no growth. I've often referred to the initial semester of classes in speech communication in ministry as "Awareness 101." If at first you achieve little more than awareness, praise God for that. And then just keep praying for grace that eventually the awareness will change over into new habit and that that good new habit will kick in when you need it.

A lot of this awareness can take place any time during any day, through the use of these exercises, with no one but you realizing that you're exercising. Just take a one-minute break in whatever you're doing and concentrate on what's happening in your abdominal area and how it functions as part of your breathing.

Remember, you're working for **diaphragmatic breathing with abdominal muscular control** (i.e., "using the belt").

1. Tummy Tucks. Stand. Bend at the waist and place your hands on your knees. Use the abdominal muscles to push inward as you *exhale*, sucking in on the abdominal wall as if you were trying to touch your spine from the inside(!). Once you've exhaled as completely as possible, *swallow, and feel the muscles tighten. Inhale*, letting the abdominal area accept the filling, and relax. Repeat.

2. Broad Jump. Stand with your arms forward at shoulder height. *Inhale*, swinging your arms down and back and crouching into a jump position. Hold this for a moment, being aware of the intense expansion of the abdominal muscles. *Exhale*, rising and lowering your arms to your sides.

3. "The Thinker". Sit forward on your chair with your elbows at your knees and your hands relaxed. Let the upper body go limp. It's okay to let the whole upper body droop towards the floor. In this position, note the strong feeling of expansion at the waist as you *inhale*.

4. Gradual Rise. Stand and let the body drop forward at the waist, as in the "Rag Doll Exercise." Observe the expansion at the waist as you *inhale*, the contraction as you *exhale*. In a series of about five steps, *gradually* raise the body upwards into a relaxed standing position, taking a moment at each stage to be aware of the expansion and contraction cycle.

Do all of these exercises in a spirit of relaxed fun. For goodness' sake, don't "take them seriously" to the extent that you add <u>more</u> tension to the mind or the body. Remember, we're trying to get <u>rid</u> of tension or at least learn how to control it. Enjoy letting your body breathe as it wants to. And enjoy the freeing voice that comes with it!

Breathing—The Motor for Voice

This is the account of the heavens and the earth when they were created.
When the Lord God made the earth and the heavens—and no shrub of the field had yet appeared on the earth and no plant of the field had yet sprung up, for the Lord God had not sent rain on the earth and there was no man to work the ground, but streams came up from the earth and watered the whole surface of the ground—the Lord God formed the man from the dust of the ground and breathed into his nostrils the breath of life, and the man became a living being. (Genesis 2:4-7)

Prayer: Holy God, Creator and Sustainer of all life, you breathed into my nostrils the breath of life that I may live and move and have my being. So breathe your Spirit into me that all I do and all I am may glorify your Holy Name. In the name of Christ. Amen.

You stand up and you're about ready to speak. What's the first thing you need to do? Right, breathe.

Okay, take a deep breath. Now freeze! Hold it! Look at yourself. How, physically, do you respond when someone says, "Okay, take a deep breath"? Chances are you chugalug a big draft of air, throwing your shoulders back, lifting your chest, and sucking in your gut as you do so. Right? Close? It's the G.I. Joe approach to breathing. We're more or less conditioned to lift the chest and pull in the tummy when we consciously *take a deep breath*. But it's all wrong, wrong, wrong—the wrong kind of breathing for *speaking*.

As I Live and Breathe. Now: *"At ease"* just for a moment. Relax. Don't even think about breathing. Gradually let yourself observe what happens *naturally* when you're not thinking of gasping in a big chunk of air to breathe. Chances are your shoulders are relaxed, your chest is relaxed, and your tummy is doing the work. Watch a little child breathe.[1] They do it so easily and so naturally, they've got the belly motion going just fine. And probably the rest of the body is already so active that shoulders and chest and neck and jaw and all that don't stand a chance of getting tensed up and ready to get into the act of speaking. Maybe when Jesus said you've got to become like a little child, one of the things he had in mind was using the body, the breathing mechanism, the right way for speaking. Okay, so there are probably millions who go ahead and do it the wrong way, and they may wind up with funny, tight, hurting voices but they don't care much because they don't have much at stake. But if you're reading Scripture, or leading worship, or preaching, or teaching a class, or singing, or using your voice in any public presentational way, you can't afford to have a funny, tight, hurting voice unless you're not very smart.

Of course, not many of us are really very aware of how we breathe in the first place. When was the last time you sat down—or stood up, or lay down or whatever—and pondered just exactly *how you breathe*? If someone told you they had spent the last half hour thinking about their breathing, you'd probably say, "Get a life!" There are some saints and mystics who do spend time focusing on their breathing as the very source of life, the center of their being, a means of one kind of communion or meditation or another. But we're not going to get into that, except to say that especially if you need to use your voice in a way that's pleasing, strong enough to be heard clearly, and isn't going to conk out on you somewhere down the line, you need to become conscious of how you breathe for speaking.

> The life-giving breath comes up through our body from the center of our being. Let it not be hindered by inefficient vocal habits or tensions that render it ineffective.

Shallow Breathing. The kind of chest-out-stomach-in-shoulders-back breathing mentioned above uses the clavicular and costal regions of the body. Your clavicle is also called your collarbone. "Costal" refers to your ribs. So you've got your collarbone and your rib cage tensed up and ready to go, and what happens to your voice? Try it! (This is *negative practice*!) Take a deep breath, be sure to "catch" it and hold it in your throat, tighten up all the muscles between the upper chest and the jaw, and try to speak. What happens? You get a very tight, very throaty sound that sounds like you're wearing your little brother's size *small* dress shirt because you couldn't find a 16½-34 of your own. Or wearing a choker necklace that's really a *choker* necklace. Sort of like you're trying to do a Donald Duck imitation. Or in need of Dr. Heimlich. *Please hear this: This kind of breathing is hazardous to your voice. Don't do it. Stop it now!*

A word about runners:
>   Several years ago, I was working with a student, Kevin, who was finding it *impossible* to master diaphragmatic breathing. I tried every trick I could think of to get him to breathe deeply and coordinate that with the speaking voice. He *couldn't help* lifting the upper chest every time he inhaled. He was frustrated. I was frustrated.
>   Finally he said, "Dr. Jacks, do you suppose it has anything to do with my being a *runner*?"

He had, it turns out, been a cross country star at Colgate, and also ran daily for his own enjoyment.

"I know when I run I lift my chest."

I began mentally and then actually running in place to see if I *had* to lift my chest when running. I *didn't.*

"Kevin," I said, "can't you *keep the chest high* so that when you inhale you let the lower part of your body expand and take a deeper breath?"

"Oh, yeah," he smiled. "You mean a *belly breath!*"

Problem solved. From that point, Kevin learned how to take a *belly breath* to support his speaking voice. And I learned how to approach diaphragmatic breathing with runners. Runners do tend to take shallow, chest-lifting breaths. But if you run with the chest *already lifted,* then you can permit the abdominal area to expand and take the deeper breath—which, I'm told by some runner friends, adds greatly to your endurance as a runner!

Just recently, I made the same "belly breath" observation to another runner, Jon. This was just before the summer break, and I suggested he try it when running during the summer months.

He returned in the fall and told me with great glee that he had mastered the "belly breath."

"Also," he told me, "I can hold my breath under water *forever!*"

Plus, he had a greatly improved heart rate. And blood pressure.

"And just in general," he added, "I've been so much more relaxed!"

Jon's joy in mastering diaphragmatic breathing is shared by many. Over the years, a great number of students have remarked how *easy* it is to speak with the proper support, and how *good and relaxed* it feels to master this kind of breathing.

DIAPHRAGMATIC BREATHING WITH ABDOMINAL MUSCULAR CONTROL.

Okay, let's master diaphragmatic breathing. Try to relax the whole body. Now just observe how the body naturally functions when you breathe. And think about how you can harness that natural function for speaking. There are several ways of discovering what your body does during natural, relaxed breathing. And they all begin by putting the body in positions you're not likely to use in public speaking. You're not likely, for example, to have your body in a bent-over doubled up position unless you're up in the rafters somewhere and your audience is down beneath you. Nor are you likely to find a situation in which you're lying on your back. But these are both good ways of beginning to monitor your breathing preparatory to harnessing the good breathing for speaking. So let's go through a couple of sequences from breathing awareness to phonation (producing vocal sounds) in which you'll wind up being upright as you probably will be in a public speaking situation.

Bend Over Approach.[2] First of all, stand slightly bent over, as if you were addressing a golf ball. (No, I don't mean, "Hi, there, golf ball!") In this position, observe that your stomach wall *expands* when you inhale, and *contracts* when you exhale. Don't *do* anything in particular; just observe what your body's doing when you stand in this position. Next, find an uncomfortable chair and sit down. Not an overstuffed comfortable one. One that makes you sit up tall. Scootch forward on the seat of the chair, and let your upper body collapse forward so that your elbows are in front of your knees. Upper chest totally relaxed. Head and neck relaxed. Body's all scrunched forward. Just sit quiet for a moment. Then begin to observe what's happening with your body. You're going to notice that there's some movement going on, and it isn't in the jaw-neck-collarbone-rib area. It's down around your belt. As you *inhale*, your abdominal area expands and pushes against your belt. And as you *exhale*, the area contracts. Your upper body is not bobbing up and down. It's not going anywhere. All the activity is at the belt line. Be aware that the inhale/expansion occurs not just in front (your belly) but all the way around your waist. Gently bring your hands up to your abdomen, and feel that movement: inhale/expand > exhale/contract. That's the way you breathe *normally* 24 hours a day. When you're relaxed. When you're asleep. When you're not doing something *abnormal* with your breathing in order to speak. Try adding a little, gentle voice to your exhaled breath: "Ahh..." and associate the exhale/contract motion with the production of voice. Notice that now there's no tension in the voice. All the tension is at your waist. The throat is relaxed. When you put your body in this position everything should work favorably and comfortably for speaking.

Move into an upright sitting position. Gradually—continuing to feel the expand/contract motion in the abdominal area—bring the body to an upright position. Feel as if you are *relaxing upwards*, and not tensing any part of the upper body. Gently bring your hands up to your lower ribs (thumbs in back, other fingers over the stomach area). *[Here's an image for you: Think of the hands-abdomen area as the cone of an ice-cream cone. Everything above that is the ice cream. The cone supports the ice cream. And the body is erect so the ice cream doesn't fall off.]*
Inhale, and feel the expansion against your hands, especially the four fingers in front. Exhale, and let the fingers monitor the abdominal contraction. Don't let the upper chest sink as you exhale.

Begin to proceed towards phonation. As you exhale, whisper "Hahhhh," observing that the inward contraction or tug of the abdominal wall is the *impetus* for the sound you're hearing. The *motor*, in other words, is down at your belt and not up in your throat. Gradually, on subsequent exhales, produce first a gentle sigh ("Aahhh") and then stronger and louder sounds. Keep the throat relaxed and let the "belt" do the work.

Add some counting exercises. As you become comfortable with this, try some easy counting exercises. You may begin by doing them on a whisper, then repeating them *sotto voce.* In the following, the double slash (//) indicates an inhale. *Observe that your abdominal wall always expands on an inhale. You always speak on the exhaled breath, as the abdominal wall contracts.*[3] Monitor that action on the following counts:

> 1 - 2 - 3 - 4 - 5 // 1 - 2 // 1 - 2 - 3 - 4 // 1 - 2 - 3 (etc., varying the count on each exhale)
> 121, 122, 123, 124, 125 // 126, 127, 128, 129, 130 // (etc.)

Lying-Down-on-the-Floor Approach.[4] Lie on your back on the floor. Place one hand on your upper chest, the other on your lower abdomen (where your belt would be). Just relax and observe the natural expansion and contraction in this position. You're not making anything happen. It just *happens.* It's all *involuntary.* The hand on the abdomen is going up on the inhale and back down on the exhale. The hand on your chest is going nowhere. It's barely moving, if it's moving at all. Go through the same procedure as above: a little audible breathing, a sigh, a little stronger sound, then stronger again—each time observing that the impetus comes from the belt (with *no activity in the upper chest area*). Gradually let the involuntary movement become *voluntary*, as you make the abdominal movements a little stronger. You ought to be able to work up to a series of loud "HO!" sounds (think drill sergeant) with a powerful sound and *no tension in the throat.* Keep all the tension in the belt region.

Shift to a standing position. Stand up. Move up against a wall, with your back to the wall, aligned as it was while you were lying on the floor. That is, everything that was touching the floor is now touching the wall. Nearly everything. Modify this posture in two ways. (1) First, *relax the head,* letting it fall gently into a normal standing posture. The front of the neck should be shortened, the back lengthened. (Notice that if your head is back against the wall you get a very tense sound if you produce, say, an "Aahh" sound. Then when you relax the head that tension disappears. Try it.) (2) Second, *tighten the gluteus maximus muscles,* feeling tension from the groin area to the floor.[5] This stance—a basic singer's stance—provides tension in the body where it can be useful in supporting the voice. At the same time, it reduces the likeliness that you'll be tensing in the throat area.

In this position, do the same things you did when you were lying on the floor. Put one hand on your chest, another at your belt, and observe the breathing. Don't let the chest rise and fall. All the movement is at the belt. Gradually add the whisper, then phonate, increasing the volume and the muscular movement each time.

Other Helpful Approaches. Anything that can keep the upper body stable, chest high but relaxed (and not heaving up and down as you breathe) can be helpful in mastering this kind of breathing. Try some of the following:

§ **Sit, grasping the underneath of the chair seat with both hands.** Trying to lift the chair from the ground (you can't), do some of the above breathing exercises or counting exercises, or a series of "HO" sounds. (Success at landing a Santa Claus position is not guaranteed.) Once again, keep the upper chest stabilized and use the <u>belt</u> to produce the sounds.

§ **Stand, holding a lightweight chair at arm's length.** Be sure to use a chair that's light enough that you don't strain. Or a stool. Or even a stack of books. The object is to keep the upper body out of commission and let the lower body do its work.

§ **Stand with your arms extended high above your head.** Same principle. I "invented" this approach one evening after about four hours of rehearsal with a band. I was getting so tired, and the tiredness started to affect my voice. When I did the "hands up" position, it lifted my chest and forced me to keep the "belt" going.

§ **Stand about four feet from the wall, facing the wall.** Lean forward, pushing against the wall until you feel the stretch in the backs of your legs. Your upper body is now immobilized. Feel the inhaled breath automatically *expand the abdomen*. (Gravity also helps!) Go through the above steps: breathing, adding sound bit by bit making the abdominal muscular movements voluntary to produce full sound. I happened upon this approach once during a workout where I was doing a chest stretch, standing in a corner facing the wall. Gravity being what it is, I don't think you can breathe any other way, when you're standing in this position.

§ **Imagine you have no vocal mechanism in the face/neck area.** Instead: (1) you have a large mouth at the *lower abdomen*; produce some strong "HO" sounds, aiming the voice towards the floor in front of you; (2) you have a large mouth at the *base of the spine*; produce "HO"s, aiming the voice towards the floor behind you. These really work. Especially if you have a weird imagination. And they're fun. You'll be producing sounds you never before experienced.

Other Breathing Exercises. There are a lot of other breathing exercises you can do. The objective, once again, is to gain breath control that will help you when you speak. Pick up any basic yoga book, and you'll find lots of good breathing exercises. (As I understand it, one of the fundamentals of yoga is to get the body doing what it should be doing normally instead of what we often do out of bad habits.) The *Alternate Nostril Breathing* exercise is particularly helpful—and relaxing. (You gently block one nostril, inhale through the other ... hold the breath

... unblock and release the breath—then alternate.) I generally do this to a 1 / 4 / 2 count: inhale (1), hold (4), release (2)—then increase the count, keeping the ratio the same.

A word about singers and musicians:

I've worked with a lot of students who have had extensive vocal training or training in playing a wind instrument, who know how to use diaphragmatic breathing in their art. Oddly, some of these people have had the worst speaking voices one could imagine. Tension in the throat, glottal shock, total lack of support, thin reedy sounds. I've likened it to the "Jim Nabors" Syndrome—a flat nasal voice for his role as Gomer Pyle, and an open rich sound for the singing voice. Don't presume that because you know how to support the voice for singing or playing an instrument you'll automatically use that support for speaking. It's not difficult, however, to make the transfer. Simply think of "singing" as you speak. Or (in practice) chant a paragraph and speak the next. Anything to make the transfer from singing to speaking. The best results have often come from a prod such as "Imagine you're singing that thought to us, but speak it instead." When you come to think about it, speaking should be sort of like singing in in a kind of monotone. This is especially important with regard to the habit of swallowing phrase endings. If you think of "singing through" to the end of the phrase, you won't let the sound go "down the drain" at the end of the phrase. So "sing out," saints!!!

BREATHING AND POSTURE

Once you have mastered the technique of diaphragmatic breathing—and while you're learning it—pay close attention to the way you stand or sit when speaking. Don't slouch.

Sitting. When you're sitting, sit tall as if you were at choir practice: rear end away from the back of the chair, sitting forward, as if you were "relaxing" towards the ceiling. Much of the time, when we're relaxed and "casual," we sit in a slouched position: rear end kind of tucked under, and spine bearing the weight of the upper body. Then when we breathe, we're most likely to bypass the diaphragmatic action and abdominal muscular control, and instead lift the chest on an inhale and let it fall as we speak. The result is a weak or strained, unsupported voice. Granted, we're not likely to do much public speaking from a sitting position, but we ought to realize this posture is not conducive to very good voice habits. When you *do* speak from a sitting position, for example, answering a phone or sitting in a conference, sit tall—and breathe right. I'll bet a penny you've done that without being told. You're on the phone, scrunched down in your chair, and the person on the other end of the line says, "I can't hear you very well—do we have a bad connection?" And you scootch up and sit tall, and say, "Is that better?" Or you're sitting in a discussion group, and people start firing questions at you like, "What was that?" or "What'd you say?" and you drag yourself up to a straighter sitting position. At times like this it's kind of an automatic reflex. It would be good if it were automatic *all the time!*

Standing. The time when diaphragmatic breathing is most crucial is when we're standing, in front of an audience, needing a voice that is supported and full, projecting to the back of the room.

"Body Blocks". Standing tall, imagine that your body is made up of a stack of blocks, one resting on top of the other. There are the *feet to knees blocks*, on top of which are the *thigh blocks*, then the *hips and upper body blocks*, and finally the *neck and head blocks*. Make sure the blocks are stacked directly on top of one another, and don't lean like the Tower of Pisa, or the upper blocks will topple. Along with this image, think of a straight line descending from the back of your head to your heels. This is the kind of alignment you want for good breath support.

Watch one part of the body in particular: the pelvic region. Many of us stand with the pelvis flared backwards, giving us a kind of swayback posture.

Imagine that stack of blocks. It's as if the *feet to knees blocks* were straight, but then the *thigh blocks* start to bow out towards the back, and then the *hips and upper body blocks* and the *neck and shoulder blocks* try to balance on top of that, and the whole thing is wobbly and out of kilter.

Try tucking in the pelvis (see the notes on tightening the *gluteus maximus* muscles), and you'll find the body coming into good alignment.

Imagine the plumb line from the top of the head down to the heels. Imagine it being held at the back of your head, running straight down your back. Now it's in front of you. Now it's at your left side. Are you still on-center? Now it moves to your right side. Be sure to keep the line as straight as possible!

Be especially careful when you stand at a lectern to read or speak. It's very tempting to relax the posture, just so you feel relaxed in front of your audience. But be careful that you don't, in the process, lose your support. It's so tempting to cross one leg in front of another, or to shift the weight to one leg, or to lean over the lectern. But in doing this, you're likely to lose the support you're more likely to gain if you stand tall. Keep your center high and your overall presence will be more positive—and your breath support should be there!

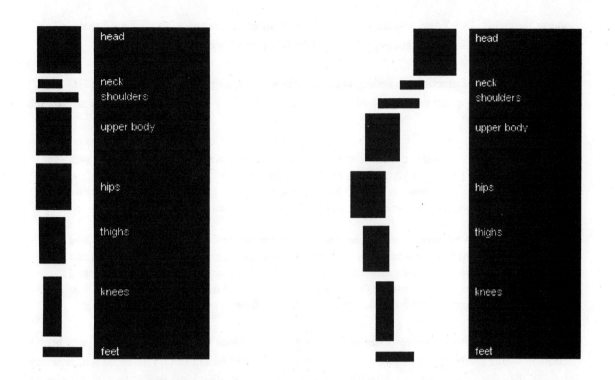

THE PAUSE THAT REPLENISHES!

Something must be said here about pauses. Many of us rush headlong into speaking without the preparation *vital* to speaking aloud, namely, *breathing*. In fact, it's probably typical in a public speaking situation to see someone rise, go to the speaker's stand and immediately begin talking. When we do that, we cheat ourselves. We haven't begun the breathing process that can get us through the next *x*-number of minutes we're going to be speaking. (Furthermore, we haven't taken that precious pre-speaking moment to graciously acknowledge our audience with a silent "Hello out there!" before we begin addressing them.) When you arrive at the lectern or pulpit or podium or wherever you're going to be standing, let your body relax (tall) into a comfortable posture, take a nice deep breath, and then begin.

And don't be afraid of pauses as you speak or read. They'll help you, giving you time to breathe adequately for speech. Furthermore, they'll give you time to get inside each thought before you start to speak it, and to think through the thought as you "think it in" from the printed page. And they'll help your listeners, giving them time to appropriate and process what you're telling them. If you're reading from a text or a manuscript, try going through it and marking it for appropriate pause moments. Don't feel you have to get through an entire sentence on a single breath. 'Tain't necessary. In fact, some sentences practically *defy* being spoken on a single breath.

Just for the sake of practicing pausing, take the following passage from Colossians 3:12-17 (NIV) and read it aloud, pausing at each of the || marks. Take your time, and don't rush any of the pauses.[6]

> Therefore, || as God's chosen people, || holy and dearly loved, || clothe yourselves with compassion, || kindness, || humility, || gentleness || and patience. || Bear with each other || and forgive || whatever grievances you may have against one another. || Forgive || as the Lord forgave you. || And over all these virtues, || put on love, || which binds them all together || in perfect unity. ||
>
> Let the peace of Christ || rule || in your hearts, || since as members of one body || you were called to peace. || And be thankful. || Let the word of Christ dwell in you richly ||as you teach and admonish one another with all wisdom, || and as you sing psalms, hymns and spiritual songs || with gratitude in your hearts || to God. || And whatever you do, || whether in word || or deed, || do it all in the name of the Lord Jesus, || giving thanks to God the Father || through him.

Try reading this into a tape recorder and playing it back. Does the pausing improve your breath control—your ability to get through longer sentences without fading out? You're no longer trying to get through too many words with too little breath. Notice how much less effort you're expending as you speak. Notice the lack of strain in the voice. You may want to add or remove some of the pauses. But notice how helpful they can be when you, now the *listener*, are on the receiving end being given time to think along with the speaker. *Just remember to stay with the thought during the pause.* And you may be pleasantly surprised to notice that your listeners don't fidget during those pauses. You're now giving them time to participate with you in the process of communicating the Word of God.

PRACTICE!

Once you get the hang of diaphragmatic breathing, don't expect it to become the "wonderful new habit" overnight. Habits take time to form. And they take time to change. Once you discover how good and relaxed it feels to speak with the supported voice, you'll want to make it a full-time habit. Have patience, and it will come.

Once, when I was taking voice lessons, my coach would say, "Well, you missed three days of practice this week!" (Or four days, or whatever.) And he was always right. He could tell whenever I didn't practice my voice work. Developing diaphragmatic breathing as a habit won't come just by wishing it, or by thinking hard about it. It will come only through practice.

Here's a suggestion to apply to *any* voice and speech work you're trying to master. Don't practice for an hour a day or a half hour a day *at a time*. Spread your practice out over several shorter periods of time. Suppose you decide it's worth half an hour a day. Find ten minutes every morning, ten every afternoon, and ten every evening to practice. Even five minutes three times a day can work wonders. If you have an assignment you need to work on specifically, spend your time with that. Otherwise, just sit and read your newspaper, your textbook, your novel—or whatever—as a means of practicing, say, your breathing. Put a hand on your abdomen and read aloud for five minutes or so, monitoring your breathing and making sure it's working right. *You don't have to take time away from other activities or responsibilities* to practice speech techniques. They can be worked into your daily routine.

Remind Yourself. Buy a packet of the little sticky paper things that you can write memos on. Find a word that serves as a reminder of what you're working on. Again, let's say you're working on mastering diaphragmatic breathing. Write the word "belt" or "breathe" or "gut" or just draw a smiley face, as a reminder to go into diaphragmatic breathing mode. Now put one on your telephone. Every time you answer the phone, put a hand on your belly, and say "Hello...!" with a nice abdominal tug.[7] Or put one on your bathroom mirror. Practice your "HO"s or "HA"s as you shave or brush your hair or whatever you do in front of your bathroom mirror. Put one on the dashboard of your car, or on the center of your steering wheel. Use your driving time to practice coordinating diaphragmatic breathing with speaking. When you get up in front of an audience to speak, paste a reminder at the top of each page of your reading or your manuscript to remind you to breathe correctly.

These reminders really work. There was a time when I was doing a lot of solo vocal work. I would be concentrating like crazy on what I was doing. As a result, even if I was singing a happy ballad or a love song or something light and bright, there would be this intense furrowed brow in the way of the happy or in-love or light and bright mood the song was supposed to convey. Someone told me about it. So I started writing "SMILE" at the top of each page of music. And it worked. I didn't start grinning like a happy idiot, but it helped me relax my facial posture so a frown didn't get in the way of the mood of the song. See if it doesn't work for you. At least try it!

---

[1] *All of us naturally breathe correctly as children. As we "grow up," we often do things that get in the way of what's "natural." Like changing our breathing habits. I have experienced that this shift frequently occurs around*

the time of puberty, when the individual becomes self-conscious about physical changes in the body and the change of voice in males. This is also, for many, a time of insecurity. "Holding back" the voice through tension in the throat can be a form of retreat into that insecurity. I have also observed that this is the age at which young people begin to mumble instead of enunciating clearly. ("I'm not too sure of myself, so if I don't speak up or speak clearly no one will get on my case....")

[2]When I was in college, one of the "neat things" (read: "stupid tricks") to do was to go to a public place, like a train station or a big store, and ask someone to page "Ben Dover." It was supposed to produce high hilarity when people heard: "Bend over, bend over." We also tried it with Ben's wife Eileen and their friend Ben Down. It was more fun than eating goldfish.

[3]All speech is produced on exhaled air. There are, however, some sounds produced on an inhale which could come under the category of speech. Among these is the imploded "Ja" uttered by many Swedes and by one young Polish gentleman who grew up in Minnesota. An inhaled sound such as this should be avoided while one is eating Swedish meatballs.

[4]This is a modification of what many people, as singers, have gone through in order to learn to breathe properly. I had a voice teacher who'd put a big stack of books on my stomach so I could feel the kind of muscular pressure necessary to engage and tighten up the abdominal muscles. At one point, he even stood on top of the books (with only one foot, thank goodness) to make me work a little harder. You can do the same thing with books with this exercise. Don't try standing on your own stomach.

[5]A couple of years ago, families gathered in the sanctuary of our church for a Family Night program. We were all going to sing some new Christmas hymns. The children's choir director, a wonderfully sweet and talented musician, announced, "If you want to be sure to hit some of those high notes, squeeze your cheeks -- and I don't mean [pointing to her face] these!"

[6]If you find it helpful, count "1 - 2" to yourself at each pause mark. But don't make the pauses mechanical. Some of them will want to be "quickies," just giving you time to take a sip of breath. Others will want to be more protracted, either because of the profundity or complexity of the thought or for the sake of emphasizing the important matters in the thought.

[7]Watch it when talking on the telephone. That little mouthpiece is so nice and close! There's nothing there that suggests "I've got to breathe right, get my voice in focus, and project." In fact the situation says practically the opposite: "Don't sweat it. Stay all slouched and don't bother to breathe or articulate, because the receiver will do all the work for you." Don't you believe it! Or am I the only person in existence who's had to say, "I'm sorry, I didn't hear what you said," or some such utterance to someone who sounded as if they were speaking to their belly button? Even the person who habitually uses the voice properly in a person-to-person situation will often fade out vocally with a little tiny unsupported voice when speaking on the telephone. Confess: Have you ever had anyone ask you to repeat yourself or "speak up" when you were on the 'phone? Those little yellow reminder sheets might not be a bad idea for all of us to use all the time. In fact, do you suppose we could get Ma Bell to put some vocal advice like "BREATHE RIGHT AND GET YOUR VOICE IN FOCUS!!!" on every telephone?

Putting Your Best Voice Forward

How beautiful on the mountains are the feet of those who bring good news,
who proclaim peace, who bring good tidings, who proclaim salvation,
who say to Zion, "Your God reigns!"
Listen! Your watchmen lift up their voices; together they shout for joy.
When the Lord returns to Zion, they will see it with their own eyes.
Burst into songs of joy together, you ruins of Jerusalem,
for the Lord has comforted his people, he has redeemed Jerusalem.
The Lord will lay bare his holy arm in the sight of all the nations,
and all the ends of the earth will see the salvation of our God.
Depart, depart, go out from there! Touch no unclean thing!
Come out from it and be pure, you who carry the vessels of the Lord
But you will not leave in haste or go in flight;
for the Lord will go before you, the God of Israel will be your rear guard. (Isaiah 52:7-12)

Prayer: I thank you and praise you, Heavenly Father, for the voice you have given me. And I thank and praise you even more for the Gospel you have given me to proclaim—the Gospel of peace, and good tidings, and salvation to a world so desperately in need of this good news—the good news that you reign over our lives to give us joy and victory. And how can I thank you enough that as you call me to speak your word you yourself go with me, to guide me and show me your way. Bless me, Lord, that my voice may be heard, strong and clear, as I go forth with you. In the strong and wonderful name of Jesus I pray. Amen.

"I Can't Stand My Voice!" Well, I can't tell you how many times in nearly three decades I've heard that sentiment expressed. I've had women tell me that whenever they answer the phone the voice on the other end asks, "Is your mother there?" What mature woman wants a little girl voice? Once when I called the home of one of my son Stephen's classmates, a mezzo-soprano voice answered, "Hello!" I said, "Mrs. Bleeker?" And the voice said, "No, this is *Mr.* Bleeker." I later met this little man with a very tight throaty voice that sounded for all the world like a little boy's voice. I don't suppose he liked his voice very much either. For years, we've done an initial tape recording of each student entering the seminary. For many years, we used audio tapes only; now we use videotapes and do the recordings in class. These tapes are used in one-on-one follow-up conferences. Most students are eager to hear (and see) how they present themselves, and to learn ways of improving what they observe. But for some, the very trauma of hearing their own voice is just short of the trauma of facing root canal work with a rusty coat hanger.

"Do I Have To?" This is the question that sometimes follows, when you start to turn on the

machine and play "The Tape." "Do I have to listen to *that*?" And you usually want to say "Yes, you do, because the rest of us have to suffer with it and you might as well join the crowd." But being kind and Christian, you usually say instead, "Oh, sure, it won't be so bad!" or something equally palliative. But the really best response of all might be to say, "No, you don't have to have a voice you don't like or a voice you think other people don't like. You can change it, and I'm here to help you do just that." And that's the truth. The good news is that you can have the most pleasant voice you're capable of producing. But it's going to take some work. And lots of awareness. And a willingness to whittle away at the bad things you don't like and focus on the goals that'll give you the voice you'd like to have.

> God loves us enough to accept us just as we are. But He loves us too much to leave us that way.

How's Your Attitude? If you have a positive attitude about yourself (God does) you'll find it a work of joy to discover the best voice you can have for your ministry. (And whether you're a lay person or a theological student or a pastor your work as a Christian is a ministry.) But it takes awareness, and time, and a willingness to work. If you have a negative attitude about yourself and about your voice, you and your voice are probably a pretty good match for each other, and your prospects for growth and change are slim. So take seriously the promise that God loves you just as you are, but loves you too much to leave you that way. Take seriously too the notion that God wants you to love yourself enough to grow in grace and be nurtured in all the good gifts God provides to enable you to fulfil your ministry. And remember that God, being a gracious God, loves to be gracious to you. That grace is running downhill towards you all the time. All you have to do is look up and accept it and say "Thank you!" So do it.

Finding Out What Habits to Change. I'm not going to try to cover all the possible vocal idiosyncrasies that exist. There are technical books you can read if you want to go into that. But I want to discuss some of the *typical* voice problems that worship leaders and other public speakers *typically* need to deal with, and try to help you work through these. And about the audio and video tapes I mentioned earlier: Don't shy away from them! They can be the very best friends you've ever had when it comes to finding out how you *really* sound and how you *really* present yourself as a public speaker. They can give you good objective feedback. And *objectivity* is one of the graces you're going to need as much as anything. *Because you never come across to your* *audience the way you think in your own head you're coming across.* So trust those tapes. Trust your friends who are trying to give you feedback. Chances are you'll feel strange the first time you come forth with a good strong voice. You'll say, "That's not me!" "But that sounds so overdone!" "But I'm going to sound phony!" and a bunch of other excuses. But take feedback seriously. It can help you come to the point where *eventually you will be able* to come across to others the way you think you're coming across.

The following is a list of some of the typical "uh-oh" things all of us need to be aware of. Once again, they are habits that *can* be changed once awareness kicks in and you tell yourself, "I ought to do something about that!" I've been there myself, and know how easy it is to settle into habits that don't serve you or your ministry very well. I'll try to describe these so you can sense whether or not they apply to you, and then offer some suggestions for working through them.

VOICE AND DICTION CONCERNS

Unsupported Sound / Throaty Production: This is one of the major concerns all of us need to deal with. We've bypassed the diaphragmatic breathing that can support the production of voice. Therefore our sounds are tense and throaty. There may be so little physical energy used in producing sound that we grind out the voice with an irritating (to us and to our listeners) glottal fry.[1] Or there may be so much energy directed towards super-clarity of enunciation and precision—in the form of tension localized in the throat area—that there's a superabundance of glottal shock. All of these indicate tension in the throat where we don't need it and where it can be detrimental. The "cure" is to learn correct breathing.[2] This probably will include a greater awareness of posture and how or bodies naturally function when we breathe normally. Prepare for any public speaking with a good period of warming up. Relax your throat and use your belt to support your voice. When you look at yourself on videotape, take a close look at your upper body. Are you lifting your shoulders and clavicular area when you inhale? If you are, your voice is probably one of those "talking heads" voices—usually a tight little squeak from the neck up. But that's not where your voice should be coming from. It should originate from "down under" (and I mean from the diaphragm and not from Australia). Get some "body" (literally!) into the voice and free it from captivity!

What you see is what you hear. My wife and I recently attended a meeting where a professional woman was addressing an august assembly. (In July!) Here we witnessed a perfect example of the *correlation between the physical and the aural* in voice production. *What we were seeing* was the following: leading with the head (especially the chin) for emphasis; head generally "busy" (with enthusiasm) from the neck up; noticeable muscular tension in the neck; chest heaving upward with every inhaled breath; much general movement of the upper body, especially the shoulders. If I had seen this on video without any sound, I would have known precisely *what we were hearing*: a tight, scratchy voice; continual tiny coughs to "clear the throat"; endings of phrases being swallowed, dying out into glottal fry. And the opposite is true. If I had heard only the audio with no video, I could have told you what I would have seen. Two other things happened during her presentation. First, after several minutes there was sympathetic throat-clearing and little coughs from the audience. Totally subconscious. It's very easy to develop a sympathetic sore throat from listening to a speaker with a sore throat. Second, general concern for her voice drew our attention away from what she had to say. What she said was incredibly interesting. But some of it got lost when our focus shifted to how she was using her voice and what was happening to it. Think about this. It happens frequently.

Throaty Placement (Back Placement): Sounds tend to be swallowed, throaty, can sound "growly," or cloudy. The voice may have a kind of "foggy" quality, as if there were a cloud cover over it. Imagine a television commercial for "HACKIES," (a soothing vaporizing throat lozenge I just made up). There on the screen the pulsing red light back down in the throat is indicating, "You've got a sore throat! You need HACKIES!" That's where the focus of your voice is. The placement, production, and energy of phonation are down there in the basement. This often happens if the pitch is too low. That deep contrabassoon sound with all the pharyngeal resonance may sound absolutely wonderful to my own ears. But that's where it's staying. To my *listeners' ears* it sounds muffled and dark. And it's not going anywhere except to my own ears. It's largely bone-carried sound being reinforced inside my own head.

Pitch Range. What I want to do with this voice is bring it upstairs and into focus. In the case of a too-deep bass growl, it will improve if I use a slightly higher register. (I sing second bass, and can hit some pretty low tones. But if I tried to use my voice down in that bottom range for teaching or preaching or just plain everyday speaking, I'd be in trouble. So I use what tends to be a fairly high baritone voice. It helps bring sounds forward, helps me focus my voice in the front of my mouth.) A voice that's consistently too near the top or too near the bottom of one's *optimal pitch range* is a voice that's likely to be strained. Imagine this page as representing your optimal pitch range. The top of the page is as high as you can go (sing or speak) and the bottom is as low as you can go. A person's *habitual pitch range* (the range you're using by habit most of the time) is usually roughly a third of the optimal range—that third lying on the lowish side of the middle of the page.

If I'm working with a too-low voice, I've got my habitual range way down at the bottom of the page. And that's where my voice is getting strained and is not likely to carry or project well to my listeners' ears. So how do I know if my pitch is too low or not? Try this. Put your fingers in your ears and hum up and down a scale until your voice sounds *loudest* inside your own head. It's supposed to sound loudest right about in the middle of where your optimal range is. If you have access to a piano or guitar or a pitch pipe or a tuning fork, check it out. See where the middle of your range is. And then check and see what range you tend to use most of the time. If the former is higher than the latter, try speaking in a *slightly* higher register. Try about three notes on a scale higher than you're habitually using. Don't strain, and don't try to sound like Squeaky the Mouse. And don't be surprised if you think it sounds weird. And don't be surprised either if nobody else notices the difference (except that they can hear you a lot better!).

Voice Focus. Be honest. Are you being very Christian by keeping that voice locked back in your throat? I don't think so. So why not share it with your listeners? Get it up out of your throat and into your face. (I just said it that way to wake you up, but it really is the case that you want to get your *face* into the act of voice production.) What you want is voice that's less bone-carried and more *air-carried* en route to your listeners' ears. So imagine the "HACKIES" commercial again. This time the pulsating red light is up on your forehead, right between your eyes. And the announcer is saying, "Now you're feeling the wonderful vaporizing action of HACKIES!" and blah-blah about your sinuses being nice and clear and all that. *Right here is where you want your voice to be focused. In the front of your face. Between your eyes.* Many of us were taught to "sing *in the mask*"—that is, to focus the voice in the middle of where your mask would be if you were the Lone Ranger. Or Tonto. Some voice teachers talk about being a unicorn and putting the voice up in the horn of the unicorn. Some voice teachers are ditzy. But the idea works. Play with it. Think of the sounds coming not from your throat, but from the middle of your forehead and going *"zing!"* right towards your listeners' ears. If you tend to focus sounds in the throat, imagine the inside of your mouth is like a big auditorium or a cathedral with a high ceiling. As you speak, try placing your voice up there on the ceiling. That should begin to get it into forward focus. Here's another image for you: Imagine a garden sprayer—one of those tank things with a hose attached and a nozzle attached to the end of the hose. The sprayer (the source or energy or power for voice production) is down in the abdomen and diaphragm area. The hose (the conduit or passageway) goes up through the body and through the neck and throat and up between your eyes. And the nozzle (the production end of things, or the focus where it all comes out) is right there *between your eyes*. Isn't that a wonderful way to represent how the voice should work and how it should be unconstrained in the throat and how it should be up in forward focus? All right, like I said, some voice teachers are ditzy. But it really *does* work. Trust me.

Visual focus. Another kind of focus that helps with voice projection is *visual focus*. Several years ago, I was planning to sing a solo in church. I was at home, sitting at the piano, working my way through Aaron Copland's terrific arrangement of *At the River*. My son Stephen, who was about eight at the time, came up and sat down next to me on the piano bench, and said, "Can I sing with you?" I said, "Sure!" And he said, "I mean in church!" So he learned the song with me. And even accomplished the phenomenal feat of coming in with the opening line "Shall we gather by the river..." on the right note without being given any pitch in the introductory measures. On Saturday, we were at the church rehearsing with the organist. Stephen's voice was a little timid. He'd never done anything like this before. The door at the front of the chancel opened, and in walked the choir director who listened for a few minutes, then said, "Stephen, sing to the pulpit." (We were standing upstairs in the choir loft at the back of the sanctuary.) So we started the song again, and out came the clearest, purest, strongest sound you could imagine! On Sunday, when he started the first few bars of the song, people down in the nave turned around and looked up, their faces beaming at the thrill of this big beautiful voice coming from this little guy. Then I came in on my line, "Yes, we'll gather at the river...." But I couldn't see their faces any more. I must have had something in my eyes. *The point of this is: give yourself a visual focus for your voice. Aim towards the clock on the back wall. And sure enough your voice will come out clear and pure and strong, and the Word you're proclaiming will be heard throughout the entire room. And I'll be back there in the back, proud as punch, with my face beaming. And probably something in my eye.*

Endings Swallowed: This a *very* common problem. It's a vocal habit you and I can get away with if we're talking to one another over a cup of coffee at a little table. Or on the phone. Or speaking something into our tape recorder, sitting there with the microphone right in front of our face doing the work for us. In any kind of casual setting, it's easy for the ends of phrases to tend to get swallowed. And in some casual setting, it's no big deal if this happens. But put me in front of a class lecturing on "the extreme importance of (*what was that she said?*)" or telling you "never to forget that (*could you repeat that please?*)" and it becomes a big deal. Or get me up in front of the congregation to do a Minute for Mission and all my listeners hear is a "Minute for Mish..." and it's a big deal. Or stand me up at the lectern to read Scrip... and all you... is the begin... and lose out on every... that comes at the end of the sent... and it's another big deal. I need to follow through to the end of each phrase. Just as I need to follow through on my golf swing. I've got to get the last part of the thought out there as surely and clearly as the first part. What if the most crucial element of my thought is in the last three or four words? I've cheated my listeners out of hearing the whole wonderful idea. And if I'm communicating my own ideas in an announcement or a message or a sermon, I've cheated myself because all the good preparation has been for naught. No one has heard what I had to say! And if I'm reading Scripture I've cheated God. And that's not nice. So it really does behoove me to project my voice and my ideas well.

"Sing Out". Remember the scene in the musical *Gypsy* where Mama Rose is coaching Louise and Baby June, saying, "Sing out...?" That's the way our listeners are talking to us when they can't hear half of what we're saying. I know they don't really sit there and say "Sing out!", but that's what they're all thinking. And it's good advice. If you're in the habit of swallowing endings, try singing the thought. Literally. Take a page of whatever you're reading and sing the first third of it on a chant. (Do this at home, not when you're speaking in public.) *You'll notice that you can't swallow the end of a sung phrase. It's impossible. You'd choke if you tried to do it.* Automatically when you *sing* you follow through to the end of the musical phrase. So apply this to your speaking. Chant through the first part of a page and be aware of how the voice is behaving when you are singing. Nothing is swallowed. It's all going forward. Then do a combination of chanting and speaking the next third of the page. Fool yourself into not knowing whether you're going to chant this phrase or speak it. Mix it up. And keep the production the same for *speaking* (nothing swallowed, all going forward) as it is for *chanting*. Finally, speak the last third of the page and keep the sounds forward. When you get up to speak or read in public, think to yourself, "Now I'm going to 'sing' this thought to my listeners."

"Call Out". One very helpful way to master voice projection is to note contexts in which we very naturally do project the voice. We do this, for example, whenever we "call out" to someone across some distance. Something inside us would tell us we'd never be heard if we kept the voice locked up in the throat or swallowed part of what we were trying to communicate. I have my students demonstrate this for themselves by standing in front of an open window and calling out to an imaginary someone on the other side of the parking lot at the back of the classroom building. Yes, I know they can be heard. Yes, I know it sounds crazy. Yes, I know it can make you feel silly and embarrassed and all that. But it does work. Try some of these "calls" for yourself. Get someplace where you can make noise without being arrested. You'll find the voice naturally comes into focus. You naturally shift into a higher register. You naturally lengthen the vowel sounds. [Note that the vowel sounds bear the primary *carrying quality* of the voice. Without them, you'd barely be heard—let alone understood. Look at one of the sentences below: "Hey, fella! Get that dog off my lawn!" Without the vowel sounds you'd be saying, "H—— f—l! G—t th—t d—g f m l—n"—a bunch of little sounds that don't go anywhere. When you call out to someone you make good, full use of the sounds that carry over a distance: the vowel sounds.]

In short, your voice naturally projects to your listeners' ears when you're calling to them. And you're not *screaming* or *yelling* at them at all. The voice isn't strained or forced, it's just come into focus.

Hey, Henry, come down from that tree!
Come on, team, let's get things moving here!
Kimberly! Come, please! Mike's on the phone!
Look! Another flying saucer way over there!
Tommy, Susan!! Dinner's on the table!
Young man, you get right back up there to bed!
Hey, fella! Get that dog off my lawn!
Park the car over on the other side of the lot!
You know I can't hear you with my Walkman on!
What'd you say? Look out for <u>what</u> manhole???

Now try the same kind of "calling out" focus with a Call to Worship. You're not screaming or yelling at people, "All right, you varmints, get with it and we're gonna worship God." You're inviting them. In a nice pleasant inviting voice. But you need to be heard. Try bringing the voice into focus on some of these kinds of "calling out" statements.

Lift up your heads, O gates! and be lifted up, O ancient doors!
that the King of glory may come in.
Who is the King of glory? The Lord, strong and mighty, the Lord mighty in battle!
Lift up your heads, O gates! and be lifted up, O ancient doors!
that the King of glory may come in!
Who is this King of glory? The Lord of hosts, he is the King of glory!

Praise the Lord! Praise the Lord, O my soul!
I will praise the Lord as long as I live; I will sing praises to my God while I have being.
The Lord will reign forever, thy God, O Zion, to all generations. Praise the Lord!

The Lord is my light and my salvation; whom shall I fear?
The Lord is the stronghold of my life; of whom shall I be afraid?
Wait for the Lord; be strong, and let your heart take courage; yea, wait for the Lord!

Grace be unto you, and peace, from God our Father, and from the Lord Jesus Christ.
It is a good thing to give thanks unto the Lord, and to sing praises unto Thy name, O Most High:
To show forth Thy loving-kindness in the morning, and Thy faithfulness every night.
Delight thyself also in the Lord; and He shall give thee the desires of thine heart.

Come now, let us reason together, says the Lord:
though your sins are like scarlet, they shall be as white as snow;

though they are red like crimson, they shall become like wool.
Let us worship God.

Other Images. Whether it's the golf swing idea of "follow through" or the Mama Rose idea of "singing out" or some other image, the important thing is to keep the thought alive to the end and make sure everyone hears what you have to say. You may conjure up some other image that will help you. Think, for example of the voice being like a little train that's always going forward towards its destination, and never sliding backwards into the roundhouse. Actors sometimes do an exercise where they pair up and while one is speaking the other is "reeling in" the words as one would reel in a garden hose or tug on the rope that ties a boat to the pier. Any such image will work for you if you're convinced it's important for us to hear every word.

One More Wor-DUH. Use singers' diction (energetic, "athletic" diction) on those final consonant sounds. Remember, most of our consonant sounds are produced right up at the front of the face by the lips or the tongue tip. You want us to "worship God" and not "Gah." To "rejoice in the Lord" and not "in the Lore." You can *use those final consonant sounds*—sounding them out clearly and energetically—as an aid to the placement and projection of the voice.

I just came from a chapel service. Heard a great example of vocal style that works in one context and doesn't work in another. This person had developed the kind of quiet, confidential, pastoral counselor sound—voice often doing a diminuendo to an intense whispery quality. In the pastor's office, sitting five or six feet from one's visitor, this voice could be very effective. Very pastoral. Very comforting. But it doesn't work in public speaking. This fellow must have halfway realized that. Because he began each statement with a nice full voice. But then he faded out from the middle of the phrase to the end, which was almost inaudible. (You could expect to see his congregation choreograph their response to his sermon as he went from loud to weak to fade-out: *sit tall—cup right hand to right ear—lean far forward // sit tall—cup right hand to right ear—lean far forward // sit tall—cup right hand to right ear—lean far forward // sit tall—cup right hand to right ear—lean far forward—cha, cha, cha.*) The "soundtrack" went something like this:

The God who made us gives us all good things to bless our lives...

Jesus Christ alone is the only hope by which the world can be saved...

Come to the table, all who truly hunger and thirst, and he will feed you...

At first, you'd be blown out of your seat, and then you'd listen and wonder, "Where'd he go? Where'd he go...?" It's disconcerting when this happens. I find myself tuned in to the speech pattern and listening to it in all its predictability, and *missing out on the content*. And from what I know of this student, and from what I *could* hear of his message, he had a hope and a promise and a powerful Gospel to proclaim. Sad to say, though, we all lost out on the last 50% of each thought he gave us! I kind of think Jesus would have been sad about it, too.

Flat or Nasal Quality: Many people are bothered by a voice that tends to be flat or nasal—whether that voice is their own or someone else's. The chapter on Resonance and the material on Open Vowel Sounds will deal more with this problem. But let's tackle it here for a moment. This book contains several "commercials" for opening one's mouth. When the mouth is open (as in "taking a bite of apple" and we focus sounds forward (against back of the upper teeth) we add warmth, resonance and carrying quality to the voice. The sounds are full and rich because we've provided them with enough space to resonate. But if I speak with my mouth nearly closed, providing a flatter space for the sounds to re-sound in, the result is going to be what's called a *flat voice quality*. The cure, simple enough, is to "open your mouth." Take seriously what the Lord says in Psalm 81:10:

> I am the Lord your God, who brought you up out of Egypt.
> Open wide your mouth and I will fill it.

Nasalized Sounds. With a flat voice quality, vowel sounds are not only going to be flat, they are also likely to be nasalized. Watch out especially for [æ] (as in *cat*) and [aʊ] (as in *how*). With the [æ] sound, focus should be more toward the mid-back of the mouth (central area of hard palate). If too far forward, takes on an "eh" quality. This easily becomes nasalized. The [aʊ] diphthong is a combination of "ah+oo" and not "æ+oo". When it becomes the latter, it too is easily nasalized. We're talking largely a matter of aesthetics. But to most ears, a warm pleasant [æ] sound is far better than a harsh [ã] sound and a resonant [aʊ] pleasanter than the whiny [æʊ] sound.

Regional "Accent". There are certain parts of the country where sounds tend to be flat and somewhat nasalized. This is not to disparage anyone who comes, for example, from New Jersey. After all, I live in New Jersey. Have for more than twenty-seven years—not counting three years here as a seminary student. (I may forever despair, however, over our having named one son "Dan"—since we've lived here he's been *Dee-yun*. But I said we wouldn't be disparaging.) If you discover a flat or nasal quality to your voice you don't have to move. Just be aware of how it sounds, and if you really want to change it it's not hard at all. Just open your mouth. If you discover that your neighbor sounds flat and nasal don't presume that you sound the same. I grew up in Indianapolis, six blocks from a fraternity brother who had a really grating Hoosier twang. Yet I was once asked if I were from England because my voice had no such twang. Go figure!

Strident or Harsh Voice Quality: Put together the throaty tension of an unsupported, right voice and the flat or nasal quality and you have a voice roughly the equivalent of fingernails caressing a blackboard. This one's no harder to "cure" than the tight voice by itself (breathe correctly) or the flat nasal voice by itself (open your mouth and focus). Since, however, it's a double-barreled phenomenon, it's likely to take longer to fix. Or twice as much awareness.

Breathy Quality: If you said, "Hi!" could you blow out all the candles on your birthday cake at once? Do you sound a little like Mae West or Vincent Price? Do you have that sultry, sexy voice quality that turns strong men into overdone pasta or causes women to swoon? If you do, you may have a breathy voice quality. If you do, you might make a wonderful matinee idol. But if you do, we probably can't hear you past the second row. Because if you do, you're *wasting* breath rather than using it for full voice. And in the process you're making yourself tireder than necessary—all that breathing for so little output. Some suggestions might help:

—Light a match or candle and hold it just a couple of inches in front of your mouth. Don't burn your nose. Say "Hi' without blowing out the candle. Cut back to the tiniest /h/ sound you can muster, and try it again. Like this: ni!" Now try the same with "Hey, Hee, Hi, Ho, Hoo"—with just a little /h/ and a lot of vowel sound. You're aiming for a lot of voice and *no wasted breath*.

—With or without the candle, repeat these words (same pairs as in the "What ELSE Happens..." chapter) keeping the /h/ sound as minimal as possible:

hear . . . ear	high . . . eye	hail . . . ail	had . . . add
head . . . Ed	hairy . . . airy	hallow . . . aloe	ham . . . am
hand . . . and	hasp . . . asp	hitch . . . itch	hike . . . Ike
hone . . . own	heart . . . art	hedge . . . edge	hod . . . odd

—Hold a hand in front of your mouth and repeat the following, allowing *as little breath as possible* to escape:

pah-pah-pah-pah—pah-pah-pah-pah—pah

tah-tah-tah-tah—tah-tah-tah-tah—tah

pah-tah-kah-tah—pah-tah-kah-tah—pah

She sees Sue's shoes. Sue sees Sherri's suits.

Children's teachers teach each other.

Fred Pitt flunks French.

Read each line on a single breath. Then read the first two lines on a single breath. Then the first three lines on a single breath. Do the same with lines four, five and six. Good breath control is a major asset. Don't waste breath. Use it for projecting power.

—Cupping a hand in front of your mouth (as if to "catch" and "contain" the sound as it comes out) feel as if you are "holding in" the sound (and, of course, not wasting any breath) on the following:

Gentle Jesus, meek and mild.

I am well. How are you?

Oh, wow! You're wonderful!

Try each of these lines on a single breath. Try all three lines together on a single breath. If someone wonders what you're up to, just tell them you're praying out loud.

—Avoid the breathy quality for emphasis or dramatic effect. The sound becomes diffuse, out of focus, loses carrying quality. Instead, try extending sounds (e.g. vowel sounds, liquid consonants such as /m, n, ŋ, l, z/) as a means of projection. Think of the breathy sound as whooshing out to the sides. The extended sound is protracted towards your listeners—quiet but zeroed in on target. Take for example the phrase:

Behold, I tell you a mystery . . . .

It so often comes out with a lot of wasted breath and a spooky effect:

BeHHHHHHHHHHHold, I tEHHHHHHHHHHHll you a mySSSSSSSSStery . . . .

It would still convey the effect of "mystery" (not something spooky but something known to God alone) if we'd extend vowel and liquid consonant sounds:

BehOHLLLd, I teLLL you a MMMystery . . . .

A tad hard to get across in the printed word, but experiment with it and I think you'll get the idea.

Control the energy. Wasted breath is wasted energy. If you're wasting breath with a whispery voice quality, you are throwing away energy. As a result, you're going to tire the voice (and yourself) quickly, and a lot of your good effort will be for naught. Consider the following "homespun" analogy, which applies to voice quality and breath control as well as to the general proclamation or reading of the Word. Suppose I have in hand a bottle of Coke.

I flip the cap off, and hold my thumb over the top and shake it up real well. Now there's lots of energy built up inside in the form of all this het up Coke wanting to do something and go somewhere. So what do I do with it? I have two choices. One: I can take my thumb off all at once and the whole mess goes sloshing to the floor right in front of me. It doesn't go anywhere, except all over my hand and shoes. It's just wasted energy. Or: I can release my thumb a little tiny bit and *aim* that stream of sticky stuff all around the room—at you, and at you, and at you. Now I'm in control of it, and I can use it and focus it and give it a purpose to go where I want it to go and do what I want it to do. Think about that Coke when you think about how you're using your voice. Is it energy all wasted, going nowhere? Or is it controlled energy, focused and purposed and going where you want it to go and doing what you want it to do?

"Teacup" Inflections: Yes, again! Not only do they botch up any sensible interpretive reading with their "boing-dy boing-dy boing-dy boing-dy boing" sound, they also tend to foment the bad voice-production habit of combining falling inflections with decreasing volumes. Imagine those upside-down "U"-shaped inflections (teacups) paired with decrescendos (like this: > > > > >) and you get a sort of "boing-dy boing-dy boing-dy boing" thing going. Again, we need to watch the tendency to give each phrase a rise-fall inflection pattern (teacups). When, with this, volume fades at the ends of phrases, everything suffers. Ideas fail to progress to their climax, and even if they did we couldn't hear them because of faulty projection. Thoughts conceived in the passion of commitment and concern die aborning.

Variables—Pitch, Rate, and Volume: If there's ever a place where a tape recorder could be a helpmeet, it's here in the area of the vocal variables. If we're not aware of it, our pitch, rate, and volume can tend towards sameness. We need to vary these vocal dynamics. Listen. And stretch.

Are you using a a too-narrow pitch range? Stretch it. Are your rate and volume the same throughout? Or do you vary rate and volume to match each thought?

Maybe you need to "take the lid off" and let it all out. "Play it again, Sam" into your tape recorder, and really overdo it. Enter into the energy of each idea feet first. How do you *feel* about the things you're saying? Let us know. Show us. Lift into mind-grabbing, heart-rending, soul-convicting prominence the good news, the important news, the new news of every thought.

Put *your* best voice forward!

[1]*See the chapter "What ELSE Happens When We Speak" for further material on the tight throaty voice, glottal shock, glottal fry and other anomalies.*
[2]*See the chapter "Breathing—The Motor for Voice" for further clarification.*

Lift Up Your Voice—Make God's Name Resound

Comfort, comfort my people, says your God.

Speak tenderly to Jerusalem, and proclaim to her that her hard service has been complete,

that her sin has been paid for, that she has received from the Lord's hand double for all her sins.

A voice of one calling: "In the desert prepare the way for the Lord;

make straight in the wilderness a highway for our God.

Every valley shall be raised up, every mountain and hill made low;

the rough ground shall become level, the rugged places a plain.

And the glory of the Lord will be revealed, and all mankind together will see it.

For the mouth of the Lord has spoken."

A voice says, "Cry out." And I said, "What shall I cry?"

"All men are like grass, and all their glory is like the flowers of the field.

The grass withers and the flowers fall, because the breath of the Lord blows on them.

Surely the people are grass.

The grass withers and the flowers fall, but the word of our God stands forever."

You who bring good tidings to Zion, go up on a high mountain.

You who bring good tidings to Jerusalem, lift up your voice with a shout,

lift it up, do not be afraid;

say to the towns of Judah, "Here is your God!" (Isaiah 40:1-9)

Prayer: Sovereign Lord, you come with power and might, and you tend your flock like a shepherd. You have created the heavens and the earth, and you teach us knowledge and show us the path of understanding. You are the everlasting God, who gives us strength and hope. Wonderful God, how can I praise you enough? As the heavens declare your glory and the skies proclaim the work of your hands, so may my voice resound in blessing your holy name. From the very foundation of my being may my whole life resound in praising you. In the Savior Jesus' name. Amen.

Let the Sound Resound. When my son Stephen was born, someone gave us a little music box to dangle from his crib. It was a little brown box, about two inches cubed, with a string that hung down that you pulled to make it play *Make Someone Happy*. Like any object hung on the side of a crib (at least any object worth more than thirty-nine cents), this little music box was subject to one of the joys of infantdom: being dislodged and thrown over the side onto the floor with sufficient force to decimate it. Thus the insides of the music box emerged and found their way into my hands and into my classroom as a demonstration of *resonance*. Holding the little musical mechanism by itself, outside of the box, you could still pull the string and it would play. But it gave out a teensy little tinkly sound almost inaudible unless you were right up next to it. It sounded something like this:

"Make someone happy, make just one person happy"

(I know, it didn't make little "word" sounds, but that *suggests* the size and tone of the sound it produced.) If I'd then take the mechanism and set it inside its original now-in-two-pieces box, the sound got a little bigger, but still wasn't really big. Sort of like this:

"Make someone happy, make just one person happy"

But then I found a nice little wooden box, about 3" x 6" x 2½", and brought it in to school. When I set the musical mechanism down in this box the sound grew tremendously. Something like this:

"Make someone happy, make just one person happy"

Okay, so I'm exaggerating a *little* bit.[1] But it was a wonderful demonstration of resonance. Without a *box* to play in, the sound dissipated into thin air. Put it in a small box, and you got a small, albeit audible, sound. Put it into a bigger box, and you got a much bigger sound.

The Human "Box". If you haven't yet recognized it, this is another thinly-veiled commercial for *opening your mouth*. The production of sound initiated by the vibration of the vocal bands is hautomatically enlarged or reinforced by the

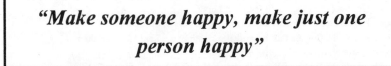

The space on the left provides a considerably larger "playroom" for the sounds, whereas the more constricted space on the right limits a lot of the various possible overtones

human "box" in which it's situated. In a sense, the whole body is such a box, giving power to the tones vibrated by the vocal bands. But the *major resonance box* is the oral chamber (your mouth) where all the *vowel sounds* are given shape and structure and, ultimately, more or less resonance. And that box, like the series of little boxes for the musical mechanism, can be enlarged. At least, we can open up and gain more resonance than we may be doing right now. (If you're sitting in a group where people are talking—say, a discussion group of some sort—watch people as they speak. Many of us don't open our mouths very noticeably at all. You can sometimes look around the whole room and wonder *who is talking* because you can see barely any animation at all!)

<u>*Vowel Sounds = Carrying Power*</u>. Bear in mind that the vowel sounds are the *carrying power* of our speech. If the space provided for producing these vowel sounds is minimal, the resulting sound is going to be minimal. (And, concomitantly, the diction is likely to be sluggish and the entire voice production lacking in energy, but that's—as they say where I grew up—"a whole 'nother matter.") If you enlarge the space for producing vowel sounds, the result is resonance: the richness and carrying power which enable a voice to project and at the same time give it warmth and beauty. If you provide a little flat playground for the sounds you produce, you're giving those sounds a little cramped space, and you'll wind up with a little flat voice. If you open and provide a bigger playground for the sounds to move around in and re-*sound* (re-*son*-ate) in, they'll be happier and more boisterous and provide you with a fuller and richer sound.

<u>**Open Vowel Sounds**</u>. To provide the optimal open space for vowel sounds, open the mouth and lift the palate as if you were going to *take a bite of apple*. This is a feeling similar to an open, relaxed yawn. The throat is free, the palate high, and the resulting sound is a pleasant, open, unconstricted one. (Notice the difference between this sound and the sound produced by the suggestion to "drop the jaw." The latter sound is much more throaty, and the dropping of the lower jaw tends to constrict the larynx.) The open "apple" space is considerably more conducive to producing sounds that are forward and in focus—sounds that will easily project to our listeners' ears. The space created is not unlike an open rectangle standing on its short side:

We'll use this figure of a rectangle to suggest the shape of the oral cavity in producing the open vowel sounds (see below).

Shaping the Open Vowel Sounds. The next step is to shape this optimal space into the various vowel sounds. There are seven vowel sounds that can be opened maximally and shaped into speech without distorting the sound or flow of speech. They are:

AH as in _odd_ or _hot_	_IPA:_ [ɑː]
AW as in _all_ or _ought_	_IPA:_ [ɔː]
OH as in _oat_ or _hoe_	_IPA:_ [əʊ]
OO as in _ooze_ or _who_	_IPA:_ [uː]
OW (= **AH** + **OO**) as in _out_ or _how_	_IPA:_ [aʊ]
A as in _add_ or _hat_	_IPA:_ [æ]
EE as in _ease_ or _heat_	_IPA:_ [iː]

Try saying these vowel sounds. Notice they go from more _open_ (as with AH and AW) to more closed (as with EE). If you voice an open yawn into an "AH" sound, you'll produce possibly the nicest, most rich, free, full, resonant sound you're capable of making. Try recreating this fullness on words such as _odd, hot, God, father, what, Mom_. It's fairly easy to maintain that open "rectangle" space with this vowel sound, and most of us _tend_ to be a little more open on that sound than we do on the others. Read down through the list: AH, AW, OH, OO, OW, A, EE. Most of us tend to close up that rectangular space as we go down the list. AW is a little more closed than AH. OH becomes more closed still. OO is a sound we can produce by barely opening the jaw. And OW, A, and EE can become very pinched and flat in their production and sound. What we're going to aim for is to keep the rectangular space the _same_ (or as nearly so as possible) for each of the vowel sounds. Even though they become more closed as you go down the list, we're going to shape that closure _with the lips only_ and not by shutting down the rectangle. The **Open Vowel Chart** will indicate how this is done. Notice that the A and EE sounds are a _little_ less open than the others. But they are still open. Don't let them become flat and pinched. Watch out for the EE sound especially. Try producing the EE with the teeth together and jaws closed and hear how pinched it sounds. Then continue producing the sound as you open the jaws and teeth as far as possible without totally distorting the vowel sound. You should be able to get the knuckle of your thumb in between the teeth.

OPEN VOWEL SOUNDS—(Take a bite of apple)

AH

AH as in *odd* or *hot*
- *Don* used *hot water* to *wash* the *jar.*
- *Arlene got* the *car* through the *yard* and *parked* in the garage.
- The *odd bard shocked* the *czar.*

AW

AW as in *all* or *hall*
- *All,* even the *bawdy* and *jaunty, mourned* at the *shores torn* by the *storm.*
- *Paul* said, "I *thought* I *warned* you not to *call* the *dorm!"*

OH

OH as in *oat* or *hoe*
- How *low* could you *go* when you *chose* that *poem*?
- *Throw* the *coal* in the *hole, Joel.*
- *No, Flo, don't go!*

OO

OO as in *ooze* or *who*
- *Who threw* the *shoe* at the *moon*?
- Did *you, Sue,* or did *you choose* a *boot*?
- *Hugh* and the *pooch* took the *crew through* the *new zoo.*

OW (AH+OO)

OW (= AH + OO) as in *out* or *how*
- How do you get *ground round* from a *cow*?
- *Now* I *found out* about a *thousand houses down town.*
- "I'm *bound* to *pounce* on a *mouse," shouted* the *owl* to the *cow.*

A

A as in *add* or *hat*
- *That chap Dan banned* the *battered slats* on the *abandoned shack.*
- *Pamela Anne can't stand that bad fat cat.*

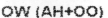

EE

EE as in *ease* or *heat*
- *She freezes peas,* then *eats* them with her *sweet niece Lucille.*
- *These* are the *keys* to *being easy* to *keep peace* with *Peter* and *Keith.*

As you practice these open vowel sounds, don't force the jaw open or do any kind of movement that contorts the face. You are trying to gently coax the oral cavity to be more open. You may find it helpful to place your hands lightly along the sides of your cheeks, just to feel the rectangular space and monitor the production of these sounds. Doing this, you should feel no muscular movement in the area of the cheeks and no movement of the lower jaw (except for a slight shift on the A and EE sounds). The only movement will be that of the lips as they shape these sounds from their rectangular "framework." Keep the face and especially the lower jaw relaxed. Keep in mind the feeling of a yawn. In fact, if you start yawning while you're doing these exercises, you're probably doing them exactly right!

Notice that not all the vowels are considered "open" vowel sounds. In the sentence "Don used hot water to wash the jar," the vowel sounds in "used," the "-er" in "water," "to," and "the" have a little less carrying power than the "open" sounds. Let them "go along for the ride" as you relax open all the rest of the sounds.

Watch out for two of the "open" sounds especially: the OW diphthong [aʊ] and the A sound [æ]. These are mentioned in the chapter *Putting Your Best Voice Forward* as being sounds easily flattened and nasalized. The A vowel sound [æ] should be produced a bit farther back in the mouth than the EH sound [e] as in *bet* but not as far back as the AH sound [ɒ] as in *bottle*. It becomes distorted and often nasalized when it's produced too far forward, approximating the [e] sound. When this happens, the word *bat* takes on the coloration of the word *bet*—sometimes prolonged and nasalized [bẽːt]. Experiment with the feeling of placement of each of the vowel sounds and you'll get it right. If you produce in turn each of these vowels:

ee (as in *beet*)	*IPA:* [iː]
i (as in *bit*)	*IPA:* [ɪ]
e (as in *bet*)	*IPA:* [e]
æ (as in *bat*)	*IPA:* [æ]
ah (as in *bottle*)	*IPA:* [ɒ]
aw (as in *bought*)	*IPA:* [ɔː]

you can feel how they move from front to back in the mouth.

The OW diphthong is a blend of a rich open AH sound plus a less accented OO sound. Phonetically, the sounds are [aʊ]. Be careful not to substitute the [æ] vowel sound (as in _hat_), creating this combination: [æʊ]. In many regions of the country this diphthong is flattened or nasalized. The well-known phrase "HOW NOW, BROWN COW?" was surely coined to correct that distortion that would make it sound like "Hay-oo nay-oo, bray-oon cay-oo" or worse. It may seem "forced" to say "Hah-oo nah-oo, brah-oon cah-oo," but that's what it's supposed to sound like. Just don't overdo it and _sound_ like a brown cow. You're working for a pleasant, natural voice, and not for the golden pear-shaped tones of an orator.

**Nasal Resonance**. In the chapter _What Happens When We Speak?_, you demonstrated that you can't produce the [m] or [n] or [ŋ] sound if you're holding your nose. These sounds depend upon open nasal passages for their resonance, their richness and their beauty. These are all three sounds upon which you could hum a tune. Any such sounds—vowel sounds or vocalic consonant sounds—should be cultivated for the beauty and carrying power they supply to the voice. Take, for example, verses such as these from Genesis 1:1-2 (NIV):

> In the beginning God created the heavens and the earth. Now the earth was formless and empty, darkness was over the surface of the deep, and the Spirit of God was hovering over the waters.

Experiment with the musical beauty realized if you sustain the [m] [n] and [ŋ] sounds where suitable. (Look too at the beauty of the sustained [z] sounds in words like "heavens" and "waters," and the [v] in "heavens" and to a lesser extent in "over" and "hovering." These are good examples of the beauty of _chest resonance_.) Humming can be a wonderful way of warming up (a lot of choirs and other musical groups do it) and of getting the voice in focus. Be sure to hum with the teeth apart (and the lips closed). If you hum with the teeth together and the jaws tight, you'll get a dark swallowed sound that's to be avoided. A good exercise for focusing the voice is to move from a hummed sound into some combination of the vowel sounds, for example:

MMay - MMee - MMi - MMoh - MMoo
MMoo - MMoh - MMah - MMay - MMee

These can be spoken or sung. Try to feel as if the vowel sounds were coming out well in front of the lips. You can do the same kind of vocalizing on the [n] and [ŋ] sounds in combination with the vowel sounds.

**Nasal Resonance and Nasality**. Nasal resonance, si! Nasality, no! Nasal resonance is a positive voice quality you want to develop—*on the [m] [n] and [ŋ] sounds only.* When excessive nasal resonance slips into vowel sounds you get the whiny, twangy voice quality known as *nasality*. Try this to see if you're too nasal on the vowel sounds. Take a sentence that doesn't contain any of the nasal consonants ([m] [n] [ŋ], on which you *want* nasal resonance), such as:

> This is the house Jack built.

Speak the sentence. Then hold your nose and repeat it. If you're excessively nasal, you'll hear a very twangy "This is the house that Jack built." If you're not nasal, there should be no difference at all whether you're holding your nose or not. Want another commercial for *opening your mouth*? If you don't open, and you step into a large setting where you need to raise your voice in order to be heard in the back row, all the sound may go sailing up into the nasal passages and destroy the eardrums of your more sensitive listeners. Listen, the sound has to go somewhere. And if you're not letting it come out of an open oral chamber it's going to seek an outlet somewhere else. And since it has a hard time coming out of your ears or eyes, its most natural means of escape is up through the nose. Open your mouth and the nasality disappears—as if by magic!!!

Assimilation Nasality. Most people are generally free from nasalized vowel sounds. But in certain phonetic contexts the vowel sounds become nasalized. For example, I can say the word "bad" holding my nose or not holding my nose, and it will be untainted by nasality. But then I might turn around and say "That stuff is so *bad* they ought to *ban* it!" Or "It's so *bad* it really makes me *mad*!" Or "The *bad* guy took a gun and it went '*Bang*'!" Or "He's a very *bad man*!"

And I'll get nasal on the words *ban, mad, bang,* and *man.* Why? Because the nasal resonance that's *supposed* to be on the nasal consonants has become *assimilated* into their neighboring vowel sounds. I've let the [n] of *ban* or the [ŋ] of *bang* become anticipated into the vowel sound. The [m] of *mad* has carried over into the vowel sound. And the [m] and [n] of *man* have caught me coming and going. To remedy this, I need to recognize the pure vowel sound I want and try not to let it become affected by the neighboring nasal consonant. I might take a word like *time,* for example. I don't want the [m] sound assimilated into the vowel sound. So I will practice, trying to fool myself into not knowing whether I'm going to say *time* or *tie* and repeat the words randomly, trying to keep the same pure vowel sound in each word:

tie - tie - tie - **tie**	tie - tie - tie - **time**	tie - tie - tie - **time**	tie - tie - tie - **tie**
tie - tie - tie - **time**	tie - tie - tie - **tie**	tie - tie - tie - **tie**	tie - tie - tie - **time**

Denasality. It's the height of the cold season, and you go to class or to work (or wherever) and say, "Oh, I wish I didn't have to speak today. I sound so *nasal*!!" Wrong. If a cold has you stopped up you don't sound nasal at all. You sound *denasal*. In other words, the sounds that *want* nasal resonance [m] [n] [ŋ] are not getting it because of your "code id the doze" that's preventing the resonance that derives from open nasal passages. You may just have to ride out the cold. Or blow your nose. Or, if you simply are slighting the nasal consonants so much that your voice quality is denasal, you may need to do a lot of humming and giving more value to the [m] [n] and [ŋ] sounds when they occur.

<u>**Chest Resonance**</u>. Chest resonance occurs on three sounds: [z] [ʒ] and [v]. If you place a hand on your upper chest and produce these sounds you'll feel vibration throughout the chest area. Since all three of these sounds are forward sounds produced by the tongue tip, lips and teeth, giving them extra value can help with projection of the voice. Like the three nasal consonants, you can carry a tune on these sounds. They should be cultivated for the beauty and carrying power they can contribute to the voice. Many of us tend to give them too little value. They are often, at ends of words, *devoiced*. That is, we cut off the vibration that gives them their "buzzing" quality too soon, rather than sustaining it through to the ends of the words. Then *endzz of wordzz* become *entss of wortss* or *enss of wortss*. We'll say more about voiced and unvoiced consonants later. Pick out phrases that contain the [z] [ʒ] and [v] sounds and experiment with the cello-like quality they can lend to the voice. There's a qualitative difference, for example in the phrase "in him we live and move and have our being," between slighting and affirming the value of the [v] sounds in *live* and *move* and *have*. Once again, experiment, and see what feels and sounds right. But get that feedback from a tape recorder, rather than depending upon your own subjective judgment!

---

[1]*My friend Lois Haydu read this, and said, "No! That's **not** exaggerated!" Then she told me about a grandfather clock mechanism she and her family had ordered. They didn't think the sound was grand enough, so they sent it back and ordered a new, more expensive one. Lois's brother-in-law came over to install it, and while it was on the kitchen table he tried it out. "I don't think they're going to like this one either," he said. "It's not much better than the other one." But he placed it inside its big wooden cabinet and finished the job. When Lois and her family got home, they telephoned him, and said, "Bob, this is beautiful!" "But it's not very loud," he said. "Oh, yes, it is! You can hear it all the way in the basement!" they answered. The difference was the tremendous difference between the mechanism uncased, lying on the kitchen table, and the mechanism inside its big wooden cabinet. That difference was **resonance**.*

The International Phonetic Alphabet

"All authority in heaven and on earth has been given to me. Therefore go and make disciples of all nations, baptizing them in the name of the Father and of the Son and of the Holy Spirit, and teaching them to obey everything I have commanded you. And surely I am with you always, to the very end of the age." (Matthew 28:18-20)

Prayer: Lord Jesus, I thank you for your Good News that has captivated my life. You told your disciples to go into all the world teaching and proclaiming your Word of salvation and new life. I know that somehow that mandate applies to me. Help me understand, Lord, how I'm to do my part—whether through reading your Word in worship, teaching or preaching it, or actually going to other lands to speak the Good News for which souls hunger. In love I surrender myself to your love and your leading. Amen. Maranatha.

Question: What do the following words have in common?

bough, cough, dough, hiccough, hough, lough, nought, rough, through

Answer: They all contain the letters "o - u - g - h". They look like they should rhyme. They don't even begin to rhyme. They're very confusing. Even though they're *spelled* the same they *sound* completely different.

Next question: What do these words have in common?

bough, bow, cow, frau, how, now, sough, sow, vow
cough, doff, off, trough
dough, beau, bow, doe, foe, go, hoe, Joe, know, low, mow, no, oh, owe, roe, row, sew, sow, tow, woe
hiccough, pickup, stickup
hough, block, cock, dock, hock, Jacques, jock, lock, mock, knock, rock, sock
lough, ach!, Bach, loch
nought, aught, bought, caught, fought, naught, ought, sought, taught, taut, water, wrought
rough, buff, cuff, enough, fluff, gruff, huff, muff, puff, ruff, sough, stuff, tough
through, blew, blue, brew, coo, coup, crew, do, ewe, froufrou, glue, gnu, goo, muumuu, ooh!, Pooh, queue, rue, Sioux, sue, to, too, true, two, who, woo, yew, you, zoo

Answer: The ones in each row *rhyme* with each other, but they're not *spelled* the same. They're very confusing.

Question: When do 5 and 21 add up to (approximately) 50?

Answer: When you add five vowels and twenty-one consonants and wind up with about fifty sounds. When you traffic in the English language. When your language can be *very* confusing.

Question: Suppose you were just learning the English language. What would you make of a story like this?

> I brushed aside a bough and swept through the rough terrain by the lough in Scotland. "I don't know how I knew that stuff by Bach," I murmured to myself. Suddenly, I heard a cough not far off from where I stood. And then, I heard someone hiccough. A tall man jumped out of the bushes. "This is a stickup," he said. "Give me all your dough," "Your mother should have taught you better, sir," I laughed. "For your robbery attempts are all for nought, you naughty rascal. It's a good thing I saw to it to bring *this* in my rucksack," I cried. And I hit him over the head with the beef hough I'd bought at the grocery that morning.

Answer: I'd say, "Help!! It's *unmercifully confusing*!"

Question: And what if someone *read* that story to you and asked you to *write* it? Remember, you're just beginning to learn this wonderful language.

Answer: It took me all day, but this is what I came up with.

> I brushed aside a bow and swept threw the ruff terrain by the lach in Scotland. "I don't no hough I gnu that stough by Bough," I murmured to myself. Suddenly, I heard a coff not far ough from where I stood. And then, I heard someone hickup. A tall man jumped out of the bushes. "This is a sticcough," he said. "Give me all your doe!" "Your mother should have taut you better, sir," I laughed. "For your robbery attempts are all for naut, you gnawty rascal. It's a good thing I sough to it to bring this in my rucksack," I cried. And I hit him over the head with the beef hock I'd bought at the grocery that morning.

Question: Well, wye knot? Why not, that is, go in for more—well, *creative* ways of spelling? Isn't spelling pretty arbitrary, anyway? And besides, there are spell-checks on our word processors, aren't there? Is there a *better* way, considering all the orthographic conundrums that exist, to know how words in the English language are supposed to be *pronounced*?

Answer: Let's face it: our spelling shenanigans are "creative" enough as it is. And yes, sometimes it seems our spelling is terribly arbitrary. But spell-checks aren't the answer. Half the words inn that last version of thee story wood slip threw unnoticed. (See??) Yes, there *is* a better way to figure out how to pronounce our words—or the words in *any* language, for that matter. It's called the International Phonetic Alphabet—the IPA. It uses symbols or characters that stand for *sounds* or *phonemes*. Even though many spellings have the same sound, there's only one phoneme symbol for each sound. Take that list up above, for example. If you were using the IPA, you could reduce the confusion of "ough" words to a list like this:

bough	/baʊ/
cough	/kɒf/
dough	/dəʊ/
hiccough	/ˈhɪkʌp/
hough	/hɒk/
lough	/lɒx/
nought	/nɔːt/
rough	/rʌf/
through	/θruː/

What may look difficult and complicated at first glance is really rather simple. And compared with your average "dictionary pronunciations" it's considerably more convenient and simpler than trying to figure out all the different "keys" to pronunciation. Some use diacritical markings. Some try to provide rhyme-words as keys. There's a great deal of inconsistency. If you spread out twenty-three different dictionaries in front of you, you could wind up with twenty-three different systems of determining pronunciation.

Besides, a lot of people whose native language is other than English already *know* the IPA. For them, it provides a consistent standard for learning pronunciation. Goodness knows, our spelling of words doesn't help. So, there are lots of reasons for learning this alphabet. You could go anywhere in the world and study any language, and teach people how to read, and share the Good News with them! Who knows what the Lord may have in mind for you?

In the process of learning the IPA, you'll notice that a lot of the sounds are the same as the letters conventionally used to represent them. Here are the ___consonant sounds___ represented that way:

b	*b*ed	/bed/
d	*d*og	/dɒg/
f	*f*an	/fæn/
g	*g*ive	/gɪv/
h	*h*ot	/hɒt/
k	*c*ow	/kaʊ/
l	*l*og	/lɒg/
m	*m*at	/mæt/
n	*n*ow	/naʊ/
p	*p*an	/pæn/
r	*r*ing	/rɪŋ/
s	*s*in	/sɪn/
t	*t*ip	/tɪp/
v	*v*ow	/vaʊ/
w	*w*in	/wɪn/
z	*z*oo	/zuː/

Some other consonant sounds are represented by special symbols. It's important to remember that these symbols aren't "letters" as we normally think of letters used to spell words. They represent _sounds_. It's very tempting, at first, to look at the /j/ and think of it as "j"—"jay" the letter. But /j/ the symbol represents the initial sound in a word such as "yes"—no particular surprise if you consider words like "Jah" in German or "Ja" in Swedish, where the "j" *letter* denotes the same sound as the "y" letter in "yes". Look too at the /ŋ/ phoneme, which stands for the "ng" in words like "ring" and "sing". There's no "g"-sound in the "ng" combination—and it's a sound produced totally different from the /n/ sound of the letter "n", being made with the back of the tongue and not the tip. So the IPA creates the /ŋ/ symbol which looks a little like the "n" with a "g" tail on it. Similarly, the /ʃ/ sound in a word like "she" is not a combination of the /s/ and the /h/ sounds but a totally different animal. And so forth. Once you've learned these few special consonant sounds they'll be second nature to you.

Here are those "special" IPA consonant symbols:

j	*yet*	/jet/
ʃ	*she*	/ʃiː/
ʒ	*vision*	/ˈvɪʒ(ə)n/
θ	*thin*	/θɪn/
ð	*then*	/ðen/
ŋ	*sing*	/sɪŋ/
x	*loch*	/lɒx/
ʍ	*where*	/ʍeə(r)/
tʃ	*chin*	/tʃɪn/
dʒ	*jaw*	/dʒɔː/

As far as *vowel sounds* are concerned, there are many more than the traditional "five or six": "a - e - i - o - u and sometimes y" *letters of the alphabet.* There are two categories of vowel sounds: the simple vowel sounds and the diphthongs. (Alert! Greek scholars: What's a *diphthong*? Most excellent!! Two sounds [or two voices]: δι-: *twice, two-, double* + φθόγγος: *voice, sound*—two vowel sounds in a single syllable.)

The following are the symbols for the *simple vowel sounds*.

æ	*hat*	/hæt/
ɑː	*art*	/ɑːt/
e	*bet*	/bet/[1]
ɜ	*her*	/hɜː(r)/[2]
ɪ	*fit*	/fɪt/
iː	*see*	/siː/
ɒ	*hot*	/hɒt/
ɔ	*paw*	/pɔː/
ʌ	*cup*	/kʌp/
ʊ	*put*	/pʊt/
uː	*do*	/duː/
ə	*ago*	/əˈgəʊ/[34]

The *diphthong* sounds have the following symbols.

aɪ	b*y*	/baɪ/
aʊ	n*ow*	/naʊ/
eɪ	s*ay*	/seɪ/[5]
əʊ	s*o*	/əʊ/[6]
eə	c*are*	/keə(r)/[7]
ɪə	h*ear*	/hɪə(r)/
ɔɪ	b*oy*	/bɔɪ/
ʊə	t*our*	/tʊə(r)/
aɪə	t*ire*	/taɪə(r)/
aʊə	s*our*	/saʊə(r)/

The character /'/ placed before a syllable indicates that that syllable has the primary stress: *pronounce* /prə'naʊns/. The character /ˌ/ placed before a syllable indicates that that syllable has a secondary stress: *pronunciation* /prəˌnʌnsɪ'eɪʃ(ə)n/.

The character /ː/ placed after a sound indicates that sound is lengthened, as with the vowels iː (*see* /siː/) and uː (d*o* /duː/).

b *bed*	d *dog*	f *fan*	g *give*	h *hot*	j *yet*
k *cow*	l *log*	m *mat*	n *now*	p *pan*	r *ring*
s *sin*	t *tip*	v *vow*	w *win*	z *zoo*	ʃ *she*
ʒ *vision*	θ *thin*	ð *then*	ŋ *sing*	x *loch*	ʍ *where*
tʃ *chin*	dʒ *jaw*				

æ *hat*	ɑː *art*	e *bet*	ɜ *her*	ɪ *fit*	iː *see*
ɒ *hot*	ɔ *paw*	ʌ *cup*	ʊ *put*	uː *do*	ə *ago*
aɪ *by*	aʊ *now*	eɪ *say*	əʊ *so*	eə *care*	
ɪə *hear*	ɔɪ *boy*	ʊə *tour*	aɪə *tire*	aʊə *sour*	

---

[1] *Some use the /ɛ/ symbol for the vowel sound in a word like "bet" and reserve the /e/ for the short unaccented sound such as the final vowel sound in a word like "rotate".*

[2] *For the unaccented "er" sound in a word such as "father" some use the /ɚ/ symbol, a schwa-type sound with "r"-quality.*

[3] *The /ə/ sound, often called <u>schwa</u>, is always an unaccented "uh" sound, as in words such as "above" and "sofa".*

[4] *The parenthetical /ə/ indicates the slight schwa sound in, e.g. "bottle" or "burden" /ˈbɒt(ə)l, ˈbɜːd(ə)n/. Some use the following mark beneath the consonant sound to indicate that the consonant is syllabic: /ˈbɒtl̩, ˈbɜːdn̩/.*

[5] *cf. note #1. The /eɪ/ symbol is used for accented syllables. Some use only the /e/ for unaccented syllables.*

[6] *For the accented sound, some use the symbol /oʊ/, and the symbol /o/ for the unaccented "o" sound in, e.g. "motel" /moˈtel/.*

[7] *The parenthetical /r/ occurs at the end of a word. When followed by a vowel sound, the /r/ is sounded: "I care a lot." When followed by a consonant sound it generally is not sounded: "I don't care for any."*

O Lord, Open My Lips: Consonant Energy

Ascribe to the Lord, O mighty ones, ascribe to the Lord glory and strength.
Ascribe to the Lord the glory due his name; worship the Lord in the splendor of his holiness.
The voice of the Lord is over the waters;
the God of glory thunders, the Lord thunders over the mighty waters.
The voice of the Lord is powerful; The voice of the Lord is majestic.
The voice of the Lord breaks the cedars; the Lord breaks in pieces the cedars of Lebanon.
He makes Lebanon skip like a calf, Sirion like a young wild ox.
The voice of the Lord strikes with flashes of lightning.
The voice of the Lord shakes the desert; the Lord shakes the Desert of Kadesh.
The voice of the Lord twists the oaks and strips the forests bare.
And in his temple all cry, "Glory!"
The Lord sits enthroned over the flood; the Lord is enthroned as King forever.
The Lord gives strength to his people; the Lord blesses his people with peace. (Psalm 29)

Prayer: Mighty, loving God, I praise you for your glory and strength, for the splendor of your holiness. I thank you that your glory, your strength, your holiness have touched my life and called me by my own voice to touch the lives of others. I pray for a touch of the creative wonder of your voice even as I lift my voice to speak of you. As in your temple I cry, "Glory!" grant that that hymn of praise may be heard clearly and ring grandly in the ears of others. All this I pray that you, Lord, may receive the praise and glory. Amen.

"You have lazy lips!"

"Oh, no!!!"

"Yes! You need to get more 'bite' into the labial sounds."

And that was the beginning of a conversation that ended with me singing lustily for several weeks:

    ma-ma-ma-ma-ma-ma-ma-ma-ma
    pa-pa-pa-pa-pa-pa-pa-pa-pa
    ba-ba-ba-ba-ba-ba-ba-ba-ba

ma-ma-ma-ma-ma-ma-ma-ma-ma

pa-pa-pa-pa-pa-pa-pa-pa-pa

ba-ba-ba-ba-ba-ba-ba-ba-ba

Up the scale and back down. In the shower. In the car. In the morning, afternoon and evening. In my dreams. It was a concerted effort to lose the "lazy lips" stigma in time for a recital. The voice coach who had castigated me with her lip-character assassination was ultimately pleased. She beamed benignly at the recital's end. "Nice job," she said. "Lips worked!!"

It's a terrible blow to be told you have lazy lips. Or lazy anything for that matter. And it's only voice coaches and speech teachers who would *ever* thus malign a person. Actually, I had worked with enough voice coaches and had enough unspeakable comments made about this and that, that I was sufficiently thick-skinned to realize she wasn't calling *me* lazy. Just my lips. So please bear that in mind if someone tells you you have lazy diction—lips, tongue, whatever. They're not being insulting to you. They're simply telling you that your speech muscles need a tune-up. They need a workout. They need to be exercised. It's very easy nowadays to come by flabby speech agents. You're familiar, probably, with the "classic" conversation consisting of "Jeet jet?" "No, jew?" which characterizes the kind of enunciation that passes muster in our day and age. In our society we have no particular fondness for elocution, a discipline relegated to the past with great-grandmother's dressmaking dummy up in the attic. Children do not recite before sitting rooms of adulating adults. Few sing the Gilbert and Sullivan tongue-challengers such as *The Mikado*'s "to sit in solemn silence in a dull dark dock." We have instead gone in with the Brando-style mumble epitomized by Stanley Kowalski. And why should we need more?

One answer to that question may be that we as worship leaders are communicating something more important that Stanley Kowalski's howling, "STELLA!!" And if we're trying to communicate the Good News about God, then we want to do it clearly and accurately. Another answer may be that—whether we like it or not—we as worship leaders are models of speech and communication. And if we don't do it right, people are likely to focus more on our speech habits than they do on our content. We are models, just as much as television personalities. And we do talk about their speech habits: "Oh, yes! She's the one with no 'r' sounds!" "Him? With those 'l' sounds he sounds like he's talking baby talk!" "Geez, his 's' sounds are so whistly he sounds like he's calling his dog!"

And what are people going to say about you when you get up on Easter morning and announce: "Jethuth Chritht ith rithen!"? Think you might want to work on that 's' sound? Familiarizing ourselves with the various sounds of speech may help us correct any problems and add energy and clarity to our speech.

Consonant Sounds.

Prolong an "ah" sound, or any other vowel sound, and the voice flows freely. Slip in any consonant sound and the voice flow will either stop momentarily or be altered. Say for example "ahpahpahp" or "ahbahbahb" and the flow stops and starts again. Try "ahmahmahm" or "ahzahzahz" and the sound continues to flow but is changed. Appropriately, the [p] and [b] are called **"stops"** and the [m] and [z] are called **"continuants."** With some sounds the voicing (vibration of the vocal bands) continues (as with [b], [m] and [z]) and with other sounds there is no vibration. The former are called **"voiced"** consonants, and the latter **"voiceless."** Try placing your fingers gently alongside the larynx and going back and forth between [s] and [z]. You'll feel the voicing, or vibration on the [z] but not on the [s]. Many consonants appear in voiced-voiceless pairs. Sounds are also described according to the **speech agent(s) where these sounds are modified**.

For example a "voiced bilabial stop" would describe the [b]. "Bilabial" means both lips are involved, "stop" indicates that the flow of voice stops for a moment, and "voiced" means there is vibration in the vocal bands. A "voiceless bilabial stop" would describe the [p]. With the [p] there is no vibration in the vocal bands. Otherwise, the two sounds are identical. *Three things, then, are to be considered in describing a consonant sound: whether it is a stop or a continuant, whether it is voiced or voiceless, and which agents modify the sounds.*

A glance at the **CONSONANT CHART** will show how the consonants are classified.

- **Stops** are sounds that briefly *stop* the flow of voice. Pressure builds up between agents and then "explodes" to produce a sound with a sudden release of breath—hence, the name *plosives*. For example, pressure between the upper and lower lips "explodes" into either a voiceless [p] or a voiced [b], depending upon whether there is vibration in the vocal bands. Pressure between the tongue tip and the gum ridge is released into either a [t] or a [d]. Pressure between the back of the tongue and the velum is released into either a [k] or a [g].

- **Nasals** are produced as the soft palate is lowered so that there is resonance in the *nasal passages*—shaped into sound by either the lips [m], the tongue tip and gum ridge [n], or the back of the tongue and the velum [ŋ].

- **Fricatives** are produced by *friction*—between lower lip and upper teeth for the [f] and [v] sounds, from tongue tip against upper teeth for the [θ] and [ð], over tongue tip at the gum ridge for [s] and [z], over tongue blade in a slightly more retroflex position at the gum ridge for [ʃ] and [ʒ], and over the partly open vocal cords to produce the [h].

- **Affricates** are combinations of a stop and fricative. The tongue tip moves from the gum ridge into a slightly retroflex position to produce [tʃ] and [dʒ], tongue tip releases at the gum ridge from [t] to [s] for the [ts] and from [d] to [z] for the [dz].

- The **lateral** sound [l] is produced with the tongue tip at the gum ridge as air is released around the *sides* of the tongue.

- **Glides** are produced by the movement of articulators. Lips move from a "whistle" position to the next sound for the [ʍ] and [w]. Sides of the tongue blade against the hard palate move to the next sound for the [j]. And sides of the tongue against the upper teeth with the tip curled and suspended at the front of the palate produce the [r] sound.

CONSONANT CHART

TYPE OF SOUND	VOICELESS	VOICED	PRODUCTION
STOPS (Plosives)	**p** (*p*ill) **t** (*t*all) **k** (*c*all, *k*ill)	**b** (*b*ill) **d** (*d*oll) **g** (*g*ill)	bilabial tongue tip/gum ridge tongue back/velum
NASALS **(Semi-Vocalic)**		**m** (*m*ail) **n** (*n*ew) ŋ (ri*ng*)	bilabial tongue tip/gum ridge tongue back/velum
FRICATIVES	**f** (*f*ull) θ (*th*in) **s** (*s*ee) ʃ (*sh*oe) **h** (*h*it)	**v** (*v*ery) ð (*th*an) **z** (*z*oo) ʒ (vi*s*ion)	labiodental tongue tip/dental tongue tip/gum ridge tongue blade/gum ridge glottis
AFFRICATES **(Stop + Fricative)**	tʃ (*ch*ew) **ts** (pi*zz*a)	dʒ (*j*oy) **dz** (be*ds*)	tongue tip/gum ridge tongue tip/gum ridge
LATERAL **(Semi-Vocalic)**		**l** (*l*et)	tongue tip/gum ridge
GLIDES **(Semi-Vocalic except** **for [ʍ])**	ʍ [or **hw**](*wh*y)	**w** (*w*ine) **j** (*y*es) **r** (*r*ed)	labial rounded tongue blade/palatal tongue tip/prepalatal

ARTICULATION PROBLEMS

A handful of the consonant sounds can create problems for us. We'll consider here only the most common difficulties. Some sounds are problematic because of *misproduction*, some because of *substitutions*, and some because of *omission*.

MISPRODUCTIONS

Certain sounds cause problems for some people due to faulty production. The three most common are the [s], [l] and [r]. Let's look at them individually.

The [s] and [z] Sounds.

If there's any sound that sends me dashing over to the radio to adjust the tuning, it's the [s]. There are so many ways of distorting the sound. You don't have to have a lisp to have problems with this sound. Just hang on to it too long or get the tongue in the wrong position and you may sound like a leaky tire or a teakettle. To produce a clear [s], align the upper and lower teeth as well as you can. A lot of people have a bit of an overbite, so this may require some forward thrusting of the lower jaw. But keep the jaw relaxed! The lips should be drawn away from the teeth. If you smile (a little more than Mona Lisa, a little less than Cheshire cat) you should get the appropriate feeling. The sides of the tongue are hugging the upper teeth, as they would if you were saying the word "yet." The tongue tip is forward, near the gum ridge and about a quarter inch behind the front teeth. There is a wee, tiny groove in the center of the tongue tip over which the air passes to produce a clean, clear [s]. Try it. If you alternate between "yet" and "yes" you should have the tongue in the right position. It will touch the gum ridge for the [t] in "yet," but not for the [s] in "yes." [Note: It's often very helpful to work on the [t] and [s] in tandem with one another, as long as the tongue tip is high for both sounds. A [t] produced with the tongue tip behind the lower teeth will usually be a dull dentalized sound, and [s] produced the same way will be correspondingly dull.]

Some [s] Problems.

- *Labial Lisp.*

Out of a class of eight to ten people, it's not surprising to find at least two or three with a "labial lisp." When this distortion is identified, one is usually somewhat horrified to have a speech problem labeled as a "lisp." But that's exactly what it is. It's easy enough to approximate, and you can tell right away if you have this culprit sound. Stand in front of a mirror and say, "The sorceress sees the sausages." Can you see both the upper and lower teeth? Only the upper? How about the lower? Are they hidden by the lower lip? Could it be that your upper teeth and *lower lip* are making contact to produce the [s]? If so, you have a labial lisp. "Labial" = lip(s). You're using the *lower lip* instead of the *lower teeth*. And the result is an indistinct fuzzy sound. Just place the articulators in position for [f] or [v] (upper teeth/lower lip) and try to say [s]. There's your problem. Now smile a little, bring the *lower teeth* into contact with the *upper teeth*, and try again. You should get a good clean sound.

- Frontal Lisp.

Here the tongue tip goes too far forward, somewhere between the front teeth, and the result is [θ] instead of [s]. The tongue tip needs to come back, the upper and lower teeth making contact as much as possible. Experiment with front to back tongue positions between [θ] [s] and [ʃ]: between the teeth ([θ]), slightly behind the upper teeth ([s]), and back slightly farther toward the back of the gum ridge. Try to fix a good clean [s] in that in-between position.

- Lateral Lisp.

Here the tongue is making approximately the same movement for the [s] sound as it does for the [l]: tongue tip stays fixed in position and the sides of the tongue release, letting the air stream flow over one or both sides. I once had a student whose name had lots of sibilants in it (we'll call him "Derek Springstone") who had a very severe lateral lisp ("*Sh*prings*h*tone"). He wanted to change it. We spent about an hour every Monday for about four weeks, and by the end of that time the lisp was gone. Awareness is half the battle. The other half is willingness. And the last half is practice.

- Whistly [s].

If the tongue tip is too *high and tense* the result will be a sharp hiss not unlike that of a radiator. The tongue needs to relax and perhaps come back a tad from the upper teeth for a cleaner sound. If the tip is too *low and lax* and too far behind the teeth, the sound may approximate a whistle somewhat like [ʃ]. See above practice for correcting the frontal lisp: distinguish between the thicker farther back [ʃ] and the cleaner farther forward [s]. When any of these sounds is too prolonged, you may attract all the neighborhood dogs. Try to keep any [s] sound as trimmed and inconspicuous as possible.

<u>*Correcting [s] Sounds*</u>.

- [s] with [t].

A friend of mine in graduate school, a wonderful German woman, was diagnosed by the speech faculty as having a whistly [s]. It was not at all unlike [ʃ]. She was given a nonsense word "TUTSEE" ['tʌtsiː] to repeat off and on throughout the day. She said she drove everyone within earshot crazy, but it did the trick. So I've recommended it to a lot of students and find it helps a great deal. The secret is in articulating the [t] twice before moving into the [s] position. Again, the tongue tip must be high for the [t] for the exercise to do its job. But if you want to clean up your [s] sound, try it. Slowly and deliberately at first. Then very lightly and briskly. It's a good exercise. Or you can *insert a [t]* before any [s], as a "reminder" to the tongue tip of where it should go. For example: "The sorceress sees the sausages" would become "The *ts*or*ts*ere*ts* *ts*ee*ts* the *ts*au*ts*age*ts*."

-[s] with other tongue tip sounds.

Look at the consonant chart and notice all the sounds where the tongue tip makes contact with the gum ridge. You'll find [t], [d], [n], [l], along with a few others where the tongue tip and gum ridge become friendly with one another. Now make up lists of words where these sounds and [s] (or [z]) naturally occur together. For example:

tots   dates   lets   notes   Tulsa   tense   dads   toads   leads   nods   dulcet   dens

Feel the position of the tongue tip on the other tongue tip sounds as you release from them into [s] or [z]. Then move gradually in to a clean [s] or [z]. Take your time, and produce the sound as precisely as you can. Once again, a tape recorder may help.

- [s] with [j] or [ʃ].

The tongue tip doesn't quite touch the gum ridge for the [j] as in "yes," but the [j] position is an ideal one from which to move into the [s]. Experiment with the [ʃ] sound, which most people will produce with the tongue high behind the gum ridge. Prolong the [ʃ] with the lips *rounded* (as if you were saying "shoe" or "show") and then change the [ʃ] to [s] *spreading the lips* broadly (as if you were saying "see") as the tongue tip moves forward.

- [s] and [z] distinction.

If you clean up any slushy [s] problems you'll probably come close to fixing any [z] problems as well. The most important thing about the [z] is to make sure it *buzzes*, giving it adequate chest resonance. Go back and forth between [s] and [z] with your fingers at your larynx and feel the vibration on the [z]. Make sure that vibration is there especially on ends of words ("endz of wordz") and that you don't cut off the voicing and give us "ents of worts." Make a distinction between the following pairs of words:

bits - bids   cats - cads   dots - Dodds   pats - pads   wets - weds
cease - seas   dice - dies   fuss - fuzz   hiss - his   loss - laws

Try making up your own [s] and [z] tongue twisters. Here's one that just came to mind (honest): "Cecil sees the seas cease." You can do better than that!

The [l] and [r] Sounds.

Let's look at these two together because they're cognates. Often if one sound is distorted the other is affected. The result is the "Elmer Fudd" speech ("you wascally wabbit") that's cute for a cartoon character but not for the rest of us. With both of these sounds (see again the Consonant Chart) the tongue tip is supposed to be high, at [l] or near [r] the gum ridge. If the tongue tip is lax and low, the lips may get into the act (this is known as labial compensation) and you get the resulting [w] sound. Sometimes the lower lip will touch the upper teeth, giving the sound a [v] quality. Pucker your lips and say "the vewy wapid wittow wabbit wan thwough the woses and wowwed awound" ("the very rapid little rabbit ran through the roses and rolled around") and you'll get the drift—these are the sounds you want to change.

Working on the [l].

Work on the awareness factor first. Chances are you may have a perfectly acceptable [l] when the sound is in the *initial position* in a word. Try the simple syllables "lay, lee, lie, law, loo" and be aware of the tongue tip in contact with the gum ridge. Now try the [l] in the *final position* in the syllables "ail, eel, isle, awl, ool". The tongue tip should still touch the gum ridge. Be sure the *back of the tongue* does not rise to produce the [l]. When this happens the entire voice production is likely to be dark and throaty. Try words with the [l] in initial, medial and final positions:

> *Initial:* lap - let - lock - live - long - line
> *Medial:* gully - blunt - felt - tally - world - Charlie
> *Final:* pull - earl - smile - until - bottle - meal

and with the [l] in combination with other tongue tip sounds:

> battle - bootleg - butler - badly - bloodless - oddly - deadly - only - inlay - insular - thistle
> alto - hilltop - filter - bolder - mildew - walnut - illness - also - else - Balzac - Beelzebub

Look back at the Open Vowel Chart. Can you maintain the open rectangle shape of the mouth on these vowel sounds and move in and out of [l] sounds without rounding the lips? Try it:

> [a-la-la, aw-law-law, oh-loh-loh, u-lu-lu, au-lau-lau, æ-læ-læ, i-li-li]

Awareness. Willingness. Practice.

Working on the [r].

Try experiencing this sound also in the *initial, medial and final positions*

> *Initial:* rob - rut - real - wrote - rhyme - rhythm
> *Medial:* plural - bride - strut - flurry - caring - array
> *Final:* father - air - dare - nor - myrrh - catarrh - far

Begin by pairing the [r] with other tongue tip sounds.

> tray - tree - try - trowel - true - dry - dray - dream - drove - drew
> unreal - enriched - en route - onward - Elroy - Ezra - astray - ashtray - strew - shrew

With the Open Vowels, try keeping the rectangular shape of the mouth without rounding the lips for the [r]:

> [a-ra-ra, aw-raw-raw, oh-roe-roe, u-ru-ru, au-rau-rau, æ-ræ-ræ, i-ri-ri]

More awareness. More willingness. More practice.

Another Word About [s], [l], and [r].

These three sounds are among the latest in a child's linguistic development. As children play with sounds, trying to learn them, there are likely to be distortions, omissions, substitutions. Our son Stephen, for example, had difficulty for a while in producing the [l]. He called his sister Lisa "Eesa." As we played with him, he eventually could produce the [l] like this: "la, la, la, la, la." But he had trouble putting it all together. He would say "la, la, la, la, Eesa!" In time he could say "la, la, la, Lisa!!" Our grandson Andrew used to say "yiddoo" for "little." He soon outgrew tha pronunciation. Ask any parents or grandparents, and they could probably give you dozens of examples of misproductions of the [s], [l] and [r] sounds. And lots of them are funny. But *please*—don't talk "baby talk" back to children. No matter how cute or funny they may seem to you. If she says, "My name is Thuthie," don't say "Hewwo, Thuthie!" Say "How are you, *Susie?*" Call Biwwy Bi*ll*y and Wobbie *R*obbie. You don't want to reinforce the misproduction, which can leave the child at that stage of language development. You want to positively reinforce the correct production, in the sure and certain hope that the child will on her or his own develop through the misproduction into the correct sounds.

SUBSTITUTIONS

Once again: speech is habit. And who knows where all the various habits come from? We may have picked them up from people in our family. They may come from the region or regions where we grew up. We may have copied them from a friend, an admired teacher, an actor. But once we become aware of our habits we can change them if we want to. The following *substitutions* of one sound for another are among the most common faulty speech habits.

[n/ŋ] Substitution.

This is the kind of substitution ya make when yer talkin' a kinda dialect an' you wanna soun' real folksy, like yer chawin' on a piece of hay. Everythin' with a "-ing" endin' comes out like yer droppin' the "g" sound. But guess what? There ain't no "g" sound involved! What you're doing is substituting the [n] sound for the [ŋ] sound. Using the tongue tip to produce the [n] instead of the tongue back to produce [ŋ]. So if you *don't* want to sound "folksy" you'll want to make the correction. It's not at all difficult. You want to distinguish between the [n] in words like "sin, kin, din" and the [ŋ] in words like "sing, king, ding." One of the easiest ways of working on this is to make up pairs of words in which you distinguish between these two sounds:

    bin - bing   kin - king   din - ding   pin - ping   sin - sing   thin - thing

Another is to remember there's a "king" in "walking" and a "thing" in "something" and a "wing" in "throwing" and so forth. Watch out for the [n/ŋ] substitution also in words like "length" and "strength"—it's not "lenth" and "strenth." One good way of correcting this is to be aware of the "long" in "leng-th" and the "strong" in "streng-th."

Substitutions for the [θ] and [ð].

[t, d]. When I spent a summer studying in Sweden, a lot of my friends wanted to "practice English" and have me "correct" them. Of course, at the same time, I wanted to "practice Swedish" and have them "correct" me—but that's another story. One of the major difficulties my *svenska vänner* had with English was in producing the [θ] and [ð] sounds, which don't exist in Swedish. They would automatically substitute a [t] for the [θ] and a [d] for the [ð] sound. I had fun telling them it was "okay" to stick out your tongue when you produced these sounds. Again, once you know how to produce the [θ] and [ð] sounds, practice them in pairs that distinguish between the two sets of sounds:

tin - thin	tank - thank	taught - thought	tie - thigh	tinker - thinker
mitt - myth	wit - with	bat - bath	boat - both	hat - hath
den - then	die - thy	dare - there	doze - those	day - they
udder - other	fodder - father	breeder - breather	wedder - weather	

[f, v]. I envy people who can recognize specific dialects. What I might call a "cockney" accent might be correctly relabeled something else. So I won't try to put a label on this one. But you've heard it, perhaps in movies or stage productions. It's the sort of thing Henry Higgins had to work with with Eliza Doolittle. It's the substitution of [f] or [v] for the [θ] and [ð] sounds, as in, "I'd go wif you, but me muvver and me favver wouldn't fink vat was such a good idea." (You won't find that line of dialogue anywhere. I just made it up.) If you're substituting sounds in this way, try the same kind of paired-words practice in order to distinguish and produce the correct sounds.

fin - thin	fink - think	fought - thought	deaf - death	miff - myth
van - than	V's - these	loaves - loathes	veil - they'll	vie - thy

[w/ʍ] Substitution.

Many of us fail to distinguish between the [ʍ] sound (in many words beginning with "wh" spelling, such as "which") and the [w] sound (in, for example, "witch"). But the [ʍ] and the [w] are two distinct different sounds. The [ʍ] is voiceless and produced with a little puff of breath that could blow out a candle. The [w] is voiced and lacks that little puff, leaving the candle still burning. As a kind of interesting aside, for folks who enjoy words and word origins: many of the "wh" words in our dictionary come from Anglo-Saxon words, and were originally spelled with "hw" instead of "wh". A few examples: "whale" comes from the Old English *hwæl*, "what" from OE *hwæt*, "wheat" from OE *hwæte*, "whether" from OE *hwæther*. So spelling-wise the words have become "wh" words, but pronunciation-wise, they've maintained the [ʍ] sound. At least, they're supposed to have maintained that sound, which is different from the [w] sound. I recall an episode on the TV comedy *Mork and Mindy*, where a very seductive blond was cuddling up to Mork, saying, "How about a little wine?" His answer was, "Okay." [And he whines.] So we don't always make the distinction, but we should. One more time, list-makers, make up some lists of pairs of words and practice making the different sounds. Here's a start:

whale - wale	what - watt	when - wen	where - wear	whet - wet	which - witch
whether - weather	while - wile	whine - wine	whit - wit	whither - wither	

[tʃ/tj] and [dʒ/dj] Substitutions

It's arguable whether these are substitutions or just casual or "sloppy" diction. *Don't you, won't you, can't you, couldn't you, wouldn't you*—all containing the [tj] combination (in the spelling "t...y") super-easily become *don'tchoo, won'tchoo,* and so forth—substituting the [tʃ] for the [tj]. The same thing happens with the [dj] in *did you, would you, could you* and their friends. They become *didjoo, wouldjoo, couldjoo*—with the [dʒ] being substituted for the [dj]. It's easy to slip over into the substituted sound. Consider the pronunciations, for example of "mature"—containing the [tj] pronunciation—and "nature" with the [tʃ] pronunciation. And do you "graduate" with a [dj] or a [dʒ]? Even dictionaries can't agree. But here we slip over from *articulation* or *diction* to *pronunciation*. Which might be a good time to try to distinguish between (among) these terms. Once more, even dictionaries are fuzzy—probably because we human beings are a little fuzzy over which word means what. For purposes of being arbitrary here, we're using *articulation* and *diction* pretty interchangeably to refer to the manner in which the sounds of speech are produced. If you say, "This is my *glub*, and I'm *berry* fond *ub* it," you have a problem with the diction or articulation of the [v]. You seem to be substituting a [b] for that sound.[1] If, however, you say, "This is my *gloove*," you would seem to be *pronouncing* the word "glove" incorrectly. In either case, people may have a bit of a problem understanding you. And that's what language is largely about.

Who Sez???

Actually, you do. You say, ultimately, what's the right and wrong pronunciation—or at least what's accepted and what's preferred. I have in my possession (honest) a dictionary published in 1951 in which the preferred pronunciation of the word "pejorative" is *PEE-jer-ay-tiv* /ˈpiːdʒəreɪtɪv/. I'm not kidding. I've been using language since long before 1951 (well, not awfully long), and I'd never heard anyone—proper or improper—pronounce the word that way. The few odd people who ever used the word at all pronounced it *pih-JOR-i-tiv* /pɪˈdʒɒrətɪv/. And the way people *actually* pronounced the word won out. Remember, language is always in a state of flux, and it will change according to usage. The way people use the language eventually becomes the acceptable, the norm. And some of us go down kicking and screaming when the changes occur. Remember, "to err is human." Now is that *air* or *urr*? When in doubt check half a dozen dictionaries and go with the flow.

DIFFICULT CONSONANT COMBINATIONS

We can't possibly leave a chapter on articulation without bringing up the fact that the English language is a veritable bear, sometimes, to put up with. One of the major difficulties is in consonant clusters that are very tricky to articulate. And so we sometimes don't even try. *And here's where the third category of articulation problems comes in: <u>omissions</u>. When we encounter consonant clusters such as the ones that lie in the road ahead, we frequently leave out sounds altogether.* But if we're going to be paragons of clarity, we ought to try perhaps just a bit harder than we do. Here's a list of some of the toughest consonant combinations we have to work with. The key to mastering these is.... Well, I suppose there's a whole key chain.

(1) *Practice.* Find out which of these combinations gives you trouble, and then go over it and then go over it and then go over it and then go over it and then go over it.

> <u>Get it right.</u> In the first parish I ever served, my little office was back in a corner just outside the sanctuary. In fact it was right outside where the organ was situated. And every day the organist would come in to practice. And whenever she came to a musical phrase that was difficult, she would go over it and over it, etc. And one day, I stuck my head through the door (I opened it first) and said, "Jan, that drives me up the wall when you repeat and repeat those passages." I said this good-naturedly, since we were buddies. And she smiled and said, "I know. Me too. But it's the only way I know to get it right." And she was, of course, right on target. So one of the keys to mastering a consonant combination problem is to practice.

(2) *Find a word or words in which you naturally and easily use the sequence of consonants without difficulty.* For example, you may have problems with the [sts] in a word like "hosts". Do you have problems saying "hostess"? Probably not. So repeat the word "hostess" several times and then drop out the vowel between the [t] and the [s] and you've got it. Then go back to "hosts" and practice it.

(3) *Take it slow.* These consonant clusters will willingly yield to you if you relax and approach them very slowly at first, picking up speed as you need to and as you incorporate words with clusters like these into your everyday speech. If you rush through, you can be pretty sure you're

going to leave out sounds or slur over them. Easy does it!

(4) *Consciously try to use in everyday speech* words that contain the clusters that bug you. The more familiar you are with them, the more comfortable they will become to you. Don't wait until you have to read or speak about the "Lord of *hosts*" or the "high *priests*" to get that consonant cluster in gear. One final word before you look at the list which follows: Don't ever write sentences like this. This is only a test. Repeat: This is only a test.

DIFFICULT CONSONANT COMBINATIONS

[SUFFERING THROUGH THE ENGLISH LANGUAGE]

1. /ts/
Flotsam and jetsam float slowly past the boats, while the footsore mates in their wet suits sit sullenly pondering the weights of life's limits, fates, and wants.
[NOTE: This isn't terribly difficult. You say it just right every time you call out and order a pizza with mozzarella cheese.]

2. /sts/
He distrusts the costs, and wastes the best stuff that coats hosts of posts and masts, resists decay and consists of resinous pastes.
[NOTE: Start with "hostess" and then try this sentence. Break the [sts] into two 'syllables' with a tiny break after the first [s], like this "hos-ts".]

3. /fts/
As the sand sifts and shifts, the swift sailor drifts into Taft's Thrift Store and lifts gifts from the lofts.
[NOTE: "My foot's asleep" will get you into this one easily. Just make sure to beware of Greeks bearing "gifts".]

4. /kts/
He reflects on the facts: he expects and exacts too much from the sects in the districts, and thus constructs and erects barriers between them.
[NOTE: If you announce on Sunday morning that the topic for discussion at the evening forum is going to be "Christian Sex," and then you start talking about "sects," you're in big trouble. And please don't read Scripture from the "Book of Ax."]

5. /s..r/

The strange Christian pastor, stressed yet usually constrained, you understand, strode across the street screaming and shrieking stridently as he was struck by the shirtless construction worker.

[NOTE: It's the retroflex position of the tongue for the [r] that presents the problem here. In that position the [s] is going to come out like [ʃ] every time. Slow down and don't "shtrike" out too hastily!]

6. /sks/

He risks doing tasks moving casks of discs, husks, and dusky tusks.

[NOTE: How are you at throwing the "discus"? Just "ask us"!]

7. /skt/

Her half-asked question was why the masked man basked in the sun.

[NOTE: Don't give us the wrong idea about her question. Try "ascot, mascot, basket" to get into the swing of this combination.]

8. /θs/

Four-fifths (or eight-tenths) of this month's statistics about births and deaths are myths, says this youth Sam, the sixth son of a soothsayer, in the depths of despair.

[NOTE: Theists reading Thessalonians should find this as easy to handle as thistledown.]

9. /ðz/

He loathes her clothes. He writhes and seethes. She breathes a sigh, mouths some truths, bathes and soothes and smooths his brow.

[NOTE: Many moons ago, people pronounced some of these [ðz] combinations as two syllables, viz.: KLO-thihz. Nowadays we tend to wear what you do to an open door that you don't want open!]

10. /dz/

Her husband Zachary builds roads towards fields of weeds, while she tends the lads and mends the shades with threads.

[NOTE: The main concern here is not to 'devoice' the final sounds so that ends of words become "ents of worts."]

11. /dθ/

The sad threnody faded then, and the hundredth psalm was sung over the width and breadth of the land thus comforted.

[NOTE: It's not so hard to do this combination in a phrase like "odd thing." But it becomes a bit tricky in the middle of a single word. Don't devoice the [d]. It's not "wit-th" but "wid-th." It might help if you think "wide-th" and "broad-th." Try this sentence: "Attila's termagant wife, Matilda the <u>Hun, dread thing</u>, made her baker slice the <u>bread thin</u>." With that you've just said, correctly, "hundredth" and "breadth." By George, I think you've got it!!!]

12. /tl/

While the cattle ate the myrtle and the beetles rattled near the kettle, he gave a gentle chortle and whittled a little whistle.

[NOTE: The tongue tip goes into place for the [t] and stays there while the sides of the tongue release into the [l], e.g.: /kætl̩/—Don't slip an "uh" sound in there. It's not KAT-tuhl.]

13. /dl/

The answer to the riddle: The noodle is in the ladle and the bridle is cradled in the middle of the saddle.

[NOTE: Tongue movement is the same for this as for the [tl]. Just remember the [t] is voiceless and the [d] is voiced. Be sure you distinguish between "mettle" and "meddle".]

14. /nt/

As he drove to the dentist's office in his Pontiac, he thought about his Auntie Flo and her continental way of doing things since she was in her twenties.

[NOTE: Don't leave out the [t] sound! In this combination it has often gone the way of the dodo. Let's bring it back!]

---

[1] *It's also possible that you have half a peanut butter and jelly sandwich in your mouth. Or that you just came from the dentist's office and are under the influence of novocaine.*

Praise On My Tongue: Pronunciation Matters

Devote yourselves to prayer, being watchful and thankful. And pray for us, too, that God may open a door for our message, so that we may proclaim the mystery of Christ, for which I am in chains. Pray that I may proclaim it clearly, as I should. Be wise in the way you act toward outsiders; make the most of every opportunity. Let your conversation be always full of grace, seasoned with salt, so that you may know how to answer everyone. (Colossians 4:2-6)

Prayer: Holy God, I need your grace. And I thank you that you're so much more willing to give me that grace than I am even to ask for it. You've called me to speak your Word, and I know I can't do it on my own. Open my mouth, guide my tongue, that I may proclaim your message clearly. And grant that as you bless me with this ministry, I may be a blessing to all who hear. In Jesus' precious name. Amen.

<u>***"Jelly Beans Filled the Sky!***</u>*"* Here's a true story. A woman was walking out of church one Sunday after the service. She stopped to shake hands with the pastor, and said to him, "I didn't understand the part where you said 'Jelly beans filled the sky'!" Can you guess what he *thought* he'd said? Clue: this was a Sunday near Christmas. You're right, he was attempting to say *"angelic beings* filled the sky."

A lot of us need to watch more than our p's and q's when it comes to articulating our thoughts clearly. I shouldn't have to say more than that. But here are some dillies I have actually heard (really!), in case you need a chuckle. *I am not making these up!*

> I will multiply your descendants as the *sand which is* on the seashore = *sandwiches* (that's what happens when you cast your bread upon the waters, isn't it?)
>
> Where is he who has been born *king of the Jews = king of the juice* (orange you glad?)
>
> Balaam went with the *princes of Moab = princess of Moab* (she was a knockout!)
>
> *Surely* goodness and mercy = (why do you keep calling me *Shirley*?)
>
> *Saul, Saul,* why do you persecute me? = *saw, saw!*
>
> Today's Scripture is from *Paul's* letter to the Romans = *Paw's letter* (and next week we'll hear from *Maw*)
>
> Be strong and *let your* heart take courage = *lecher heart!*

I will make three *booths* here, one for you and one for Moses and one for Elijah = *booze*
or *"boo"s* (take your choice)

And he made a trench about the altar ...*And he* put the wood in order ...*And he* said, "Fill
four jars with water...."

You can figure out that last one on your own. All I'm going to says is, Andy and Annie are two of
the busiest critters in the whole Bible. Sounds like it, anyway. (You do remember that wonderful
song, don't you, that goes "Andy walks with me, Andy talks with me..."?) Groan.

Not all of the bloopers come from poorly articulated consonant sounds. I've heard my share
about shepherds a*bah*ddin' in the *fi*lled, and I'm sure you have too. You get to a point where you
no longer have problems with regional accents because they—well, they're a part of that person
God made and Jesus loves. The only problems arise when something really *wrong* comes out of
the mouth. And that happens. The most recent time it happened was in a class where everyone
was reading from Luke 1 (KJV). It was a good class, terrific rapport, had a good sense of
Christian community to it. We came to the part in Luke where the angel Gabriel gets sent from
God unto a city of Galilee, named Nazareth. You know that part. He's sent to greet Mary like
this:

> And the angel came in unto her, and said, Hail....

Well, John was up front reading. John had one of these accents you couldn't put a finger on. It
wasn't quite regional, it was just sort of eclectic. And John got to verse 28, and read, "And the
angel came in unto her, and said, Hell ...." Pause. Laughter. Uncontrollable laughter. And the
class was over. We got it on videotape, and had the best time playing that moment over and over:

> And the angel came in unto her, and said, Hell... And the angel came in unto her, and said,
> Hell... And the angel came in unto her, and said, Hell... And the angel came in unto her, and
> said, Hell ....

What are you going to do when a whole class breaks up and gets silly? I think probably God got a
kick out of it too. John ("but I didn't say 'hell,' I said 'hell'") got a bunch of hugs.

It's important that we speak clearly, if we really want people to understand us. And I'd say it's
terribly important when it comes to our reading Scripture. We don't want to sound like a dear
child I knew very well who didn't like peas and would sit at the table with a mouthful of them that
she wouldn't swallow. Chipmunk cheeks. You can imagine what happened when she opened her
mouth to protest. I mean besides the mess. "I don't like these" sounded like "My known ike eed."

Fortunately, she grew up and learned to like peas and now has the privilege of assuring her children that peas are good for you!

Precise, But Not Punctilious. Before I move on into some exercises you may find helpful and some other notes on clear diction, I want to issue a caveat: *Avoid over-precise diction.* You don't want to sound prissy. Or as if you were doing a very bad rendition of some sort of foreign accent ("Thissa issa the Worda ofa Godda"). Best example I've ever heard was with the three words: felt tip pen. *Over-precision* would render this something like "feltuh tippuh pennuh"—with a little plosion on each of the final consonant sounds. That's too much. You don't want to be *under-precise* and make it "fel tih pen" (almost as if it were a single word). What you do want is a sort of double-consonant sound that links the two like consonant sounds together without releasing (or plosion) between them. For example, the /t/ from "felt" releases into the /t/ of "tip," then the /p/ from "tip" releases into the /p/ of "pen." It might *look* something like: "felttippen." A rule of thumb would be to let the words flow with as much precision as possible without crumbling phrases into too-precise fragments.

I once worked with a man who was a rising star in a big corporation. Make that "who *was* a rising star." He kept getting overlooked for promotion because his bosses thought he was an embarrassment whenever he made a presentation. His diction was terribly slurred. He was aware of that. And now he wanted to do something about it. I gave him the *teeth-together exercise*, and it worked incredibly well. In fact, the first time he tried it he amazed himself! The diction was clear, he opened up and got some resonance, and he sounded like a different person. Then he started doing this exercise just minutes before he had to make a presentation, and he amazed some other people. Amazed them so much he started getting promotions. Now I'm not going to promise you a better job or anything if you try this exercise, but I do think you'll find it helpful.

The teeth-together exercise. Imagine you've gone to the dentist, and she's wired your teeth together—upper teeth directly above the lowers. Can't talk very well, and the only thing you can eat is what you can sip through a straw. You get home, and there on your answering machine is a message that you've got to address a big audience *tonight.* Have to do it. Can't get out of it. And it's a big room. And there's no sound system. So you figure out you have to do your best with what you've got to work with, and that means you'll have to *overdo the movement of tongue and lips.* Super energize them. But remember, you can't separate your teeth. Can't open your jaws at all. All you have to work with is very, very energetic consonant sounds.

That's it. That's the setup for the exercise. Try it. You can read anything. This page. The telephone directory. Anything. Read aloud about the equivalent of two-thirds of a typed page.

Now, the dentist appears like magic (she moonlights as a fairy godmother) and cuts away the wires. You can open up again. So keep reading aloud, and see what happens now. Keep up the energy with the lips and tongue-tip. It really works! Your consonants are clearer. You're opening the mouth more (because it feels so good after having had lockjaw) so you're getting more resonance. The placement of your voice is forward, rather than being swallowed, because so much of the consonant energy is up at the front. It's a little like swinging around three baseball bats before you go up to the plate, then putting two away and going up to bat. Your energy is focused.

Not only does it generally improve diction and resonance, but this exercise is also good for cleaning up the /s/ and /l/ sounds. Your teeth are positioned for a clear /s/ sound. And with the teeth together it's difficult *not* to get the proper placement of the tongue for the /l/ sound.

Read backwards. This is an old actor's trick. I don't mean a trick for old actors. Again, read aloud anything you want, but read it *backwards*. The first sentence in this paragraph, for example, would read: "trick actor's old an is this." This exercise is also a really helpful one. It does several things for you. (1) It slows you down, just in case you're one of the millions of people who tend to talk too fast. (2) It helps your enunciation, because you're concentrating on *sounds* rather than on *sense*. (By the way, that word is "enunciation" and *not* "annunciation," which is the way I've seen some people spell it, and which is what Gabriel did to Mary and doesn't have anything to do with the way you speak.) Once you've read this way for a few minutes, try reading forward at approximately the same speed and with the same kind of energy. You'll be pleasantly surprised.

Final Consonants. One thing that's important to remember is that what I can get away with in private conversation may not work well for me when it comes to speaking in public. If there's any one particular articulation problem I've heard over the years, it's *weak final consonant sounds*. I don't want to come across sounding prissily precise, but I do need to follow through to the ends of my words. And it may seem to me as if I'm "overdoing" it a bit. What I want to work for is "singer's diction," and that's just a little more athletic than I'm used to. A singer wouldn't (shouldn't) sing "Praise the Lord" with an ordinary final /d/ sound, but rather follow through with a little schwa sound[1] that will make it sound like "Lord-uh." I'm probably going to have to "overdo" a bit the final consonant when I announce I'm reading "from the book of Job." In order to make that distinct to my listeners, I'll probably *feel* as if I'm saying "...the book of Jo-**_BUH_**." But in reality my listeners will simply be hearing "...the book of *Job*" instead of "...the book of *Joe*." It's incredible how many worshipers have suffered through "Hear the Word of the Lore" (not to mention "Almighty Gah" and "Jesus Chrissss"). People will sit in their pews and silently (we hope) say to themselves, "-duh," "-duh," "-tuh," and lose all their concentration on who they're worshipping. This very recently happened to me. In the middle of a sermon, I heard the phrase, "We believe in a God in whose hands our lives are hell." Now, since that particular tenet is not in my theological ballpark—and not, as I recall, a part of my Reformed heritage—I stopped listening for a moment to try to figure out why my life had been consigned into the hands of some fiendish deity. Of course, what I was *supposed* to have heard was "We believe in a God in whose hands our lives are hel_d_." That missing final consonant may have thrown a large part of the congregation for a loop. Sure, most of us second-guess what we're *supposed* to have heard. But wouldn't it be better if we actually *heard* it right the first time? In any case, a tape recorder or a friend sitting in the back of the sanctuary can provide great feedback to let us know whether or not what we're actually doing is coming across the way we *think* it is or would like it to be.

Probably the single greatest mispronunciation I've heard over the years is the /sts/ cluster in words like "hosts" and "priests." People will eliminate the /t/ sound and speak of the Lord of "hos" or the high "preece," or drop the final /s/ sound and say "host" and "priest." I've found the easiest way to master this combination of sounds is to think of the cluster as having two "beats": "s" and "ts". The latter is the sound we make when we imitate the sound of a hot coal falling into a pail of water. (And we've all done that, haven't we?) Or the sound of a pair of high hat cymbals. This would turn "hosts" into "hos-ts" and "priests" into "pries-ts." The very fact that we'd have to slow down a tad in order to enunciate this way would probably help. I think the separation into two beats makes it very easy to say these words clearly. And I think it occurs naturally in childhood language development when we try to master a cluster like this. My younger son used to say things like "this tas-tus good" or "that cos-tus a lot" when he was learning words like "tastes" and "costs." The little schwa sound was a natural bridge for him to get through that consonant combination.

Just for your own edification, you might make a list of words you hear mispronounced. If we sharpen our critical skills in listening to the way others speak, we often wind up being more careful speakers ourselves. The following is a list of words often mispronounced. Use it for starters, if you want, and add to it your own discoveries.

Words Frequently Mispronounced

The following words are often either mispronounced or poorly articulated. Identify the *correct* pronunciation and the *incorrect* version. Always use the correct pronunciation, or people will look at you funny. Refer to the Appendix for preferred pronunciations, or to your most up-to-date good quality dictionary. Better still, work through the list of IPA pronunciations following this list.

a
accept
across
Acts
Arctic, Antarctic
asked
asterisk
athlete, athletic
aye (yes)
aye (ever, always)
baptize, baptism, baptist
because
blasphemy, blaspheme
catch
Christian
couldn't, wouldn't, shouldn't
denarius, denarii
did you, would you, could you
don't you, won't you, can't you
duty
err
escape
et cetera
for
fulfill
gesture
government
grievous

height
human, huge, humid
Jesus
Jesus's
just
larynx
length, strength
lest
liberty, mighty, battle
lineage
magi
medieval
mischievous
new, knew
nuclear
often
our
picture
poor - pour, pore
prerogative
principal, principle
probably
pronunciation
psalm, almond, alms, balm, calm, palm
realtor
recognize
saith
Sheol
sherbet
strong
sure, surely
the
to
tumult
twenty
upon
weather/whether, wine/whine, watt/what

Words Frequently Mispronounced—IPA Pronunciation

a: /ə/²

accept: /ək'sept/   except: /ɪk'sept/

across: /ə'krɒs/

Acts: /ækts/

Arctic: /'ɑːktɪk/ Antarctic: /ænt'ɑːktɪk/

asked: /ɑskt/

asterisk: /'æstərɪsk/

athlete: /'æθliːt/ athletic: /æθ'letɪk/

aye (yes): /aɪ/

aye (ever, always): /eɪ/

baptize: /bæp'taɪz/

because: /bɪ'kɒz/

blasphemy: /'blæsfəmɪ/ blaspheme: /blɑs'fiːm/

catch: /kætʃ/

Christian: /'krɪstɪən, 'krɪstʃ(ə)n/

couldn't: /'kʊd(ə)nt/ shouldn't. /'ʃʊd(ə)nt/

denarius: /dɪ'neərɪəs/ denarii: /dɪ'neərɪˌaɪ/

did you: /dɪd juː/

don't you: /dəʊnt juː/

duty: /'djuːtɪ/

err: /ɜː(r)/

escape: /ɪ'skeɪp/

et cetera: /et 'setərə, 'setrə/

for: /fɔː(r)/ forgive: /fə'gɪv/ forget: /fə'get/

fulfill: /fʊl'fɪl/

gesture: /'dʒestʃə(r)/

government: /'gʌvənmənt/

grievous: /ˈgriːvəs/

height: /haɪt/

human: /ˈhjuːmən/ huge: /hjuːdʒ/ humid: /ˈhjuːmɪd/

Jesus: /ˈdʒiːzəs/

Jesus's: /ˈdʒiːzəs/

just: /dʒʌst/

larynx: /ˈlærɪŋks/

length: /leŋθ, leŋkθ/ strength: /streŋθ, streŋkθ/

lest: /lest/

liberty: /ˈlɪbətɪ/ mighty: /ˈmaɪtɪ/ battle: /ˈbæt(ə)l/

lineage: /ˈlɪnɪɪdʒ/

magi: /ˈmeɪdʒaɪ/

medieval: /ˌmedɪˈiːv(ə)l/

mischievous: /ˈmɪstʃɪvəs/

new: /njuː/

nuclear: /ˈnjuːklɪə(r)/

often: /ˈɒf(ə)n/

our: /ˈaʊə(r)/

picture: /ˈpɪktʃə(r)/

poor: /ˈpʊə(r)/ pour, pore: /pɔː(r)/

prerogative: /prɪˈrɒgətɪv/

principal, principle: /ˈprɪnsɪp(ə)l/

probably: /ˈprɒbəblɪ/

pronunciation: /prəˌnʌnsɪˈeɪʃ(ə)n/ pronounce: /prəˈnaʊns/

psalm: /saːm/ almond: /ˈaːmənd/   alms: /aːmz/ balm: /baːm/ calm: /kaːm/ palm: /paːm/

realtor: /ˈriːəltə(r)/

recognize: /ˈrekəgˌnaɪz/

saith: /seθ/

Sheol: /ˈʃiːəʊl/

sherbet: /ˈʃɜːbət/

strong: /strɒŋ/

sure: /ʃʊə(r)/   surely: /ʃʊəlɪ/   shirt: /ʃɜːt/

the: /ðɪ before a vowel, ðə before a consonant, ðiː when stressed³

to: /tə, before vowel tʊ, emph. tuː/

tumult: /'tjuːmʌlt/

twenty: /'twentɪ/

upon: /ə'pɒn/

weather: /'weðə(r)/   whether: /'ʍeðə(r)/   wine: /waɪn/   whine: /ʍaɪn/

watt: /wɒt/   what: /ʍɒt/

b bed	d dog	f fan	g give	h hot	j yet
k cow	l log	m mat	n now	p pan	r ring
s sin	t tip	v vow	w win	z zoo	ʃ she
ʒ vision	θ thin	ð then	ŋ sing	x loch	ʍ where
tʃ chin	dʒ jaw				

æ hat	ɑː art	e bet	ɜ her	ɪ fit	iː see
ɒ hot	ɔ paw	ʌ cup	ʊ put	uː do	ə ago
aɪ by	aʊ now	eɪ say	əʊ so	eə care	
ɪə hear	ɔɪ boy	ʊə tour	aɪə tire	aʊə sour	

¹The "schwa" sound is that short, unaccented sound occurring on a phrase like "the boys and the girls" on the "e"s in "the," or like the "a" sounds in a word like "ammonia."

²The indefinite article "a" is almost always a short, unaccented schwa sound /ə/: "I saw a boy and a girl and a dog." Only when the intention is to stress singularity should it be a long /eɪ/ sound: "Did you see two boys?" "No, I saw a boy." To say "I saw a boy and a girl and a dog" sounds artificial, as if one were learning to read. The indefinite article becomes "an" before a vowel sound: "a boy and a girl, an apple and an orange."

³cf. the definite article "the" with the indefinite "a." The short schwa /ə/ occurs before a consonant: "the boy and the girl." The longer /ɪ/ occurs before a vowel sound: "the apple and the orange." The long /iː/ occurs only when stressed: "You are the most excellent person!" To use the stressed /ðiː/ as in "I saw the boy and the girl" sounds as artificial as using the long /eɪ/ as the indefinite article.

APPENDICES

I - Belshazzar Revisited
II - Check Yourself Out
III - In a Nutshell
IV - What Makes the Story Tick?
V - Words Frequently Mispronounced

Appendix One—Belshazzar Revisited

The following are three different versions (or formats, if you will) of the story of Belshazzar's Feast. This is an abridged version of the King James translation of Daniel 5:1-30.

The first is the **_paragraph version_**, set up in approximately the kind of format and type size of an average Bible. Try reading it, or a portion of it, aloud. Notice how the eyes have to move like a typewriter (oops! word processor) across the page. Note too that ideas are broken up arbitrarily by the length of the line on the page. There are no indications of where a new character enters, or a new scene begins. There are no indications of shifts from narrative line to dialogue. There is nothing to help with the pacing, the flow, or the movement of the story. Nothing to indicate what, among all the words, are the important elements in the story.

And this is the format from which most of us read Scripture. When we read silently to ourselves, we have the leisure to be able to sort things out and figure out such things as new characters introduced, scene changes, mood changes, what's important, and so forth. But when we read aloud in a worship service, we don't have that leisure. It happens now. Now it begins, now it's over. And it's pretty tough trying to read it in this format and do justice to it. Of course, we would have spent time with it. And we probably would have marked it up with all kinds of slashes for pauses and underlines for emphases and notes in the margin and maybe different colored marking pens to indicate characters, moods, scenes, and the like. And by the time that's done, the manuscript is so marked up that we go just a little bit batty trying to make sense of it all when we do get up to read.

The second version is the **_phrased version_**. The format is quite different in many respects. For one thing, I've been able to use a full-sized 8½x11" sheet of paper, larger type, and a font that's just a bit "cleaner" and easier to read. The eyes no longer have to move back and forth across the page. They can move down the page and take in the ideas which are clustered together. The ideas now are not broken up because of line length. They are broken up in a way which helps facilitate the way I want to phrase the reading when I read it aloud. For example, I would probably read something like this:

Belshazzar the king _[slight pause]_

made a great feast *[slight pause]*
    to a thousand of his lords, *[longer pause]*
        and drank wine before the thousand.
[space - back to the margin - new idea]
Belshazzar, *[very slight pause]*
whiles he tasted the wine, *[slight pause]*
    commanded to
[shift into character mode, suggesting dialogue]
        bring the golden and silver vessels
[lengthy parenthetical idea]
            which his father Nebuchadnezzar
            had taken out of the temple
            which was in Jerusalem;
[run with this, all in one breath]
        that the king, and his princes,
            his wives, and his concubines
                        might drink therein.

[bigger space - something happens after they start drinking]
They drank wine, *[slight pause]*
[set off to suggest more dialogue, and run with it]
        and praised the gods of gold, and of silver,
            of brass, of iron,
                of wood, and of stone.

[BIG SPACE—BIG SHIFT OF MOOD]

    In the same hour *[pause long enough to visualize the scene]*
        came forth fingers of a man's hand . . . .

And so forth. My lines break down my ideas into chunks that go together. My spaces suggest pauses, shifts of scene or mood, or changes of ideas. New ideas begin back at the left margin. If I want to "run" without pausing through things like the lists of the people drinking from the sacred vessels (no need to itemize them—the idea is simply that "everybody there" was doing the partying) I can do it by "running" my words across the page. Visually, it tells me to keep going without pauses. And if, in addition to this layout, I want to do color-coding or underlining or make significant squiggles to guide my reading, the space permits without my ending up with a great lot of clutter.

The third sample is a ***version including phrasing and emphasis***. The format is exactly the same as the one used in sample number two. Here I've "built in" some additional visual guidelines, something very easy to do using a word processor. *Larger type* sets off the initial naming of the main character Belshazzar. (I'm going to use larger type too as I present each other character for the first time.) I want to grab people's attention and let them know right off the bat what the story's about. The rest of the opening sentence, giving us the setting and the situation, are also slightly larger type. I might even highlight this opening with a yellow fluorescent marker just to make sure I "highlight" it *vocally* as I read. Next, I've gone through and *italicized* what I want to emphasize within each phrase. After the "partying" sequence in the first three clusters there's that major mood shift as the reader observes the appearance of the hand. I've set that off in *boldface*, just as a reminder that something new has happened here and I don't want to continue merrily reading as though the party were still going strong. *Underlining* helps further set off important moments in the story. For example, Belshazzar's "Can You Top This?" offer of a third of the kingdom, after the offers of a red robe and a gold chain have been turned down. Underlining also sets off the disappointing turn in the story when all the wise men have gathered to reading the writing ...and ...alas, they can't do it. The story takes another important turn at the pint where Daniel says "I will read the writing" and begins his proclamation of judgment with a page from Nebuchadnezzar's history. Italics, underlining and boldface together indicate the building up of things that led to Nebuchadnezzar's downfall: *first,* his heart was lifted up and his mind hardened in pride; *next,* he was deposed and his glory taken away from him, so that *finally* he would know that there was a God and he wasn't it. (A beautiful example of how an idea builds—here in three clear steps—to a climax. And it should be read so that it *does* climax where it ought to.) And at the conclusion of Daniel's pronouncement comes the wonderful "poker player's moment" where Daniel lays down his cards one at a time:

> Then was the part of the *hand* sent from him:
> and *this writing* was written.
>> And *this* was the writing that was written:

Here it is—the moment we've been waiting for since the beginning of the story:

MENE,	*[ACE]*
MENE,	*[ACE]*
TEKEL,	*[ACE]*
UPHARSIN.	*[ACE]*

And now we *know*—only that we *don't know* because we don't know Aramaic. And we're still at the mercy of the storyteller as he continues with Daniel's words—words that amount to a *word study* (e.g. *MENE* = "to number") followed by a judgment (e.g. "and finished it").

This is the *interpretation* of the thing:

    MENE: God hath ***numbered*** thy kingdom

               and <u>*finished*</u> it.

    TEKEL: Thou art ***weighed*** in the balances

               and art <u>*found wanting*</u>.

    PERES: Thy kingdom is ***divided***

               and <u>*given to the Medes and Persians*</u>.

And this is followed by a good healthy pause. Daniel has finished his proclamation and goes home and goes to bed. And Belshazzar also goes to bed. Permanently:

    In that night
        was **Belshazzar**
            the king of the Chaldeans
               <u>SLAIN</u>.

And he met his fate in italics, boldface and underlined. And finally in capital letters. God wins again!!

All of the "decorating" of the "script" you read from is up to you. If it works for you, do it. I find that the spacing, the phrasing, the various shenanigans you can play with regarding ways you can set things off by italicizing or whatever—all of these are very helpful to me. And they make the ministry of reading God's Word a lot easier than trying to use the paragraph format. As far as I can tell, the only drawback is that it takes a bit more paper.

I have used this third format for years as a means of putting both my Scripture readings and my sermons in a form that makes delivery easier. Compared with reading the King James in tiny print and narrow columns—compared with using manuscripts typed in paragraph form on my old Underwood dinosaur with elite type and a ribbon that always needed to be changed—compared with those things I put up with for at least the first fifteen years of my ministry—this format makes the doing easy. As easy (as my friend Lucy from Knightstown, Indiana, used to say) as "fresh hog liver slippin' through a paper bag."

Try it. Play with it. See what works for you. God bless!

DANIEL—Chapter 5: BELSHAZZAR'S FEAST

PARAGRAPH VERSION

Belshazzar the king made a great feast to a thousand of his lords, and drank wine before the thousand.

Belshazzar, whiles he tasted the wine, commanded to bring the golden and silver vessels which his father Nebuchadnezzar had taken out of the temple which was in Jerusalem; that the king, and his princes, his wives, and his concubines, might drink therein.

They drank wine, and praised the gods of gold and of silver, of brass, of iron, of wood, and of stone.

In the same hour came forth fingers of a man's hand, and wrote over against the candlestick upon the plaister of the wall of the king's palace: and the king saw the part of the hand that wrote.

Then the king's countenance was changed, and his thoughts troubled him, so that the joints of his loins were loosed, and his knees smote one against another.

The king cried aloud to bring in the astrologers, the Chaldeans, and the soothsayers. And the king spake and said to the wise men of Babylon, Whosoever shall read this writing, and show me the interpretation thereof, shall be clothed with scarlet, and have a chain of gold about his neck and shall be the third ruler in the kingdom.

Then came in all the king's wise men: but they could not read the writing, nor make known to the king the interpretation thereof.

Now the queen, by reason of words of the king and his lords came into the banquet house: and the queen spake and said, O king, live forever: let not thy thoughts trouble thee, nor let thy countenance be changed:

There is a man in thy kingdom in whom is the spirit of the holy gods; and in the days of thy father
light and understanding and wisdom, like the wisdom of the gods, was found in him.

Then was Daniel brought in before the king. And the king spake and said unto Daniel, Art thou that Daniel which art of the children of the captivity of Judah, whom the king my father brought out of Jewry?

I have even heard of thee, that the spirit of the gods is in thee, and that light and understanding and excellent wisdom is found in thee.

Now if thou canst read the writing, and make known to me the interpretation thereof, thou shalt be clothed with scarlet and have a chain of gold about thy neck, and shall be the third ruler of the kingdom.

Then Daniel answered and said before the king, Let thy gifts be to thyself, and give thy rewards to another; yet I will read the writing unto the king, and make known to him the interpretation.

O thou king, the most high God gave Nebuchadnezzar thy father a kingdom, and majesty, and glory, and honor:

But when his heart was lifted up, and his mind hardened in pride, he was deposed from his kingly throne, and they took his glory from him till he knew that the most high God ruled in the kingdom of men.

And thou his son, O Belshazzar, hast not humbled thine heart, though thou knewest all this:

But hast lifted up thyself against the Lord of heaven; and they have brought the vessels of his house before thee, and thou, and thy lords, thy wives and thy concubines, have drunk wine in them; and thou hast praised the gods of silver, and gold, of brass, iron, wood, and stone, which see not, nor hear, nor know; and the God in whose hand thy breath is, and whose are all thy ways hast thou not glorified:

Then was the part of the hand sent from him: and this writing was written.

And this was the writing that was written: MENE, MENE, TEKEL, UPHARSIN.

This is the interpretation of the thing:

MENE: God hath numbered thy kingdom and finished it.

TEKEL: Thou art weighed in the balances and art found wanting.

PERES: Thy kingdom is divided and given to the Medes and Persians.

In that night was Belshazzar the king of the Chaldeans slain.

DANIEL—Chapter 5: BELSHAZZAR'S FEAST

PHRASED VERSION

Belshazzar the king
   made a great feast
      to a thousand of his lords,
            and drank wine before the thousand.

Belshazzar,
whiles he tasted the wine,
   commanded to
         bring the golden and silver vessels
           which his father Nebuchadnezzar
         had taken out of the temple
         which was in Jerusalem;
      that the king, and his princes,
            his wives, and his concubines
                  might drink therein.

They drank wine,
     and praised the gods of gold, and of silver,
         of brass, of iron,
            of wood, and of stone.

In the same hour
    came forth fingers of a man's hand
       and wrote over against the candlestick
         upon the plaister of the wall of the king's palace:

            and the king saw the part of the hand that wrote.

Then the king's countenance was changed,
  and his thoughts troubled him,
    so that the joints of his loins were loosed,
    and his knees smote one against another.
The king cried aloud
   to bring in the astrologers,
    the Chaldeans,
     and the soothsayers.

And the king spake
 and said to the wise men of Babylon,
   Whosoever shall read this writing,
   and show me the interpretation thereof,
    shall be clothed with scarlet,
     and have a chain of gold about his neck
      and shall be the third ruler in the kingdom.

Then came in all the king's wise men:

but they could not read the writing,
   nor make known to the king the interpretation thereof.

Now the queen,
 by reason of words of the king and his lords
   came into the banquet house:
 and the queen spake
  and said, "O king, live forever!"

   "Let not thy thoughts trouble thee,
   nor let thy countenance be changed.
    There is a man in thy kingdom
    in whom is the spirit of the holy gods;

and in the days of thy father,
>   light
>   and understanding
>   and wisdom,
>   like the wisdom of the gods,
>   was found in him."

Then was Daniel brought in before the king.

And the king spake
and said unto Daniel,
>   Art thou that Daniel
>   which art of the children of the captivity of Judah,
>   whom the king my father brought out of Jewry?

>   I have even heard of thee,
>   that the spirit of the gods is in thee,
>   and that light and understanding
>   and excellent wisdom is found in thee.

>   Now if thou canst read the writing,
>   and make known to me the interpretation thereof,
>   thou shalt be clothed with scarlet
>   and have a chain of gold about thy neck,
>   and shall be the third ruler of the kingdom.

Then Daniel answered
and said before the king,
>   Let thy gifts be to thyself, and give thy rewards to another;
>   yet I will read the writing unto the king,
>   and make known to him the interpretation.

O thou king,
the most high God gave Nebuchadnezzar thy father
    a kingdom, and majesty, and glory, and honor:

But when his heart was lifted up,
and his mind hardened in pride,
    he was deposed from his kingly throne,
    and they took his glory from him
        till he knew that the most high God
        ruled in the kingdom of men.

And thou his son, O Belshazzar,
    hast not humbled thine heart,
        though thou knewest all this:

But hast lifted up thyself against the Lord of heaven;
    and they have brought the vessels of his house before thee,
        and thou, and thy lords, thy wives and thy concubines,
        have drunk wine in them;
and thou hast praised the gods
    of silver, and gold, of brass, iron, wood, and stone,
        which see not, nor hear, nor know;
and the God in whose hand thy breath is,
    and whose are all thy ways
        hast thou not glorified:

Then was the part of the hand sent from him:
and this writing was written.
    And this was the writing that was written:
        MENE,
        MENE,
        TEKEL,
        UPHARSIN.

This is the interpretation of the thing:

    MENE: God hath numbered thy kingdom
                        and finished it.
    TEKEL: Thou art weighed in the balances
                        and art found wanting.
    PERES: Thy kingdom is divided
                        and given to the Medes and Persians.

In that night
        was Belshazzar
          the king of the Chaldeans
                    slain.

DANIEL—Chapter 5: BELSHAZZAR'S FEAST

VERSION INCLUDING PHRASING & EMPHASIS

Belshazzar the king

made a *great feast*
to a *thousand of his lords,*
and *drank wine* before the thousand.

Belshazzar,
whiles he *tasted* the wine,
commanded to
bring the golden and silver vessels
which his *father Nebuchadnezzar*
had taken out of the *temple*
which was in Jerusalem;
that the king, and his princes,
his wives, and his concubines
might drink therein.

They drank wine,
and *praised the gods of gold, and of silver,*
of brass, of iron,
of wood, and of stone.

In the same hour
came forth fingers of a man's hand
and wrote over against the candlestick
upon the plaister of the wall of the king's palace:

and the *king saw* the part of the hand that wrote.

Then the king's *countenance* was changed,
    and his *thoughts troubled* him,
        so that the *joints of his loins* were loosed,
        and his *knees smote* one against another.
The king cried aloud
      to *bring in the astrologers,*
        the Chaldeans,
          and the soothsayers.

And the king spake
   and said to the wise men of Babylon,
      Whosoever shall *read this writing,*
      and show me the *interpretation* thereof,
        shall be clothed with *scarlet,*
          and have a chain of <u>gold</u> about his neck
            and shall be the ***<u>third ruler in the kingdom</u>***.

Then came in all the king's wise men:

<u>but they could not read the writing,</u>
      <u>nor make known to the king the interpretation thereof.</u>

Now the **<u>queen</u>**,
   by reason of words of the king and his lords
      came into the banquet house:
and the queen spake
   and said, *"O king, live forever!"*

      "Let not thy thoughts trouble thee,
      nor let thy countenance be changed.
        There is a *man* in thy kingdom
        in whom is the *spirit of the holy gods;*

and in the days of thy father,
        light
               and understanding
                and wisdom,
                  like the wisdom of the gods,
was found in him."

Then was ***Daniel*** brought in before the king.

And the king spake
and said unto Daniel,
        Art thou that Daniel
                which art of the children of the *captivity of Judah*,
                  whom the king my father brought out of Jewry?

        I have even heard of thee,
        that the spirit of the gods is in thee,
                and that light and understanding
                  and excellent wisdom is found in thee.

        Now if thou canst read the writing,
        and make known to me the interpretation thereof,
                thou shalt be clothed with scarlet
                  and have a chain of gold about thy neck,
                    and shall be the third ruler of the kingdom.

Then Daniel answered
and said before the king,
        Let thy gifts be to thyself, and give thy rewards to another;
                yet I will read the writing unto the king,
                  and make known to him the interpretation.

O thou king,
the most high God gave _Nebuchadnezzar thy father_
     a kingdom, and majesty, and glory, and honor.

But when his _heart was lifted up_,
and his _mind hardened in pride_,
  he was _deposed from his kingly throne_,
  and they _took his glory from him_
    till he knew that the most high God
    ruled in the kingdom of men.

And thou his _son_, O Belshazzar,
  hast not humbled _thine_ heart,
    though thou _knewest all this_:

But hast _lifted up thyself against the Lord of heaven_;
  and they have brought the _vessels of his house_ before thee,
    and thou, and thy lords, thy wives and thy concubines,
     have drunk wine in them;
and thou hast _praised the gods_
  of silver, and gold, of brass, iron, wood, and stone,
    which _see not, nor hear, nor know_;
and the God in whose hand thy _breath is,_
  and whose are all thy ways
    hast thou not glorified:

Then was the part of the _hand_ sent from him:
and _this writing_ was written.
  And _this_ was the writing that was written:
    MENE,
    MENE,
    TEKEL,
    UPHARSIN.

This is the *interpretation* of the thing:

    MENE: God hath ***numbered*** thy kingdom

                                    and <u>*finished*</u> it.

    TEKEL: Thou art ***weighed*** in the balances

                                    and art <u>*found wanting*</u>.

    PERES: Thy kingdom is ***divided***

                                  and <u>*given to the Medes and Persians*</u>.

In that night

        was ***Belshazzar***

            the king of the Chaldeans

                  <u>***SLAIN***</u>.

Appendix Two—Check Yourself Out

The following _**Self-Discovery Critique**_ sheet can be helpful in keeping you "honest" about yourself as a communicator. Now please don't take umbrage that I'm suggesting you need to be kept honest. It's simply a fact of human nature that we'll get by on what we can get by on as long as we can get away with it. So please don't think that if you've gone through this book once or taken a semester or a year or even more to work on speech communication that you're through working on yourself. It's a sure thing the Lord isn't through trying to shape any of us up, and that includes you and me.

Bear in mind that it's very easy to fall back into bad habits or even get real creative and make up some new bad habits for ourselves. All you need is to find yourself standing in the chancel facing a congregation, and you'll start thinking, "Well, this is a holy place and I'm doing a holy ministry so I'd better sound holy," and out comes the monastery moan or the stained-glass voice. And if you start thinking "I'm important!" you're probably going to come across as pompous. But I'm sure you realize this. So, since it's easy to do things that get in our way and in the way of communicating God's Word, you'll want to use this as a check-list now and then. Essentially it's a little compendium of everything covered in this book. If you need to brush up on some item on the list, it's easy enough to go back to the appropriate chapter.

To use this, you'll need one of two things: a friend who's not afraid to be honest with you and whom you won't resent for telling you you're not perfect, or a VCR that can record you so you can play it back and critique yourself. (Remember, though: you can argue or disagree with your friend, but the video playback is showing it like it is!) If you're working with a friend, take a few moments to explain what each of the items means and what kinds of things you want to check for. Be sure to do this. Because people asked to become "critics" can easily go off half-cocked and miss the mark when it comes to helpful and constructive criticism. Pastors can use this check sheet to help "rehearse" lay readers. (But watch it, Rev! That astute layperson might be sitting there in church next Sunday checking _you_ out. And why not? It mightn't be a bad idea for a pastor to give copies of this critique sheet to a small cadre of lay persons in order to provide objective feedback! Let's face it. We're all in this together, to learn from one another, to grow with one another, to minister to one another. So why shouldn't the critiquing and openness and honesty go both ways?) Pastors in churches with large staffs could ask colleagues to critique them on a regular basis.

Another suggestion: this critique sheet is pretty impartial. It's not meant to make you feel negative about yourself (or for you as critic to make someone feel negative). So, whether you're critiquing someone else or critiquing yourself, be kind and gentle and affirming. How about giving a _critique sandwich_? Begin with a positive affirming comment, give a constructive suggestion of something that could be improved or needs attention, and conclude with another affirmation. (This idea of a critique sandwich, by the way, came from a wonderful sister, Jacqui Lewis Melsness, who gives so much of herself as teacher and minister. When she gives a critique, you feel as if you'd just been blessed by all the angels in heaven!) I think this helps keep us all in the right frame of mind when it comes to "offering suggestions" regarding our performance. Please remember that a person's speech communication is an intensely personal thing and that it's awfully easy to hurt someone deeply in the process of "just trying to help." Keep in mind these words of Paul to the church at Ephesus (Ephesians 4:3,14-16):

> Make every effort to keep the unity of the Spirit through the bond of peace. ... Then we will no longer be infants, tossed back and forth by the waves, and blown here and there by every wind of teaching and by the cunning and craftiness of men in their deceitful scheming. Instead, speaking the truth in love, we will in all things grow up into him who is the Head, that is, Christ. From him the whole body, joined and held together by every supporting ligament, grows and builds itself up in love, as each part does its work.

What we're after is growth. Growth in grace, growth in the Spirit, growth in wisdom, growth in ministry, growth in trusting and obeying, and above all growth every day and every moment in surrendering ourselves to the Lord who can use our lives to His eternal glory.

SELF-DISCOVERY CRITIQUE

1. INITIAL IMPRESSION

2. VOICE
     Voice quality appropriate
     Focused sound
     Resonance

3. DICTION
     Specific problem sounds
     Consonant endings

4. PRONUNCIATION PROBLEMS

5. PHYSICAL PRESENCE
     General bearing
          alert to the moment

     Eye contact

     Face: revealing
          neutral
          contradictory

     Breathing
          supported
          visible upper chest breathing

     Facial posture / sounds
          open mouth
          flat sounds

6. VOCAL GESTURE
     Logical content (clear/blurred)
          Phrasing
          Emphasis
               New/important ideas
               Sufficient inflection
     Progression of ideas
          Move to climax
          Teacups
     Varied dynamics   Pitch
                                Volume
                                  Rate
     Use of pauses

     Emotional content   Revealed
     (word color,   Obscure
     connotation)   Absent

7. PRESENCE TO THE WORD
     Involved - internalized material
     Detached - merely reported
     Sense of "now-ness" imparted to
          listeners

8. LASTING IMPRESSION
     expression = impression
     expression > impression
     expression < impression

9. GENERAL COMMENTS

Appendix Three—In a Nutshell

Here in a nutshell (as they say) is a listing of voice and diction concerns most of us are most likely to face. This is a kind of quick-diagnosis quick-cure chart you can use as a reminder of what things to work on. If you want to deal with any of these items in greater depth, you can refer back to the appropriate chapters. This is simply a distillation of the *most common* things that plague the *most people.* So you shouldn't be terribly surprised to find one of your habits on this list.

I'm going to say it again: SPEECH IS HABIT. And once you've identified the habits (good and not so good) you're halfway to achieving the kind of speech communication you want to be doing. Zero in on the habit that you want to change, and then dig in. It will take time. It will take some effort. Most of all it will take a willingness to do something about whatever needs to be done. But considering Who you're doing it for, I think it's worth it all. Don't be content with less than your best when it comes to serving Jesus Christ. (I know, that sounds preachy, but maybe if I didn't say it you wouldn't bother. And I really do want you to be the best you you can be.) (And so does He.)

So use these "nutshell" items as reminders. Identify the ones you want to work on and then write notes to yourself to keep nibbling away at the stuff you want to get rid of and to keep growing in the right direction. Those little yellow stick-up memo sheets are really helpful. Or write things on the back of your hand. Or tape record notes to yourself and put a speaker under your pillow. It's worth the effort. Really it is. And once again: God bless you!!

voice and diction concerns

<u>unsupported sound / throaty production</u>: Sounds are tense and throaty. Glottal fry and/or glottal shock indicate tension. Relax the throat and use the belt to support the voice. Be careful not to lift shoulders and clavicular area when inhaling.

<u>throaty placement (back placement)</u>: Sounds tend to be swallowed, throaty, can sound "growly," or cloudy. Sometimes "pitch breaks" occur. This often happens if pitch is too low, and improves if one uses a slightly higher register. Bring sounds forward, focus voice in front of mouth—up into the "cathedral ceiling." Involve the face in voice production. Keep sounds away from your own ears, aiming it towards the ears of listeners. Aim for the back row.

<u>endings swallowed</u>: Ends of phrases tend to be swallowed. Follow through to end of each phrase. Think of "singing out" towards your listeners. <u>Use</u> final consonant sounds (sound them out clearly and energetically) as an aid to placement and projection.

<u>flat / nasal quality</u>: Voice quality tends to be flat / nasal. Open the mouth and focus sounds forward (against back of upper teeth). Opening adds warmth, resonance and carrying quality.

<u>(*nasalized sounds*)</u>: Watch out especially for [æ] (as in *cat*) and [aʊ] (as in *how*). With the [æ] sound, focus should be more toward the mid-back of the mouth (central area of hard palate). If too far forward, takes on an "eh" quality. The [aʊ] diphthong is a combination of "ah+oo" and not "æ+oo".

<u>strident / harsh quality</u>: Combination of flat sound & tension in throat produce harsh, strident voice quality.

breathy: At times voice becomes breathy—often for emphasis or dramatic effect. The sound becomes diffuse, out of focus, loses carrying quality. Instead, try extending sounds (e.g. vowel sounds, liquid consonants such as [m, n, ŋ, l, z]) as a means of projection.

"teacup" inflections: Watch tendency to give each phrase a rise-fall inflection pattern. Occasionally with this, volume fades at the ends of phrases. Projection suffers, ideas fail to progress to their climax. "Sing out," following through vocally to the end of each phrase.

variables - pitch, rate, volume: Pitch, rate, and volume tend to be the same throughout. Need to vary vocal dynamics. Stretch. Avoid a too-narrow pitch range. Vary rate and volume to match thought. Enter into the energy of each idea, reveal how you feel about what you're saying, lift into prominence what's new / important in each thought.

special diction concerns:

Appendix Four—What Makes the Story Tick?

When you first start out reading aloud, it's awfully easy to get "stuck" with the words to the point where you're reading words more than telling the story or sharing the thought. But it's important to realize that the substance—the thought or the story—is not in inky words on paper. What we need to do is to look at the words and then *through* the words to the substance or reality to which the words give voice. Let's focus here on the task of <u>*reading a story*</u>—such as the Belshazzar story or the Naaman story, which we've talked about throughout these pages.

Knowing that it can be a somewhat sensitive issue to "play with" a story from Scripture, I've used another story, *How the Finch Got Her Colors*, to demonstrate what makes a story "tick" and how a reader relates to the story and to the audience. This is an activity that works well with a class of, say, eight or so people. If you're reading this on your own, go through it in your imagination!

The story, an old Flemish legend, goes something like this:

How the Finch Got Her Colors

There was a time, long, long ago, when the birds of the forest all were gray. They hadn't a bit of color. Nothing but gray. One day the Mighty Bird, their master and ruler, called them into his presence. He pointed up into the sky, and showed them a rainbow—a beautiful rainbow full of reds and yellows and greens and blues and violets. "I'm going to give each of you one of those marvelous colors," he said. And immediately they began jostling and crowding and pressing and pushing around him.

"I get to choose first," squawked the parrot. "I want green!"

"I'll take blue! Blue! Blue!" chirped the bluebird.

The canary twittered, "Oh, give me yellow! I would like yellow!"

But in the meanwhile, during all the commotion, there was a tiny bird who sat by herself in a corner, waiting for her turn. That little bird was the Finch.

"Well, now, don't you each look superb in your colors!" chortled the Mighty Bird. "And well you should, for all the rainbow's colors are gone!"

But just then, the Mighty Bird heard a sound from the corner.

"Peep!" It was the little Finch.

"Little Finch!" cried the Mighty Bird. "Come here! Come here! Why didn't you ask for one of the colors?"

"I was waiting my turn," peeped the little Finch.

"But the colors are all gone now," sighed the Mighty Bird.

"Alas," cried the Finch. "Then I must always be gray!"

"Gray, little Finch?" he said. "Just because you waited your turn? Just because you did not jostle and crowd and press and push like the others? We'll see about that!"

And he called to all the other birds, before they could fly away, "Come stand before me now!"

And as all the birds passed in front of him, he took from each a bit of their colors. A bit of red from the cardinal, a bit of yellow from the canary, some green from the parrot, some blue from the bluebird, and a touch of purple from the jackdaw. And he gave all these colors to the little Finch. And now the little Finch smiled, glittering with all the hues of the rainbow, all blending beautifully together.

So it came to pass that the loveliest bird of the forest was the tiny little Finch. And all because she had waited her turn.

It's a pleasant little story and fun to play with. Try going through it three times, three different ways, as a means of entering into the story and discovering all its component parts.

First Read-Through. First, one person will be the *narrator*. A second person is "cast" as the Mighty Bird, a third as the *parrot*, a fourth as the *bluebird*, a fifth as the *canary*, and a sixth as the little *Finch*. In this *first read-through* (it's usually sufficient to go just as far as the line "'I was waiting my turn,' peeped the little Finch" rather than the whole story) the *narrator* will read all the *narrative lines* and each of the *characters* will read his or her own *dialogue*. From this, it's helpful to point out that it took seven people to bring the story to life. There was a consistent narrative element. And there were six "character" elements that were all different—none of them looking or sounding a bit alike. *When only one person is reading the story, that person has to step in and out of all these roles*, performing as narrator, then as Mighty Bird, and as each of the other birds in turn. There can be no sameness throughout, with all these variations built into the weave of the story itself.

Second Read-Through. In a *second run-through* all of the characters act out their parts, speak their own dialogue, and *narrate their own narrations*. All of the action takes place *in scene* (that is, in the "stage" area) and all of the dialogue is directed from one character to another—also in scene. But all the narration is directed towards the "audience" (usually a few people left standing at the back of the room). The story, therefore, is being "told" (through the narration to the audience) and "enacted" ("on stage"). It's easy enough to do following the printed story, but if it were scripted, it would look something like this:

ALL BIRDS IN UNISON *(in place, to audience):*   There was a time, long, long ago, when the birds of the forest all were gray. They hadn't a bit of color. Nothing but gray.

MIGHTY BIRD *(to center stage, to audience):*   One day the Mighty Bird, their master and ruler, called them into his presence. *(motions to birds to come to him; addresses audience as he points to sky and relates to other birds):* He pointed up into the sky, and showed them a rainbow—a beautiful rainbow full of reds and yellows and greens and blues and violets. *(To the birds):* "I'm going to give each of you one of those marvelous colors," *(to the audience):* he said.

BIRDS IN UNISON *(to audience, as they push and shove):* And immediately they began jostling and crowding and pressing and pushing around him.

PARROT *(to Mighty Bird):* I get to choose first, *(to audience)*: squawked the parrot. *(To audience)*: I want green!

BLUEBIRD *(to Mighty Bird):* I'll take blue! Blue! Blue! *(to audience):* chirped the bluebird.

CANARY *(to audience):* The canary twittered, *(to Mighty Bird):* Oh, give me yellow! I would like yellow!

FINCH *(in corner, to audience):* But in the meanwhile, during all the commotion, there was a tiny bird who sat by herself in a corner, waiting for her turn. That little bird was the Finch.

MIGHTY BIRD *(to birds):* Well, now, don't you each look superb in your colors! *(to audience):* chortled the Mighty Bird. *(To birds):* And well you should, for all the rainbow's colors are gone!

MIGHTY BIRD *(to audience):* But just then, the Mighty Bird heard a sound from the corner.

LITTLE FINCH: Peep! *(To audience):* It was the little Finch.

MIGHTY BIRD *(to little Finch):* Little Finch! *(to audience):* cried the Mighty Bird. *(To Finch):* Come here! Come here! Why didn't you ask for one of the colors?

LITTLE FINCH *(to Mighty Bird):* I was waiting my turn, *(to audience):* peeped the little Finch.

MIGHTY BIRD *(to Finch):* But the colors are all gone now, *(to audience):* sighed the Mighty Bird.

LITTLE FINCH *(to Mighty Bird):* Alas, *(to audience):* cried the Finch. *(To Mighty Bird):* Then I must always be gray!

MIGHTY BIRD *(to Finch):* Gray, little Finch? *(to audience):* he said. *(To Finch):* Just because you waited your turn? Just because you did not jostle and crowd and press and push like the others? We'll see about that!

MIGHTY BIRD *(motioning to other birds, speaks to audience):* And he called to all the other birds, before they could fly away, *(to birds):* Come stand before me now!

MIGHTY BIRD *(addresses audience as he performs actions; birds pass in front of him in order):* And as all the birds passed in front of him, he took from each a bit of their colors.

CARDINAL *(to audience):* A bit of red from the cardinal.

CANARY *(to audience):* A bit of yellow from the canary.

PARROT *(to audience):* Some green from the parrot.

BLUEBIRD *(to audience):* Some blue from the bluebird.

GRACKLE *(to audience):* And a touch of purple from the jackdaw.

MIGHTY BIRD *(to audience, gives colors to Finch):* And he gave all these colors to the little Finch.

FINCH *(to audience, smiling, preening):* And now the little Finch smiled, glittering with all the hues of the rainbow, all blending beautifully together. So it came to pass that the loveliest bird of the forest was the tiny little Finch. And all because she had waited her turn.

Now look at all the mechanisms of "story telling" as you've gone through them. There's been _narration_—enhanced in this "telling" because each of the characters has narrated his/her own part. That usually brings a good deal of *empathy* into each narrative line, because the characters are relating that part of the story telling of *their own role* in the story. Individual story tellers, unfortunately, often overlook that element of empathy in their narrative voices. There has also been _action and interaction_. The story is not just something reduced to a sequence of words. It is a living entity, characters talking to each other, acting out their roles "on stage" and interacting with all the other characters—all to weave together a story. The story, then, is *the telling of something that's alive and happening right now*. There has also been the element of _space_—the arena in which the story has been acted out. First there's an array of birds "waiting in the wings" to be called together by the Mighty Bird. When he calls, they move from their space to another space, around the Mighty Bird. They *respond* when he shows them the rainbow, and they *react* to what he has told them by puddling around in their space. The little Finch, at the beginning of the story, is in her own space, outside that of the rest of the birds. When the Mighty Bird calls her to come to him, there is a moment of waiting until she moves from her distant space into the center of the scene. There is now a tightening of _focus_ on the conversation between the Mighty Bird and the little Finch, and with it a greater intensity in the story itself. As the Mighty Bird resolves "We'll see about that!" and the focus broadens to take in the whole scene, the story moves into its resolution and finale. The movements are broad and carefully paced as the birds pass in front of Mighty Bird, who takes colors from them and then presents them to the little Finch. Finally the little Finch takes center stage in the spotlight and the curtains close.

Third Read-Through. This time one person is given the task of reading the story. This person should stand at a lectern facing the audience. Between the reader and the audience will be the "stage" area. In this intermediate area, the other characters do everything they had done in the second read-through. *Now they do it in silence.* We see only the mimed action of the story as it unfolds. The reader has to *wait for the story* to unfold action by action before any particular action or element can be told. For example, the reader must look into the "stage" area and see the gray birds before saying

There was a time, long, long ago, when the birds of the forest all were gray.

The reader "looks into the story" again, and verifies

They hadn't a bit of color. Nothing but gray.

Then the reader sees the Mighty Bird move into his position and motion the other birds to come to him.

One day the Mighty Bird, their master and ruler, called them into his presence.

The reader waits until the birds are in their places. Then the reader sees Mighty Bird gesturing towards the sky and then towards the other birds.

He pointed up into the sky, and showed them a rainbow—a beautiful rainbow full of reds and yellows and greens and blues and violets. "I'm going to give each of you one of those marvelous colors," he said.

Now the reader sees the birds crowding around the Mighty Bird.

And immediately they began jostling and crowding and pressing and pushing around him.

The reader sees the parrot addressing the Mighty Bird.

"I get to choose first," squawked the parrot. "I want green!"

Then the reader sees the bluebird.

"I'll take blue! Blue! Blue!" chirped the bluebird.

The reader sees the canary.

The canary twittered, "Oh, give me yellow! I would like yellow!"

The reader sees the little Finch.

But in the meanwhile, during all the commotion, there was a tiny bird who sat by herself in a corner, waiting for her turn. That little bird was the Finch.

The reader looks back and sees the Mighty Bird.

"Well, now, don't you each look superb in your colors!" chortled the Mighty Bird. "And well you should, for all the rainbow's colors are gone!"

The reader sees the Mighty Bird responding to a sound.

> But just then, the Mighty Bird heard a sound from the corner.

The reader sees the little Finch.

> "Peep!" It was the little Finch.

The reader sees the Mighty Bird motioning for the little Finch.

> "Little Finch!" cried the Mighty Bird. "Come here! Come here!

Now the reader sees the little Finch leave her spot in the corner. The reader waits as she walks up to where the Mighty Bird is standing.

> Why didn't you ask for one of the colors?"

The reader sees the little Finch again.

> "I was waiting my turn," peeped the little Finch.

And so forth throughout to the end of the story.

The important principle here is:

> ## THE STORY TELLER DOES NOT MOVE THE STORY.
> ## THE STORY MOVES THE STORY TELLER.

In other words, *the story teller has to wait for the story to unfold before relating the story*. For example, the reader has to wait until all the birds have come onstage before telling us about them. Reader must see Mighty Bird in action before telling about those actions. Reader must *wait* until the little Finch moves from her space into the center of action. It's as if the story were written:

> MIGHTY BIRD: But just then, the Mighty Bird heard a sound from the corner.

> LITTLE FINCH: "Peep!" It was the little Finch.

> MIGHTY BIRD: "Little Finch!" cried the Mighty Bird. "Come here! Come here!"

(The little Finch moves from her spot in the corner over to where the Mighty Bird is standing.)

MIGHTY BIRD: "Why didn't you ask for one of the colors?"

LITTLE FINCH: "I was waiting my turn," peeped the little Finch.

The little Finch's action (the italicized, boldface line) is as much a part of the story as any of the written words. And the story teller must wait for that action to take place. (Without it, you'd have the Mighty Bird and the little Finch shouting to each other across the distance between them!)

This element of waiting for something to happen is crucial when relating a story. The story will pace the reading (not vice versa). Those of us who tend to speak too quickly can let a story spew forth like an old silent movie played on fast speed with everyone darting about all over the place. If we'll let the story control our pacing it can monitor our rate, our pauses, our general sense of timing.

Another important point here is that the *reality of the story* is not in words on a page. The story teller could tell it from memory in his or her own words. The reality that's being told about is the story acted out in that "stage" area. Presuming that we as readers or story tellers are not going to carry around our own little strolling troupe of players, we then must see that story reality *in the arena of our imaginations.* In run-through number three, the reader had to enter into the story action before telling it to the audience. Whenever we read or tell a story, we have to make that same entry into the story before we can relate it. Without doing that we're speaking only a string of words that talk *about* the story without experiencing its life substance.

Appendix Five—Words Frequently Mispronounced

a: short schwa sound before a consonant (uh boy and uh girl); long /a/ only when stressed); becomes "an" before a vowel

accept: don't confuse with "except"

across: no final /t/ sound—not "acrost"

Acts: not "ax"

Arctic, Antarctic—not "artic, antartic"—there's an "ark" in there somewhere

asked: not "ast" or "axed" or "ask"; try saying "ascot" and then dropping the last vowel sound

asterisk: not "astericks"

athlete, athletic: not "athalete" or "athaletic"

aye (yes): rhymes with "eye"—("Aye, matey, that's a patch on me eye!")

aye (ever, always): long "a" as in "forever and a 'day'"

baptize: "bap-TIZE" (cf. βαπτίζω), not "BAP-" or "BAB-"—cf. "BAP-tism, BAP-tist"

because: not "becuz"—rhymes with "pause" and not with "fuzz"

blasphemy, blaspheme: the noun is "BLAS-phemy", the verb "blas-PHEME"

catch: not "ketch"

Christian: not "chrish-ten"

couldn't: not "cooten" or "coodunt" (same with "wouldn't" and "shouldn't")

denarius: di-NAIR-i-us; [plural denarii: di-NAIR-i-eye]

did you: not "didjoo" or "didja" (same with "would you" and "could you")

don't you: not "dontchoo" (same with "won't you" and "can't you")

duty: not "dooty"; there's a tiny /y/ sound after the /d/—"d(y)ootee" (same with "new," "knew")

err: count me an old fogey on this one. I know "air" is currently considered acceptable, but "ur" is preferred

escape: please, not "excape"

et cetera: "eck cetera" need not apply

for: not "fur" (same with "forgive" and "forget")

fulfill: the initial /l/ sound is often missing

gesture: the first syllable is "jess" and not "guess"

government: not "guvverment"

grievous: never "grev*ious*"

height: not "height*th*"

human: not *"you*man"—cf. also "huge" and "humid"

Jesus: two distinct syllables—"JEE-zus"—rhymes with "frees us!!!!" (think about that)

Jesus's: just "JEE-zus" (same as without the "apostrophe-s")—not "JEE-zus-suz"

just: not "jist"

larynx: not "larnicks"

length: not "lenth"—cf. also "strength" (think of *long* and *strong* as parts of these words)

lest: don't make it "least"

liberty: not "liberdy" (watch out also for "mighdy" and "baddle")

lineage: three syllables (LIN-ny-idge)

magi: MAY-jigh (not MADG-igh or MAG-ee)

medieval: not "middy-EVIL"—the first two syllables went to *"medi"*-cal school

mischievous: not "mischeevious"

new, knew: cf. duty

nuclear: not "nucular"

often: leave out the /t/ sound

our: it's not "Are Father..."

picture: don't confuse with "pitcher"

poor: rhymes with "tour"; and "pour" and "pore" rhyme with "tore"

prerogative: not "perrogative"

principal, principle: not "princible"

probably: not "probbly" or "prolly"

pronunciation: even though the verb is "pronounce," the noun is *not* "pronounciation"

psalm: leave out the /l/ sound (cf. "almond," "alms," "balm," "calm," "palm")

realtor: not "reelator"

recognize: not "reckonize"

saith: it's "seth" and not "sayeth"

Sheol: two distince syllables (SHEE-ohl)

sherbet: it's not "sherbert," Herbert

strong: a lot of people (erroneously) say "shtrong" because of the retroflex position of
the tongue for the /r/ sound

sure: has the vowel sound of "sugar" and not that of "shirt"; same with "surely," Shirley the: short schwa sound before a consonant ("the boy and the girl"); becomes longer "thih" before a vowel sound; long "THEE" only when stressed

to: not a heavy "tuh" sound

tumult: no "tum"-my sound in this; it's "TYOO-mult"

twenty: not "twenny"

upon: sometimes you hear "a pun"

weather/whether: blow out a candle on *wh*ether," not on *w*eather"—same with "wine/whine," "watt/what"